Rick Steves®

SNAPSHOT

Scottish Highlands

CONTENTS

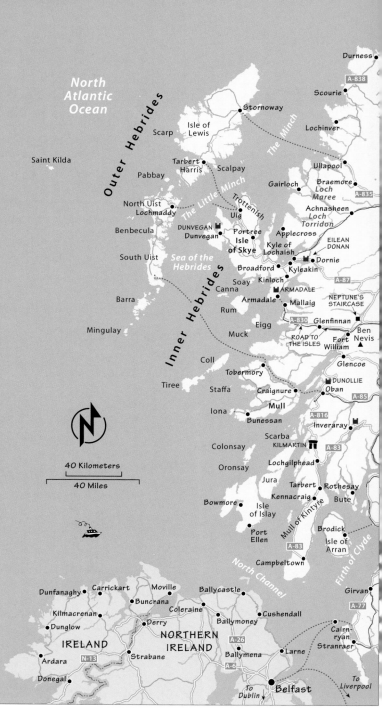

Inverness

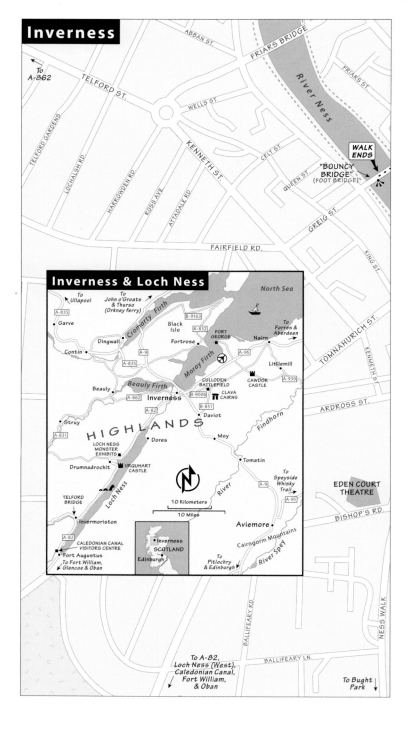

To A-862

TELFORD ST.

ABBAN ST.

FRIARS BRIDGE

FRIARS ST.

River Ness

WELLS ST.

TELFORD GARDENS

LOCHALSH RD.

HARROWDEN RD.

ROSS AVE.

ATTADALE RD.

KENNETH ST.

CELT ST.

QUEEN ST.

WALK ENDS

"BOUNCY BRIDGE" (FOOT BRIDGE)

GREIG ST.

KING ST.

FAIRFIELD RD.

Inverness & Loch Ness

To Ullapool

To John o'Groats & Thurso (Orkney ferry)

Cromarty Firth

North Sea

A-835

Garve

B-9163

A-832

Black Isle

FORT GEORGE

Nairn

To Forres & Aberdeen

Dingwall

Fortrose

Contin

A-9

A-835

Moray Firth

A-96

Littlemill

A-939

CULLODEN BATTLEFIELD

CAWDOR CASTLE

Beauly

Beauly Firth

A-862

Inverness

B-9006

CLAVA CAIRNS

A-82

B-851

Struy

Daviot

A-831

H I G H L A N D S

Findhorn

ARDROSS ST.

TOMNAHURICH ST.

KENNETH ST.

Dores

Moy

LOCH NESS MONSTER EXHIBITS

Drumnadrochit

URQUHART CASTLE

Tomatin

To Speyside Whisky Trail

EDEN COURT THEATRE

River

A-9

TELFORD BRIDGE

Loch Ness

10 Kilometers

10 Miles

A-95

BISHOP'S RD.

Invermoriston

Aviemore

A-82

CALEDONIAN CANAL VISITORS CENTRE

Fort Augustus

To Fort William, Glencoe & Oban

SCOTLAND

Inverness

Edinburgh

Cairngorm Mountains

River Spey

To Pitlochry & Edinburgh

BALLIFEARY RD.

NESS WALK

BALLIFEARY LN.

To A-82, Loch Ness (West), Caledonian Canal, Fort William, & Oban

To Bught Park

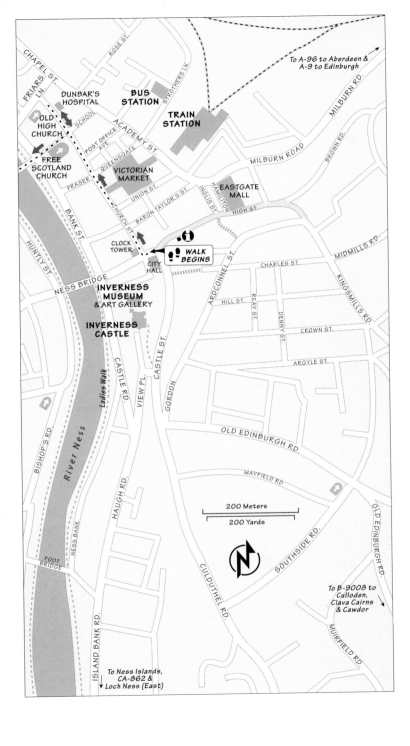

INTRODUCTION

This Snapshot guide, excerpted from my guidebook *Rick Steves Scotland*, introduces you to the Highlands, the rugged, windswept north of Scotland that's a picture-perfect setting for romantic novels and epic films. Filled with more natural and historical mystique than people, the rocky Highlands are where Scottish dreams are set. In this land of mountains and glens, you can march across legendary battlefields, taste a dram of the finest whisky, or even search for the Loch Ness monster. And along the west and north coasts lay a smattering of some of Europe's most intriguing islands—mountainous, scenic, romantic, and indelibly Scottish. On these remote outposts of Scottish life, mist drifts across craggy hillsides, grizzled islanders man the drizzly ferry crossings, and midges can make life miserable.

In the Highlands you'll find Scottish culture distilled to its most potent brew. Whenever I want a taste of traditional Scotland, this is where I come.

To help you have the best trip possible, I've included the following topics in this book:

• **Planning Your Time,** with advice on how to make the most of your limited time

• **Orientation,** including tourist information (abbreviated as TI), tips on public transportation, local tour options, and helpful hints

• **Sights** with ratings:

▲▲▲—Don't miss

▲▲—Try hard to see

▲—Worthwhile if you can make it

No rating—Worth knowing about

- **Sleeping** and **Eating,** with good-value recommendations in every price range
- **Connections,** with tips on trains, buses, ferries, and driving

Practicalities, near the end of this book, has information on money, staying connected, hotel reservations, transportation, and other helpful hints.

To travel smartly, read this little book in its entirety before you go. It's my hope that this guide will make your trip more meaningful and rewarding. Traveling like a temporary local, you'll get the absolute most out of every mile, minute, and dollar.

Happy travels!

Rick Steves

SCOTLAND

One of the three countries that make up Great Britain, rugged, feisty, colorful Scotland stands apart. Whether it's the laid-back, less-organized nature of the people, the stony architecture, the unmanicured landscape, or simply the haggis, go-its-own-way Scotland is distinctive.

Scotland encompasses about a third of Britain's geographical area (30,400 square miles), but has less than a tenth of its population (about 5.4 million). This sparsely populated chunk of land stretches to Norwegian latitudes. Its Shetland Islands, at about 60°N (similar to Anchorage, Alaska), are the northernmost point of the British Isles. You may see Scotland referred to as "Caledonia" (its ancient Roman name) or "Alba" (its Gaelic name). Scotland's fortunes were long tied to the sea; all of its leading cities are located along firths (estuaries), where major rivers connect to ocean waters.

The southern part of Scotland, called the Lowlands, is relatively flat and urbanized. The northern area—the Highlands—features a wild, severely undulating terrain, punctuated by lochs (lakes) and fringed by sea lochs (inlets) and islands.

The Highland Boundary Fault that divides Scotland geologically also divides it culturally. Historically, there were two distinct identities: rougher Highlanders in the northern wilderness and the more refined Lowlanders in the southern

Scotland Almanac

Official Name: Scotland.

Population: About 5.4 million. Scotland is mostly English-speaking, though about 1.5 million people use the Scots "language," and about 60,000 speak Scottish Gaelic.

Latitude and Longitude: 57°N and 4°W. The Shetland Islands are Scotland's northernmost point, at 60°N (similar to Anchorage, Alaska).

Area: 30,400 square miles, about the size of South Carolina.

Geography: Scotland's flatter southern portion is the Lowlands; the Highlands to the north are more wild and hilly, and the country boasts over 6,000 miles of coastline and more than 790 islands (only about 130 are inhabited). Ben Nevis in western Scotland (at 4,406 feet) is Great Britain's highest peak.

Biggest Cities: Glasgow has 600,000 people, Edinburgh 490,000.

Economy: The gross domestic product is about $142 billion, and the GDP per capita is $26,500. The Scottish service sector (including retail and financial services) has become an increasingly significant part of its economy, producing over 60 percent of all economic activity in 2015.

Scotland's main exports include food and drink, as well as chemicals and petroleum products. Scotch whisky comprises a quarter of all UK food and drink exports; exports to the US represent the biggest market for Scotch by value, though France is the biggest market by volume.

Scotland uses the same currency as the other UK countries of England, Wales, and Northern Ireland: the pound sterling.

Government: Queen Elizabeth II officially heads the country—but for Scots she is simply Queen Elizabeth, not Queen Elizabeth II. (Scotland and England were separate monarchies when England had their first Elizabeth.) Theresa May is the UK's prime minister, and Nicola Sturgeon is Scotland's first minister.

Flag: The Saltire, with a diagonal, X-shaped white cross on a blue field, is meant to represent the crucifixion of Scotland's patron saint, the apostle Andrew.

The Average Scot: The average Scottish person will live to age 79 and doesn't identify with an organized religion. He or she has free health care, gets 28 vacation days a year (versus 16 in the US), lives within a five-minute walk of a park or green space, and gets outdoors at least once a week.

flatlands and cities. Highlanders represented the stereotypical image of "true Scots," speaking Gaelic, wearing kilts, and playing bagpipes, while Lowlanders spoke languages of Saxon origin and wore trousers. After the Scottish Reformation, the Lowlanders embraced Protestantism, while most Highlanders stuck to Catholicism. Although this Lowlands/Highlands division has faded over time, some Scots still cling to it.

The Lowlands are dominated by a pair of rival cities: Edinburgh (on the east coast's Firth of Forth) and Glasgow (on the west

coast's Firth of Clyde) mark the endpoints of Scotland's 75-mile-long "Central Belt," where three-quarters of the country's population resides. Edinburgh, the old royal capital, teems with Scottish history and is the country's most popular tourist attraction. Glasgow, once a gloomy industrial city, is becoming a hip, laid-back city of art, music, and architecture. In addition to these two cities—both of which warrant a visit—the Lowlands' highlights include the medieval university town and golf mecca of St. Andrews, the small city of Stirling (with its castle and many nearby historic sites), and selected countryside stopovers.

Generally, the Highlands are hungry for the tourist dollar, and everything overtly Scottish is exploited to the kilt; you need to spend some time here to get to know the area's true character. You can get a feel for the Highlands with a quick drive to Oban, through Glencoe, then up the Caledonian Canal to Inverness. With more time, the Isles of Iona, Staffa, and Mull (an easy day trip from Oban); the Isle of Skye; the handy distillery town of Pit-

lochry; and countless brooding countryside castles will flesh out your Highlands experience. And for those really wanting to get off the beaten path, continue north—all the way up the dramatic west coast (called Wester Ross) to John O'Groats, at Britain's northeastern tip. To go farther, cross the Pentland Firth to Orkney, with its own unique culture and history.

At these northern latitudes, cold and drizzly weather isn't uncommon—even in midsummer. The blazing sun can quickly be covered over by black clouds and howling wind. Your B&B host will warn you to prepare for "four seasons in one day." Because Scots feel personally responsible for bad weather, they tend to be overly optimistic about forecasts. Take any Scottish promise of "sun by the afternoon" with a grain of salt—and bring your raincoat, just in case.

Americans and Canadians of Scottish descent enjoy coming "home" to Scotland. If you're Scottish, your surname will tell you which clan your ancestors likely belonged to. The prefix "Mac" (or "Mc") means "son of"—so "MacDonald" means the same thing as "Donaldson." Tourist shops everywhere are happy to help you track down your clan's tartan (distinctive plaid pattern).

Scotland shares a monarchy with the rest of the United Kingdom, though to Scots, Queen·Elizabeth II is just "Queen Elizabeth"; the first Queen Elizabeth ruled England, but not Scotland. (In this book, I use England's numbering.) Scotland is not a sovereign state, but it is a "nation" in that it has its own traditions, ethnic identity, languages (Gaelic and Scots), and football league. To some extent, it even has its own government.

Recently, Scotland has enjoyed its greatest measure of political autonomy in centuries—a trend called "devolution." In 1999, the Scottish parliament convened in Edinburgh for the first time in almost 300 years; in 2004, it moved into its brand-new building near the foot of the Royal Mile. Though the Scottish parliament's powers are limited (most major decisions are still made in London), the Scots are enjoying the refresh-

ing breeze of increased self-governance. In a 2014 independence referendum, the Scots favored staying in the United Kingdom by a margin of 10 percent. The question of independence will likely remain a pivotal issue in Scotland for many years to come.

Scotland even has its own currency...sort of. Scots use the same coins as England, Wales, and Northern Ireland, but Scotland also prints its own bills (featuring Scottish rather than English people and landmarks). Just to confuse tourists, three different banks print Scottish pound notes,

each with a different design. In the Lowlands (around Edinburgh and Glasgow), you'll receive both Scottish and English pounds from ATMs and in change. But in the Highlands, you'll almost never see English pounds. Bank of England notes are

legal and widely used; Northern Ireland bank notes are legal but less common.

The Scottish flag—a diagonal, X-shaped white cross on a blue field—represents the cross of Scotland's patron saint, the Apostle Andrew (who was crucified on an X-shaped cross). You may not realize it, but you see the Scottish flag every time you look at the Union Jack: England's flag (the red St. George's cross on a white field) superimposed on Scotland's (a blue field with a white diagonal cross). The diagonal red cross (St. Patrick's cross) over Scotland's white one represents Northern Ireland. (Wales gets no love on the Union Jack.)

Here in "English-speaking" Scotland, you may still encounter a language barrier. First is the lovely, lilting Scottish accent—which may take you a while to understand. You may also hear an im-

British, Scottish, and English

Scotland and England have been tied together politically for more than 300 years, since the Act of Union in 1707. For a century and a half afterward, Scottish nationalists rioted for independence in Edinburgh's streets and led rebellions ("uprisings") in the Highlands. In this controversial union, history is clearly seen through two very different filters.

If you tour a British-oriented sight, such as Edinburgh's National War Museum Scotland, you'll find things told in a "happy union" way, which ignores the long history of Scottish resistance—from the ancient Picts through the time of Robert the Bruce. The official line: In 1706-1707, it was clear to England and certain parties in Scotland (especially landowners from the Lowlands) that it was in their mutual interest to dissolve the Scottish government and fold it into the United Kingdom, to be ruled from London.

But talk to a cabbie or your B&B host, and you may get a different spin. Scottish independence is still a hot-button issue. Since 2007, the Scottish National Party (SNP) has owned the largest majority in the Scottish Parliament. During a landmark referendum in September 2014, the Scots voted to remain part of the union—but many polls, right up until election day, suggested that things could easily have gone the other way.

The rift shows itself in sports, too. While the English may refer to a British team in international competition as "English," the Scots are careful to call it "British." If a Scottish athlete does well, the English call him "British." If he screws up... he's a clumsy Scot.

penetrable dialect of Scottish English that many linguists consider to be a separate language, called "Scots." You may already know several Scots words: lad, lassie, wee, bonnie, glen, loch, aye. On menus, you'll see neeps and tatties (turnips and potatoes). And in place names, you'll see ben (mountain), brae (hill), firth (estuary), and kyle (strait). Second is Gaelic (pronounced "gallic" here; Ireland's closely related Celtic language is pronounced "gaylic")—the ancient Celtic language of the Scots. While only one percent of the population speaks Gaelic, it's making a comeback—particularly in the remote and traditional Highlands. For more on Scots words— see page 14.

While soccer ("football") is as popular here as anywhere, golf is Scotland's other national sport. But in Scotland, it's not necessarily considered an exclusively upper-class pursuit; you can generally play a round at a basic course for about £15. While Scotland's best scenery is along the west coast, its best golfing is on the east coast—home to many prestigious golf courses. Most of these are links courses, which use natural sand from the beaches for the bunkers. For tourists, these links are more authentic, more challenging, and more fun than the regular-style courses (with artificial landforms) farther inland. If you're a golfer, St. Andrews—on the east coast—is a pilgrimage worth making.

Outside of the main cities, Scotland's sights are subtle, but its misty glens, brooding countryside castles, and warm culture are plenty engaging. Whether toasting with beer, whisky, or Scotland's favorite soft drink, Irn-Bru, enjoy meeting the Scottish people. It's easy to fall in love with the irrepressible spirit and beautiful landscape of this faraway corner of Britain.

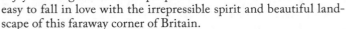

THE SCOTTISH HIGHLANDS

Filled with more natural and historical mystique than people, the Highlands are where Scottish dreams are set. Legends of Bonnie Prince Charlie linger around crumbling castles as tunes played by pipers in kilts swirl around tourists. Intrepid Munro baggers scale bald mountains, grizzled islanders man the drizzly ferry crossings, and midges make life miserable (bring bug spray). The Highlands are the most mountainous, least inhabited, and—for many—most scenic and romantic part of Scotland.

The Highlands are covered with mountains, lochs, and glens, scarcely leaving a flat patch of land for building a big city. Geographically, the Highlands are defined by the Highland Boundary Fault, which slashes 130 miles diagonally through the middle of Scotland just north of the big cities of the more densely populated "Central Belt" (Glasgow and Edinburgh).

This geographical and cultural fault line is clearly visible on maps, and you can even see it in the actual landscape—especially around Loch Lomond and the Trossachs, where the transition from rolling Lowland hills to bald Highland mountains is almost too on-the-nose. Just beyond the fault, the Grampian Mountains curve across the middle of Scotland; beyond that, the Caledonian Canal links the east and west coasts (slicing diagonally through the Great Glen, another geological fault, from Oban to Inverness), with even more mountains to the north.

Though the Highlands' many "hills" are technically too short to be called "mountains," they do a convincing imitation. (Just don't say that to a Scot.) Scotland has 282 hills over 3,000 feet. A list of these was first compiled in 1891 by Sir Hugh Munro, and to this day the Scots still call their high hills "Munros." (Hills

Hiking the Highlands

Scotland is a hiker's paradise...as long as you bring rain gear. I've recommended a few hikes of varying degrees of difficulty throughout this book. Remember: Wear sturdy (ideally waterproof) shoes, and be prepared for any weather. For serious hikes, pick up good maps and get advice at local TIs or from a knowledgeable resident (such as your B&B host). A good resource for hiking route tips is www.walkhighlands.co.uk.

For a more in-depth experience, consider one of Scotland's famous multiday walks. These are the most popular:

West Highland Way: 95 miles, 5-10 days, Milngavie to Fort William by way of Loch Lomond, Glencoe, and Rannoch Moor

Great Glen Way: 79 miles, 5-6 days, Fort William to Inverness along the Caledonian Canal, Fort Augustus, and Loch Ness

John Muir Way: 134 miles, 9-10 days, newer route—from 2014—that runs coast to coast through the Central Belt of Scotland, from Helensburgh to Dunbar via Falkirk, the Firth of Forth, and Edinburgh

from 2,500-3,000 feet are known as "Corbetts," and those from 2,000-2,500 are "Grahams.") Avid hikers—called "Munro baggers"—love to tick these minimountains off their list. According to the Munro Society, more than 5,000 intrepid hikers can brag that they've climbed all of the Munros. (To get started, you'll find lots of good information at www.walkhighlands.co.uk/munros).

The Highlands occupy more than half of Scotland's area, but are populated by less than five percent of its people—a population density comparable to Russia's. Scotland's Hebrides Islands (among them Skye, Mull, Iona, and Staffa), while not, strictly speaking, in the Highlands, are often included simply because they share much of the same culture, clan history, and Celtic ties. (Orkney and Shetland, off the north coast of Scotland, are a world apart—they feel more Norwegian than Highlander.)

Inverness is the Highlands' de facto capital, and often claims to be the region's only city. (The east coast port city of Aberdeen—Scotland's third largest, and quadruple the size of Inverness—has its own Doric culture and dialect, and is usually considered its own animal.)

The Highlands are where you'll most likely see Gaelic—the old Celtic language that must legally accompany English on road signs. While few Highlanders actually speak Gaelic—and virtually no one speaks it as a first language—certain Gaelic words are used as a nod of respect to their heritage. *Fàilte* (welcome), *Slàinte mhath!* (cheers!—literally "good health"), and *tigh* (house—featured in many business names) are all common. If you're making friends in a Highland pub, ask your new mates to teach you some Gaelic words.

The Highlands are also the source of many Scottish superstitions, some of which persist in remote communities, where mischievous fairies and shape-shifting kelpies are still blamed for trouble. Many superstitions surround babies. New parents were gripped with a fear that their newborn could be replaced by a devilish imposter called a changeling. Well into the 20th century, a midwife called a "howdie" would oversee key rituals: Before a birth, doors and windows would be unlocked and mirrors would be covered. And the day of the week a baby is born was charged with significance ("Monday's child is fair of face, Tuesday's child is full of grace...").

Many American superstitions and expressions originated in Scotland (such as "black sheep," based on the idea that a black sheep was terrible luck for the flock). Just as a baseball player might refuse to shave during a winning streak, many perfectly modern Highlanders carry a sprig of white heather for good luck at their wedding (and are careful not to cross two knives at the dinner table). And let's not even start with the Loch Ness monster...

In the summer, the Highlands swarm with tourists...and midges. These miniature mosquitoes—like "no-see-ums"—are bloodthirsty and determined. They can be an annoyance from late May through September, depending on the weather. Hot sun or a stiff breeze blows the tiny buggers away, but they thrive in damp, shady areas. Locals suggest blowing or brushing them off, rather than swatting them—since killing them only seems to attract more (likely because of the smell of fresh blood). Scots say, "If you kill one midge, a million more will come to his funeral." Even if you don't usually travel with bug spray, consider bringing or buying some for a summer visit. Locals recommend Avon's Skin So Soft, which is effective against midges, but less potent than DEET-based bug repellants.

Keep an eye out for another Scottish animal: shaggy Highland cattle called "hairy coos." They're big and have impressive horns, but are best known for their adorable hair falling into their eyes (the hair protects them from Scotland's troublesome insects and unpredictable weather). Hairy coos graze on sparse vegetation that other animals ignore, and, with a heavy coat (rather than fat) to keep them insulated, they produce a lean meat that resembles venison. (Highland cattle meat is not commonly eaten, and the relatively few hairy coos you'll see are kept around mostly as a national symbol.)

While the prickly, purple thistle is the official national flower, heather is the unofficial national shrub. This scrubby vegetation blankets much of the Highlands. It's usually a muddy reddish-brown color, but it bursts with purple flowers in the late summer; the less common bell heather blooms in July. Heather is one of the few things that will grow in the inhospitable terrain of a moor, and it can be used to make dye, rope, thatch, and even beer (look for Fraoch Heather Ale).

Highlanders are an outdoorsy bunch. For a fun look at local athletics, check whether your trip coincides with one of the Highland Games that enliven Highland communities in summer (see the sidebar on page 20). And keep an eye out for the unique Highland sport of shinty: a brutal, fast-paced version of field hockey, played for keeps. Similar to Irish hurling, shinty is a full-contact sport that encourages tackling and fielding airborne balls, with players swinging their sticks (called camans) perilously through the air. The easiest place to see shinty is at Bught Park in Inverness (see page 81), but it's played across the Highlands.

PLANNING YOUR TIME

Here are three recommended Highland itineraries: two days, four days, or a full week or more. These plans assume you're driving, but can be done (with some modifications) by bus.

Two- to Three-Day Highland Highlights Blitz

This ridiculously fast-paced option squeezes the maximum Highland experience out of a few short days, and assumes you're starting from Glasgow or Edinburgh.

The Scottish Highlands

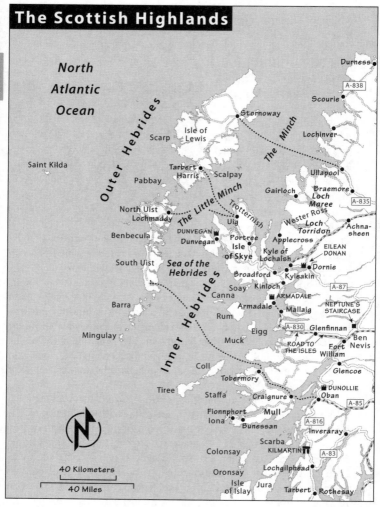

North
Atlantic
Ocean

Durness

A-838

Scourie

Stornoway

Lochinver

Isle of
Lewis

Scarp

The Minch

Ullapool

Saint Kilda

Tarbert
Harris   Scalpay

Pabbay

Gairloch   Braemore
Loch
Maree

A-835

North Uist
Lochmaddy

The Little Minch

Trotternish

Wester Ross

Loch
Torridon

Achna-
sheen

Benbecula

Uig

DUNVEGAN

Portree

Applecross

EILEAN
DONAN

Dunvegan

Isle
of Skye

Kyle of
Lochalsh

Dornie

South Uist

Sea of the
Hebrides

Broadford

Kyleakin

A-87

Soay   Kinloch

Barra

Canna

ARMADALE

Armadale   Mallaig

NEPTUNE'S
STAIRCASE

Rum

Inner Hebrides

Eigg

A-830   Glenfinnan

Mingulay

Muck

ROAD TO
THE ISLES

Ben
Fort   Nevis
William

Coll

Glencoe

Tobermory

DUNOLLIE

Tiree

Staffa   Craignure   Oban

A-85

Fionnphort   Mull
Iona   Bunessan

A-816

Inveraray

Scarba

KILMARTIN   A-83

Colonsay

Lochgilphead

Oronsay

Isle   Jura   Tarbert   Rothesay
of Islay

40 Kilometers

40 Miles

Day 1: In the morning, head up to the Highlands. (If coming from Edinburgh, consider a stop at Stirling Castle en route.) Drive along Loch Lomond and pause for lunch in Inveraray. Try to get to Oban in time for the day's last distillery tour (see hours on page 29; smart to book ahead). Have dinner in Oban.

Day 2: Get an early start from Oban and make a beeline for Glencoe, where you can visit the folk museum and enjoy a quick, scenic drive up the valley. Then drive to Fort William and follow the Caledonian Canal to Inverness, stopping at Fort Augustus to see the locks (and have a late lunch). Drive along Loch Ness to search for monsters, then wedge in a visit to the Culloden Battle-field (just outside Inverness) in the late afternoon. Finally, make

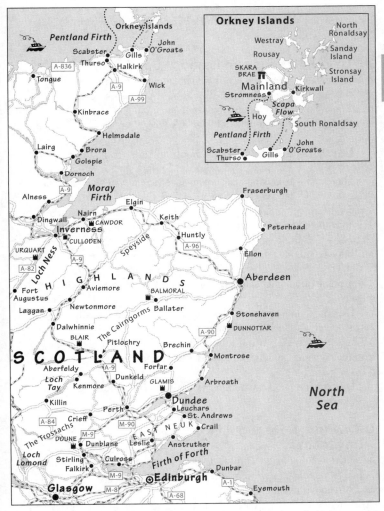

good time southward on the A-9 back to Edinburgh (3 hours, arriving late).

Day 3: To extend this plan a bit, take your time getting to Inverness on Day 2 and spend the night there. Follow my self-guided Inverness Walk either that evening or the next morning. Leaving Inverness, tour Culloden Battlefield, visit Clava Cairns, then head south, stopping off at any place that appeals: The best options near the A-9 are Pitlochry and the Scottish Crannog Centre on Loch Tay, or take the more rugged eastern route to see the Speyside whisky area, Balmoral Castle and Ballater village, and Cairngorms mountain scenery. Or, if this is your best chance to see Stirling

Castle or the Falkirk sights (Falkirk Wheel, Kelpies sculptures), fit them in on your way south.

Six-Day Highlands and Islands Loop

While you'll see the Highlands on the above itinerary, you'll whiz past the sights in a misty blur. This more reasonably paced plan is for those who want to slow down a bit.

Day 1: Follow the plan for Day 1, above, sleeping in Oban (2 nights).

Day 2: Do an all-day island-hopping tour from Oban, with visits to Mull, Iona, and (if you choose) Staffa.

Day 3: From Oban, head up to Glencoe for its museum and valley views. Consider lingering for a (brief) hike. Then zip up to Fort William and take the "Road to the Isles" west (pausing in Glenfinnan to see its viaduct) to Mallaig. Take the ferry over the sea to Skye, then drive to Portree to sleep (2 nights).

Day 4: Spend today enjoying the Isle of Skye. In the morning, do the Trotternish Peninsula loop; in the afternoon, take your pick of options (Talisker Distillery, Dunvegan Castle, multiple hiking options).

Day 5: Leaving Portree, drive across the Skye Bridge for a photo-op pit stop at Eilean Donan Castle. The A-87 links you over to Loch Ness, which you'll follow to Inverness. If you get in early enough, consider touring Culloden Battlefield this evening. Sleep in Inverness (1 night).

Day 6: See the Day 3 options for my Highlands Highlights Blitz, earlier.

10-Day (or More) Highlands Explorer Extravaganza

Using the six-day Highlands and Islands Loop as a basis, pick and choose from these possible modifications (listed in order of where they'd fit into the itinerary):

• Add an overnight in **Glencoe** to make more time for hiking there.
• Leaving the Isle of Skye, drive north along **Wester Ross** (the scenic northwest coast). Go as far as Ullapool, then cut back down to Inverness, or...
• Take another day or two (after spending the night in Ullapool) to carry on northward through remote and rugged scenery to Scotland's **north coast.** Drive east along the coast all the way to John O'Groats; then either take the ferry from Scrabster across to Orkney, or shoot back down to Inverness on the A-9 (about 3 hours).
• Visit **Orkney** (2-night minimum). This can fit into the above plan after John O'Groats. Or, to cut back on the remote driving,

simply zip up on the A-9 from Inverness (about 3 hours)—or fly up from Inverness, Edinburgh, or Aberdeen.

- On the way south from Inverness, follow the **Speyside whisky trail,** cut through the **Cairngorms,** visit **Balmoral Castle,** and sleep in **Ballater.** Between Balmoral and Edinburgh, consider visiting Glamis Castle (Queen Mum's childhood home), Dundee (great industrial museums), or Culross (scenic firth-side village).
- Add an overnight wherever you'd like to linger; the best options are the **Isle of Skye** (to allow more island explorations) or **Inverness** (to fit in more side-trips).

GETTING AROUND THE HIGHLANDS

By Car: The Highlands are made for joyriding. There are a lot of miles, but they're scenic, the roads are good, and the traffic is light. Drivers enjoy flexibility and plenty of tempting stopovers. Be careful, but don't be too timid about passing; otherwise, diesel fumes and large trucks might be your main memory of driving in Scotland. The farther north you go, the more away-from-it-all you'll feel, with few signs of civilization. Even on a sunny weekend, you can go miles without seeing another car. Don't wait too long to gas up—village gas stations are few and far between, and can close unexpectedly. Get used to single-lane roads: While you can make good time when they're empty (as they often are), don't let your guard down, and slow down on blind corners—you never know when an oncoming car (or a road-blocking sheep) is right around the bend. If you do encounter an oncoming vehicle, unspoken rules of the road dictate that the driver closest to a pullout will use it—even if they have to back up. A little "thank-you" wave (or even just an index finger raised off the steering wheel) is the customary end to these encounters.

By Public Transportation: Glasgow is the gateway to this region (so you'll most likely have to transfer there if coming from Edinburgh). The **train** zips from Glasgow to Fort William, Oban, and Kyle of Lochalsh in the west; and up to Stirling, Pitlochry, and Inverness in the east. For more remote destinations (such as Glencoe), the bus is better.

Most of the **buses** are operated by Scottish Citylink. You can pay the driver in cash when you board. But in peak season—when these buses fill up—it's smart to buy tickets at least a day in advance: Book at www.citylink.co.uk, call 0871-216-3333, or stop by a bus station or TI.

Glasgow's Buchanan Station is the main Lowlands hub for reaching Highlands destinations. From Edinburgh, it's best to transfer in Glasgow (fastest by train, also possible by bus)—though there are direct buses from Edinburgh to Inverness, where you can

Scottish Highland Games

Throughout the summer, Highland communities host traditional festivals of local sport and culture. These Highland Games (sometimes called Highland Gatherings) combine the best elements of a track meet and a county fair. They range from huge and glitzy (such as Braemar's world-famous games, which the Queen attends, or the Cowal Highland Gathering, Scotland's biggest) to humble and small-town. Some of the more modern games come with loud pop music and corporate sponsorship, but still manage to celebrate the Highland spirit.

Most Highland Games take place between mid-June and late August (usually on Saturdays, but occasionally on weekdays). The games are typically a one-day affair, kicking off around noon and winding down in the late afternoon. At smaller games, you'll pay a nominal admission fee (typically around £5-7). Events are rain or shine (so bring layers) and take place in a big park ringed by a running track, with the heavy events and Highland dancing stage at opposite ends of the infield. Surrounding the whole scene are junk-food stands, a few test-your-skill carnival games, and local charities raising funds by selling hamburgers, fried sausage sandwiches, baked goods, and bottles of beer and Irn-Bru. The emcee's running commentary is a delightful opportunity to just sit back and enjoy a lilting Scottish accent.

The day's events typically kick off with a **pipe band** parading through town—often led by the local clan chieftain—and ending with a lap around the field. Then the sporting events begin.

In the **heavy events**—or feats of Highland strength—brawny, kilted athletes test their ability to hurl various objects of awkward shapes and sizes as far as possible. In the weight throw, competitors spin like ballerinas before releasing a 28- or 56-pound ball on a chain. The hammer throw involves a similar technique with a 26-pound ball on a long stick, and the stone put (with a 20- to 25-pound ball) has been adopted in American sports as the shot put. In the "weight over the bar" event, Highlanders swing a 56-pound weight over a horizontal bar that begins at 10 feet high and ends at closer to 15 feet. (That's like tossing a 5-year-old child over a double-decker bus.) And, of course, there's the caber toss: Pick up a giant log (the caber), get a running start, and release it end-over-end with enough force to (ideally) make the caber flip all the way over and land at the 12 o'clock position. (Most competitors wind up closer to 6.)

Meanwhile, the **track events** run circles around the muscle:

the 90-meter dash, the 1,600-meter, and so on. The hill race adds a Scottish spin: Combine a several-mile footrace with the ascent of a nearby summit. The hill racers begin with a lap in the stadium before disappearing for about an hour. Keep an eye on nearby hillsides to pick out their colorful jerseys bobbing up and down a distant peak. This custom supposedly began when an 11th-century king staged a competition to select his personal letter carrier. After about an hour—when you've forgotten all about them—the hill racers start trickling back into the stadium to cross the finish line.

The **Highland dancing** is a highlight. Accompanied by a lone piper, the dancers (in groups of two to four) toe their routines

with intense concentration. Dancers remain always on the balls of their feet, requiring excellent balance and stamina. While some men participate, most competitors are female—from wee lassies barely out of nappies, all the way to poised professionals. Common steps are the Highland fling (in which the goal is to keep the feet as close as possible to one spot), sword dances (in which the dancers step gingerly over crossed swords on the stage), and a variety of national dances.

Other events further enliven the festivities. The pipe band periodically assembles to play a few tunes, often while marching around the track (giving the runners a break). Larger games may have a massing of multiple pipe bands, or bagpipe and drumming competitions. You may also see re-enactments of medieval battles, herd-dog demonstrations, or dog shows (grooming and obedience). Haggis hurling—a relatively new event in which participants stand on a whisky barrel and attempt to throw a cooked haggis as far as possible—has caught on recently. And many small-town events end with the grand finale of a town-wide tug-of-war, during which everybody gets bruised, muddy, and hysterical.

If you're traveling to Scotland in the summer, check online schedules to see if you'll be near any Highland Games before locking in your itinerary. Rather than target the big, famous gatherings, I make a point of visiting the smaller clan games. One helpful website—listing dates for most but not all of the games around Scotland—is www.shga.co.uk. For many travelers to Scotland, attending a Highland Games can be a trip-capping highlight. And, of course, many communities in the US and Canada also host their own Highland Games.

connect to Highlands buses. Once in the Highlands, Inverness and Fort William serve as the main bus hubs.

Note that bus frequency can be substantially reduced on Sundays and in the off-season (Oct-mid-May). Unless otherwise noted, I've listed bus information for summer weekdays. Always confirm schedules locally.

These buses are particularly useful for connecting the sights in this book:

Buses **#976** and **#977** connect Glasgow with Oban (5/day, 3 hours).

Buses **#914, #915,** and **#916** go from Glasgow to Fort William, stopping at Glencoe (8/day, 2.5 hours to Glencoe, 3 hours total to Fort William). From Fort William, these buses continue all the way up to Portree on the Isle of Skye (3/day, 7 hours for the full run).

Bus **#918** goes from Oban to Fort William, stopping en route at Ballachulish near Glencoe (2/day, 1 hour to Ballachulish, 1.5 hours total to Fort William).

Bus **#44** (operated by Stagecoach) is a cheaper alternative for connecting Glencoe to Fort William (hourly Mon-Sat, fewer on Sun, www.stagecoachbus.com).

Buses **#19** and **#919** connect Fort William with Inverness (7/day, 2 hours).

Buses **#M90** and **#G90** run from Edinburgh to Inverness (express #G90, 2/day, 3.5 hours; slower #M90, some stop in Pitlochry, 6/day, 4 hours).

Bus **#917** connects Inverness with Portree, on the Isle of Skye (3/day, 3 hours).

Bus **#G10** is an express connecting Inverness and Glasgow (5/day, 3 hours). National Express **#588** also goes direct (1/day, 4 hours, www.nationalexpress.com).

OBAN & THE INNER HEBRIDES

Oban • Isles of Mull, Iona and Staffa • Near Oban (Inveraray and Kilmartin Glen)

For a taste of Scotland's west coast, the port town of Oban is equal parts endearing and functional. This busy little ferry-and-train terminal has no important sights, but makes up the difference in character, in scenery (with its low-impact panorama of overlapping islets and bobbing boats), and with one of Scotland's best distillery tours. But Oban is also convenient: It's midway between the Lowland cities (Glasgow and Edinburgh) and the Highland riches of the north (Glencoe, Isle of Skye). And it's the "gateway to the isles," with handy ferry service to the Hebrides Islands.

If time is tight and serious island-hopping is beyond the scope of your itinerary, Oban is ideally situated for a busy and memorable full-day side-trip to three of the most worthwhile Inner Hebrides: big, rugged Mull; pristine little Iona, where buoyant clouds float over its historic abbey; and Staffa, a remote, grassy islet inhabited only by sea birds. (The best of the Inner Hebrides—the Isle of Skye—is covered in its own chapter.) Sit back, let someone else do the driving, and enjoy a tour of the Inner Hebrides.

This chapter also includes a few additional sights near Oban, handy for those connecting the dots: the most scenic route between Glasgow and Oban (along the bonnie, bonnie banks of Loch Lomond and through the town of Inveraray, with its fine castle); and the faint remains of Kilmartin Glen, the prehistoric homeland of the Scottish people.

PLANNING YOUR TIME

If you're on a speedy blitz tour of Scotland, Oban is a strategic and pleasant place to spend the night. But you'll need two nights to enjoy Oban's main attraction: the side-trip to Mull, Iona, and

Staffa. There are few actual sights in Oban itself, beyond the distillery tour, but—thanks to its manageable size, scenic waterfront setting, and great restaurants—the town is an enjoyable place to linger.

Oban

Oban (pronounced OH-bin) is a low-key resort. Its winding promenade is lined by gravel beaches, ice-cream stands, fish-and-chip joints, a tourable distillery, and a good choice of restaurants. Everything in Oban is close together, and the town seems eager to please its many visitors: Wool and tweed are perpetually on sale, and posters announce a variety of day tours to Scotland's wild and wildlife-strewn western islands. When the rain clears, sun-starved Scots sit on benches along the Esplanade, leaning back to catch some rays. Wind, boats, gulls, layers of islands, and the promise of a wide-open Atlantic beyond give Oban a rugged charm.

Orientation to Oban

Oban, with about 10,000 people, is where the train system of Scotland meets the ferry system serving the Hebrides Islands. As "gateway to the isles," its center is not a square or market, but its harbor. Oban's business action, just a couple of streets deep, stretches along the harbor and its promenade.

TOURIST INFORMATION

Oban's TI, located at the North Pier, sells bus and ferry tickets, is well stocked with brochures, and has free Wi-Fi (generally daily July-Aug 9:00-19:00; April-June 9:00-17:30; Sept-March 10:00-17:00; 3 North Pier, tel. 01631/563-122, www.oban.org.uk).

HELPFUL HINTS

Bookstore: Waterstones, a huge bookstore overlooking the harborfront, offers maps and a fine collection of books on Scotland (Mon-Sat 9:00-17:30, Sun 11:00-17:00, longer hours in July-Aug, 12 George Street, tel. 0843/290-8529).

Baggage Storage: The train station has pay luggage lockers, but is open limited hours (Mon-Sat 5:00-20:30, Sun 10:45-18:00)—confirm the closing time before committing.

Laundry: You'll find **Oban Quality Laundry** tucked a block behind the main drag just off Stevenson Street (same-day drop-off service, no self-service, Mon-Fri 9:00-17:00, Sat until 13:00, closed Sun, tel. 01631/563-554). The recommended **Backpackers Plus Hostel** (page 35) will also do laundry for nonguests.

Supermarket: The giant **Tesco** is a five-minute walk from the train station (Mon-Sat until 24:00, Sun until 20:00, walk through Argyll Square and look for entrance to large parking lot on right, Lochside Street).

Bike Rental: Oban Cycles is on the main drag (£25/day, Tue-Sat 10:00-17:00, closed Sun-Mon, 87 George Street, tel. 01631/566-033).

Bus Station: The "station" is just a pullout, marked by a stubby clock tower, at the roundabout in front of the train station. In peak season, it's wise to book bus tickets the day before—either at the TI, or at the West Coast Tours office (see next).

Bus and Island Tour Tickets: West Coast Tours, a block from the train station in the bright-red building along the harbor, sells bus- and island-tour tickets (Tue-Sat 6:30-17:30, Sun-Mon 8:30-17:30, 17 George Street, tel. 01631/566-809, www.westcoasttours.co.uk).

Highland Games: Oban hosts its touristy Highland Games every August (www.obangames.com), and the more local-oriented Lorne Highland Games each June (www.lorne-highland-games.org.uk). Nearby Taynuilt, a 20-minute drive east, hosts their sweetly small-town Highland Games in mid-July (www.taynuilthighlandgames.com).

Tours from Oban

For the best day trip from Oban, tour the islands of Mull, Iona, and/or Staffa (offered daily Easter-Oct, described later)—or consider staying overnight on remote and beautiful Iona. With more time or other interests, consider one of many other options you'll see advertised.

Wildlife Tours

If you just want to go for a boat ride, the easiest option is the one-hour seal-watching tour (£10, various companies—look for signs at the harbor). But to really get a good look at Scottish coastal wildlife, several groups—including **Coastal Connection** (based in Oban) and **Sealife Adventures** and **SeaFari** (based in nearby coastal towns)—run whale-watching tours that seek out rare minke

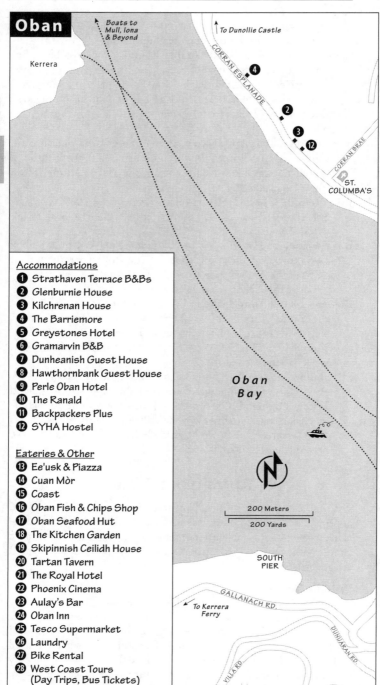

Oban

OBAN & INNER HEBRIDES

Kerrera

Boats to Mull, Iona & Beyond

To Dunollie Castle

CORRAN ESPLANADE

CORRAN BRAE

❹

❷

❸

⓬

ST. COLUMBA'S

Oban Bay

N

200 Meters

200 Yards

SOUTH PIER

GALLANACH RD.

To Kerrera Ferry

VILLA RD.

DUNUARAN RD.

Accommodations

❶ Strathaven Terrace B&Bs
❷ Glenburnie House
❸ Kilchrenan House
❹ The Barriemore
❺ Greystones Hotel
❻ Gramarvin B&B
❼ Dunheanish Guest House
❽ Hawthornbank Guest House
❾ Perle Oban Hotel
❿ The Ranald
⓫ Backpackers Plus
⓬ SYHA Hostel

Eateries & Other

⓭ Ee'usk & Piazza
⓮ Cuan Mòr
⓯ Coast
⓰ Oban Fish & Chips Shop
⓱ Oban Seafood Hut
⓲ The Kitchen Garden
⓳ Skipinnish Ceilidh House
⓴ Tartan Tavern
㉑ The Royal Hotel
㉒ Phoenix Cinema
㉓ Aulay's Bar
㉔ Oban Inn
㉕ Tesco Supermarket
㉖ Laundry
㉗ Bike Rental
㉘ West Coast Tours
    (Day Trips, Bus Tickets)

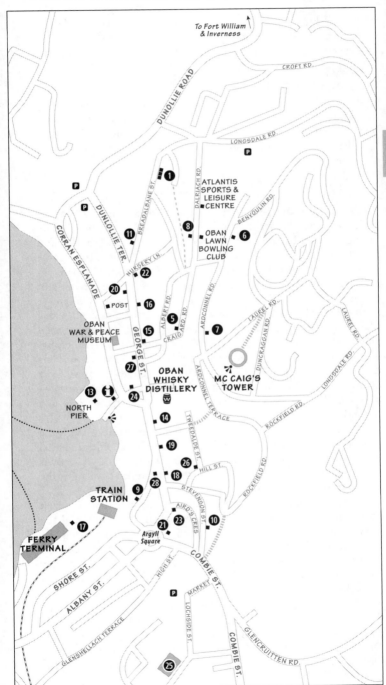

whales, basking sharks, bottlenose dolphins, and porpoises. For an even more ambitious itinerary, the holy grail is Treshnish Island (out past Staffa), which brims with puffins, seals, and other sea critters. Options abound—check at the TI for information.

Open-Top Bus Tours

If the weather is good and you don't have a car, you can go by bus for a spin out of Oban for views of nearby castles and islands, plus a stop near McCaig's Tower with narration by the driver (£7, departs train station 4/day June-Sept only, 1.5 hours, www.citysightseeingoban.com).

Sights in Oban

▲The Burned-Out Sightseer's Visual Tour from the Pier

If the west-coast weather permits, get oriented to the town while taking a break: Head out to the North Pier, just past the TI, and find the benches that face back toward town (in front of the recommended Piazza restaurant). Take a seat and get to know Oban.

Scan the harborfront from left to right, surveying the mix of grand Victorian sandstone buildings and humbler modern storefronts. At the far-right end of town is the **ferry terminal** and—very likely—a huge ferry loading or unloading. Oban has always been on the way to somewhere, and today is no different. (A recent tourism slogan: Oban...it's closer than you think.) The townscape seems dominated by Caledonian-MacBrayne, Scotland's biggest ferry company. CalMac's 30 ships serve 24 destinations and transport over 4 million passengers a year. The town's port has long been a lifeline to the islands.

Hiding near the ferry terminal is the **train station.** With the arrival of the train in 1880, Oban became the unofficial capital of Scotland's west coast and a destination for tourists. Close by is the former Caledonian Hotel, the original terminus hotel (now the Perle Oban Hotel) that once served those train travelers.

Tourism aside, herring was the first big industry. A dozen boats still fish commercially—you'll see them tucked around the ferry terminal. The tourist board, in an attempt to entice tourists to linger longer, is trying to rebrand Oban as a "seafood capital" rather than just the "gateway to the isles." As the ocean's supply has become depleted, most local fish is farmed. There's still plenty of shellfish.

After fishing, big industries here historically included tobacco (imported from the American colonies), then whisky. At the left end of the embankment, find the building marked *Oban Whisky Distillery.* It's rare to find a distillery in the middle of a town, but Oban grew up around this one. With the success of its whisky, the town enjoyed an invigorating confidence, optimism, and, in 1811, a royal charter. Touring Oban's distillery is the best activity in Oban.

Above the distillery, you can't miss the odd mini-Colosseum. This is **McCaig's Tower,** an employ-the-workers-and-build-me-a-fine-memorial project undertaken by an Oban tycoon in 1900. McCaig died before completing the structure, so his complete vision for it remains a mystery. This is an example of a "folly"—that uniquely British notion of an idiosyncratic structure erected by a colorful aristocrat. Building a folly was an in-your-face kind of extravagance many extremely wealthy people enjoyed when surrounded by struggling working-class people (an urge that survives among some of the one percent to this day). While the building itself is nothing to see up close, a 10-minute hike through a Victorian residential neighborhood leads you to a peaceful garden and a commanding view (nice at sunset).

Now turn and look out to sea, and imagine this: At the height of the Cold War, Oban played a critical role when the world's first two-way transatlantic telephone cable was laid from Gallanach Bay to Newfoundland in 1956—a milestone in global communication. This technology later provided the White House and the Kremlin with the "hotline" that was created after the Cuban Missile Crisis to avoid a nuclear conflagration.

▲▲Oban Whisky Distillery Tours

Founded in 1794, Oban Whisky Distillery produces more than 25,000 liters a week, and exports much of that to the US. Their exhibition (upstairs, free to all) gives a quick, whisky-centric history of Oban and Scotland.

The distillery offers serious and fragrant one-hour tours explaining the process from start to finish, with two smooth samples of their signature product: Oban whisky is moderately smoky ("peaty") and characterized by notes of sea salt, citrus, and honey. You'll also receive a whisky glass and a discount coupon for the shop. This is the handiest whisky tour you'll encounter—just a block off the harbor—and one of the best. Come 10 minutes before your tour starts to check out the exhibition upstairs. Then your guide will walk you through each step of the process: malting, mashing, fermentation, distillation, and maturation. Photos are not allowed inside.

Cost and Hours: Tours cost £10, are limited to 16 people and depart every 20 to 30 minutes. Tours fill up, so book in advance by phone, online, or in person to get a firm spot. Unless it's really a busy day, you should be able to drop in and pay for a tour leaving in the next hour or so, then easily pass time in the town center. Generally open July-Sept Mon-Fri 9:30-19:30, Sat-Sun until

17:00; March-June and Oct-Nov daily 9:30-17:30; Dec-Feb daily 12:30-16:00; last tour 1.25 hours before closing, Stafford Street, tel. 01631/572-004, www.discovering-distilleries.com.

Serious Tasting: Connoisseurs can ask about their "exclusive tour," which adds a visit to the warehouse and four premium tastings in the manager's office (£40, 2 hours, likely July-Sept, Mon, Wed, and Fri at 16:00 only, reservation required).

Oban War & Peace Museum

Opened in 1995 on the 50th anniversary of Victory in Europe Day, this charming little museum focuses on Oban's experience during World War II. But it covers more than just war and peace. Photos show Oban through the years, and a 15-minute looped video gives a simple tour around the town and region. Volunteer staffers love to chat about the exhibit—or anything else on your mind (free; May-Oct Mon-Sat 10:00-18:00, Sun until 16:00; off-season daily until 16:00; next to Regent Hotel on the promenade, tel. 01631/570-007, www.obanmuseum.org.uk).

Dunollie Castle and Museum

In a park just a mile up the coast, a ruined castle and an old house hold an intimate collection of clan family treasures. This spartan, stocky castle with 10-foot walls offers a commanding, windy view of the harbor—a strategic spot back in the days when transport was mainly by water. For more than a thousand years, clan chiefs ruled this region from this ancestral home of Clan MacDougall, but the castle was abandoned in 1746. The adjacent house, which dates from 1745, shows off the MacDougall clan's heritage with a handful of rooms filled with a humble yet fascinating trove of treasures. While the exhibit won't dazzle you, the family and clan pride in the display, their "willow garden," and the walk from Oban make the visit fun.

To get there, head out of town along the harborfront promenade. At the war memorial (with inviting seaview benches), cross the street. A gate leads to a little lane, lined with historic and nature boards along the way to the castle.

Cost and Hours: £5.50, April-Oct Mon-Sat 10:00-16:00, Sun from 13:00, closed Nov-March, free tours given most days at 11:00 and 14:00, tel. 01631/570-550, www.dunollie.org.

ACTIVITIES IN OBAN

Atlantis Leisure Centre

This industrial-type sports center is a good place to get some exercise on a rainy day or let the kids run wild for a few hours. It has a rock-climbing wall, tennis courts, indoor "soft play centre" (for kids under 5), and an indoor swimming pool with a big water slide. The outdoor playground is free and open all the time (pool only-

£4.20, no rental towels or suits, fees for other activities; open Mon-Fri 6:30-21:30, Sat-Sun 9:00-18:00; on the north end of Dalriach Road, tel. 01631/566-800, www.atlantisleisure.co.uk).

Oban Lawn Bowling Club
The club has welcomed visitors since 1869. This elegant green is the scene of a wonderfully British spectacle of old men tiptoeing wishfully after their balls. It's fun to watch, and—if there's no match scheduled and the weather's dry—anyone can rent shoes and balls and actually play (£5/person; informal hours, but generally daily 10:00-12:00 & 14:00-16:00 or "however long the weather lasts"; just south of sports center on Dalriach Road, tel. 01631/570-808, www.obanbowlingclub.com).

ISLANDS NEAR OBAN
The isles of Mull, Iona, and Staffa are farther out, require a full day to visit, and are described later in this chapter. For a quicker glimpse at the Inner Hebrides, consider these two options.

Isle of Kerrera
Functioning like a giant breakwater, the Isle of Kerrera (KEH-reh-rah) makes Oban possible. Just offshore from Oban, this stark but very green island offers a quick, easy opportunity to get that romantic island experience. While it has no proper roads, it offers nice hikes, a ruined castle, and a few sheep farms. It's also a fine place to bike (ask for advice at bike-rental shop). You may see the Kerrera ferry filled with sheep heading for Oban's livestock market.

Getting There: You have two options for reaching the island. A boat operated by the Oban Marina goes from Oban's North Pier to the Kerrera Marina in the northern part of the island (£5 round-trip, every two hours, book ahead at tel. 01631/565-333, www.obanmarina.com).

A ferry departs from Gallanach (two miles south of Oban) and goes to the middle of the island. This is the best option if you want to hike to Kerrera's castle (passengers only, £4.50 round-trip, bikes free, runs 10:30-18:00 with a break 12:30-14:00, none in off-season, 5-minute ride, tel. 01475/650-397, www.calmac.co.uk). To reach Gallanach, drive south, following the coast road past the ferry terminal (parking available).

Eating and Sleeping on Kerrera: $$ Waypoint Bar & Grill has a laid-back patio with a simple menu of steak, burgers, and seafood; on a nice day the open-air waterside setting is unbeatable (late May-Sept Tue-Sun 18:00-21:00, bar opens at 17:00, closed Mon and in winter, reservations highly recommended, tel. 01631/565-333, www.obanmarina.com). For lodging, your only option is the **$ Kerrera Bunkhouse,** a refurbished 18th-century stable that can sleep up to seven people in a small, cozy space (1 double and 5 single bunks, 2-night minimum, includes bedding but not towels, open Easter-Oct but must book ahead, kitchen, tel. 01631/566-367, www.kerrerabunkhouse.co.uk, info@kerrerabunkhouse.co.uk, Martin and Aideen). They also run a tea garden that serves meals (Easter-Sept daily 10:30-16:30, closed Oct-Easter).

Isle of Seil

Enjoy a drive, a walk, some solitude, and the sea. Drive 12 miles south of Oban on the A-816 to the B-844 to the Isle of Seil (pronounced "seal"), connected to the mainland by a bridge (which, locals like to brag, "crosses the Atlantic"...well, maybe a small part of it).

Just over the bridge on the Isle of Seil is a pub called **Tigh-an-Truish** ("House of Trousers"). After the Jacobite rebellions, a new law forbade the wearing of kilts on the mainland. Highlanders on the island used this pub to change from kilts to trousers before they made the crossing. The pub serves great meals and good seafood dishes to those either in kilts or pants (pub generally open daily—call ahead, tel. 01852/300-242).

Seven miles across the island, on a tiny second island and facing the open Atlantic, is **Easdale,** a historic, touristy, windblown little slate-mining town—with a slate-town museum and an egomaniac's incredibly tacky "Highland Arts" shop (shuttle ferry goes the 300 yards). Expensive wildlife/nature tours plus tours to Iona and Staffa also run from Easdale (www.seafari.co.uk).

Nightlife in Oban

Little Oban has a few options for entertaining its many visitors; check www.obanwhatson.co.uk. Fun low-key activities may include open-mic, disco, or quiz theme nights in pubs; occasional Scottish folk shows; coffee meetings; and—if you're lucky—duck races. On Wednesday nights, the Oban Pipe Band plays in the square by the train station. Here are a few other ways to entertain yourself while in town.

Music and Group Dancing: On many summer nights, you can climb the stairs to the **Skipinnish Ceilidh House,** a sprawling venue on the main drag for music and dancing (the owners are professional musicians Angus and Andrew). There's *ceilidh* (KAY-lee) dancing a couple of times per week, where you can learn some group dances to music performed by a folk band (including, usually, a piper). These group dances are a lot of fun—wallflowers and bad dancers are warmly welcomed, and the staff is happy to give you pointers (£8, May-Sept Mon & Thu at 21:00). They also host concerts by folk and traditional bands (check website for schedule, 34

George Street, tel. 01631/569-599, www.skipinnishceilidhhouse.com).

Traditional Music: Various pubs and hotels in town have live traditional music in the summer; as specifics change from year to year, ask your B&B host or the TI for the latest. Try the **Tartan Tavern,** a block off the waterfront at 3 Albany Terrace or **The Royal Hotel,** just above the train station on Argyll Square.

Cinema: The Phoenix Cinema closed down for two years and then was saved by the community. It's now volunteer-run and booming (140 George Street, tel. 01631/562-905, www.obanphoenix.com).

Characteristic Pubs: Aulay's Bar, with decor that shows off Oban's maritime heritage, has two sides, each with a different personality (I like the right-hand side). Having a drink here invariably comes with a good "blether" (conversation), and the gang is local (daily 11:00-24:00, 8 Airds Crescent, just around the corner from the train station and ferry terminal). The **Oban Inn,** right on the harborfront, is also a fun and memorable place for a pint and possibly live music.

Sleeping in Oban

Oban's B&Bs offer a much better value than its hotels.

ON STRATHAVEN TERRACE

The following B&Bs line up on a quiet, flowery street that's nicely located two blocks off the harbor, three blocks from the center, and a 10-minute walk from the train station. Rooms here are more compact than those on the Esplanade and don't have views, but the location can't be beat.

By car, as you enter town from the north, turn left immediately after King's Knoll Hotel, and take your first right onto Breadalbane Street. ("Strathaven Terrace" is actually just the name for this row of houses on Breadalbane Street.) The alley behind the buildings has tight, free parking for all of these places.

$$ Rose Villa Guest House has six crisp and cheery rooms (at #5, tel. 01631/566-874, stuartcameronsmith@yahoo.co.uk, Stuart and Jacqueline).

$ Raniven Guest House has five simple, tastefully decorated rooms and gracious, fun-loving hosts Moyra and Stuart (cash only, 2-night minimum in summer, continental breakfast, at #1, tel. 01631/562-713, www.ranivenoban.com, bookings@ranivenoban.com).

$ Sandvilla B&B rents five pleasant, polished rooms (2-night minimum in summer, at #4, tel. 01631/564-483, www.

holidayoban.co.uk, sandvilla@holidayoban.co.uk, Josephine and Robert).

ALONG THE ESPLANADE

These are along the Corran Esplanade, which stretches north of town above a cobble beach; they are a 10-minute walk from the center. For the most part, they offer much more spacious rooms than places in town (and many rooms have beautiful bay views). Walking from town, you'll reach them in this order: Kilchrenan, Glenburnie, and Barriemore.

$$ Glenburnie House, a stately Victorian home, has an elegant breakfast room overlooking the bay. Its 12 spacious, comfortable, classy rooms feel like plush living rooms. There's a nice lounge and a tiny sunroom with a stuffed "hairy coo" head (closed mid-Nov-March, tel. 01631/562-089, www.glenburnie.co.uk, stay@glenburnie.co.uk, Graeme).

$$ Kilchrenan House, the turreted former retreat of a textile magnate, has 16 large rooms, most with bay views. The stunning rooms #5, #9, and #15 are worth the few extra pounds, while the "standard" rooms in the newer annex are a good value (2-night minimum in summer, welcome drink of whisky or sherry, different "breakfast special" every day, family rooms, closed Nov-Feb, tel. 01631/562-663, www.kilchrenanhouse.co.uk, info@kilchrenanhouse.co.uk, Colin and Frances).

$$ The Barriemore, at the very end of Oban's grand waterfront Esplanade, is a welcome refuge after a day of exploration. Its 14 well-appointed rooms come with robes, sherry, etc. It has a nice front patio, spacious breakfast room, and glassed-in sun porch with a view of the water (family suite, tel. 01631/566-356, www.barriemore.co.uk, info@barriemore.co.uk, Jan and Mark).

ABOVE THE TOWN CENTER

These places perch on the hill above the main waterfront zone—a short (but uphill) walk from all of the action. Many rooms come with views, and are priced accordingly.

$$$ Greystones is an enticing splurge. It fills a big, stately, turreted mansion at the top of town with five spacious rooms that mix Victorian charm and sleek gray-and-white minimalism. Built as the private home for the director of Kimberley Diamond Mine, it later became a maternity hospital, and today Mark and Suzanne have turned it into a stylish and restful retreat. The lounge and breakfast room offer stunning views over Oban and the offshore isles (closed Nov-mid-Feb, 13 Dalriach Road, tel. 01631/358-653, www.greystonesoban.co.uk, stay@greystonesoban.co.uk).

$$ Gramarvin B&B feels a little more homey and personal, with just two rooms and warm host Mary. Window seats in each room provide a lovely view over Oban, but be warned—the climb up from town and then up their stairs is steep (skip breakfast to save a few pounds, cash only, 2-night minimum in summer preferred, on-street parking, Benvoulin Road, tel. 01631/564-622, www. gramarvin.co.uk, mary@gramarvin.co.uk, Mary and Joe).

$$ Dunheanish Guest House offers six pleasant rooms (two on the ground floor) and wide-open views from its perch above town, which you can enjoy from the front stone patio, breakfast room, and several guest rooms (parking, Ardconnel Road, tel. 01631/566-556, www.dunheanish.com, info@dunheanish.com, William and Linda).

$ Hawthornbank Guest House fills a big Victorian sandstone house with seven traditional-feeling rooms. Half of the rooms face bay views, and the other half overlook the town's lawn bowling green (2-night minimum in summer, Dalriach Road, tel. 01631/562-041, www.hawthornbank.co.uk, info@hawthornbank. co.uk).

HOTELS IN THE TOWN CENTER

A number of hotels are in the center of town along or near the main drag—but you'll pay heavily for the convenience.

$$$$ Perle Oban Hotel is your luxury boutique splurge. Right across from the harbor, it has 59 super-sleek rooms with calming sea-color walls, decorative bath tile floors, and rain showers (suites, fancy restaurant, bar with light bites, pay parking, Station Square, tel. 01631/700-301, www.perleoban.com, stay@ perleoban.com).

$$$ The Ranald is a modern change of pace from the B&B scene in Oban. This narrow, 17-room, three-floor hotel has a budget-boutique vibe going (family rooms, bar, no elevator, street or off-site parking, a block behind the Royal Hotel at 41 Stevenson Street, tel. 01631/562-887, www.theranaldhotel.com, info@ theranaldhotel.com).

HOSTELS

¢ Backpackers Plus is central, laid-back, and fun. It fills part of a renovated old church with a sprawling public living room, 47 beds, and a staff generous with travel tips. Check out the walls as you go up to the reception desk—they're covered with graffiti messages from guests (includes breakfast, great shared kitchen, pay laundry service, 10-minute walk from station, on Breadalbane Street, tel. 01631/567-189, www.backpackersplus.com, info@ backpackersplus.com, Peter). They have two other locations nearby with private rooms.

¢ The official **SYHA hostel,** on the scenic waterfront Esplanade, is in a grand building with 87 beds and smashing views of the harbor and islands from the lounges and dining rooms. While institutional, this place is quite nice (all rooms en suite, private rooms available, also has family rooms and 8-bed apartment with kitchen, breakfast extra, pay laundry, kitchen, tel. 01631/562-025, www.syha.org.uk, oban@syha.org.uk).

Eating in Oban

Oban brags that it is the "seafood capital of Scotland," and indeed its sit-down restaurants (listed first) are surprisingly high-quality for such a small town. For something more casual, consider a fish-and-chips joint.

SIT-DOWN RESTAURANTS

These fill up in summer, especially on weekends. To ensure getting a table, you'll want to book ahead. The first four are generally open daily from 12:00-15:00 and 17:30-21:00.

$$$ Ee'usk (Scottish Gaelic for "fish") is a popular, stylish place on the waterfront. It has a casual-chic, yacht-clubby atmosphere, with a bright and glassy interior and sweeping views on three sides—fun for watching the ferries come and go. They sometimes offer an early-bird special until 18:45, and their seafood platters are a hit. Reservations are recommended (no kids under age 12 at dinner, North Pier, tel. 01631/565-666, www.eeusk.com, MacLeod family).

$$$ Cuan Mòr is a popular, casual restaurant that combines traditional Scottish food with modern flair—both in its crowd-pleasing cuisine and in its furnishings, made of wood, stone, and metal scavenged from the beaches of Scotland's west coast (brewery in back, 60 George Street, tel. 01631/565-078). Its harborside tables on the sidewalk are popular when it's warm.

$$$$ Coast proudly serves fresh local fish, meat, and veggies in a mod pine-and-candlelight atmosphere. As everything is cooked to order and presented with care by husband-and-wife team Richard and Nicola—who try to combine traditional Scottish elements in innovative new ways—this is no place to dine and dash (two- and three-course specials, closed Sun for lunch, 104 George Street, tel. 01631/569-900, www.coastoban.co.uk).

$$ Piazza, next door to Ee'usk, is a casual, family-friendly place serving basic Italian dishes with a great harborfront location. They have some outdoor seats and big windows facing the sea (smart to reserve ahead July-Aug, tel. 01631/563-628, www.piazzaoban.com).

$$ Oban Fish and Chips Shop—run by Lewis, Sammy, and their family—serves praiseworthy haddock and mussels among other tasty options in a cheery cabana-like dining room. Consider venturing away from basic fish-and-chips into a world of more creative seafood dishes—like their tiny squat lobster. You can bring your own wine for no charge (daily, sit-down restaurant closes at 21:00, takeaway available later, 116 George Street, tel. 01631/567-000).

LUNCH

$ **Oban Seafood Hut,** in a green shack facing the ferry dock, is a finger-licking festival of cheap and fresh seafood. John and Marion regularly get fresh deliveries from local fishermen—this is the best spot to pick up a seafood sandwich or a snack. They sell smaller bites (such as cold sandwiches), as well as some bigger cold platters and a few hot dishes (picnic tables nearby, daily from 10:00 until the boat unloads from Mull around 18:00).

$ **The Kitchen Garden** is fine for soup, salad, or sandwiches. It's a deli and gourmet-foods store with a charming café upstairs (daily 9:00-17:30, 14 George Street, tel. 01631/566-332).

Oban Connections

By Train from Oban: Trains link Oban to the nearest transportation hub in **Glasgow** (6/day, fewer on Sun, 3 hours); to get to **Edinburgh,** you'll have to transfer in Glasgow (5/day, 4.5 hours). To reach **Fort William** (a transit hub for the Highlands), you'll take the same Glasgow-bound train, but transfer in Crianlarich (3/day, 4 hours)—the direct bus is easier (see next). Oban's small train station has a ticket window and lockers (both open Mon-Sat 5:00-20:30, Sun 10:45-18:00, train info tel. 0845-748-4950, www.nationalrail.co.uk).

By Bus: Bus #918 passes through Ballachulish—a half-mile from **Glencoe**—on its way to **Fort William** (2/day, 1 hour to Ballachulish, 1.5 hours total to Fort William). Take this bus to Fort William, then transfer to reach **Inverness** (4 hours) or **Portree** on the Isle of Skye (5 hours)—see page 137 for onward bus information. A different bus (#976 or #977) connects Oban with **Glasgow** (5/day, 3 hours), from where you can easily connect by bus or train to **Edinburgh** (figure 4.5 hours). Buses arrive and depart from a roundabout, marked by a stubby clock tower, just before the entrance to the train station (tel. 0871-266-3333, www.citylink.co.uk). You can buy bus tickets at the West Coast shop near the bus stop, or at the TI across the harbor. Book in advance during peak times.

By Boat: Ferries fan out from Oban to the **southern Hebrides** (see information on the islands of Iona and Mull, later). Caledonian MacBrayne Ferry info: Tel. 01631/566-688, free booking tel. 0800-066-5000, www.calmac.co.uk.

ROUTE TIPS FOR DRIVERS

From Glasgow to Oban via Loch Lomond and Inveraray: For details on the most scenic route from Glasgow to Oban, see "Near Oban" on page 49.

From Oban to Glencoe and Fort William: It's an easy one-hour drive from Oban to Glencoe. From Oban, follow the coastal A-828 toward Fort William. After about 20 miles—as you leave the village of Appin—you'll see the photogenic **Castle Stalker** marooned on a lonely island (you can pull over at the Castle Stalker View Café for a good photo from just below its parking lot). At North Ballachulish, you'll reach a bridge spanning Loch Leven; rather than crossing the bridge, turn off and follow the A-82 into the Glencoe Valley for about 15 minutes. (For tips on the best views and hikes in Glencoe, see the next chapter.) After exploring the dramatic valley, make a U-turn and return through Glencoe village. To continue on to Fort William, backtrack to the bridge at North Ballachulish (great view from bridge) and cross it, following the A-82 north.

For a scenic shortcut directly back to Glasgow or Edinburgh, continue south on the A-82 after Glencoe via Rannoch Moor and Tyndrum. Crianlarich is where the road splits, and you'll either continue on the A-82 toward Loch Lomond and Glasgow or pick up the A-85 and follow signs for Stirling, then Edinburgh.

Isles of Mull, Iona, and Staffa

For the easiest one-day look at a good sample of the dramatic and historic Inner Hebrides (HEB-rid-eez) islands, take a tour from Oban to Mull, Iona, and Staffa. Though this trip is spectacular when it's sunny, it's worthwhile in any weather (but if rain or rough seas are expected, I'd skip the Staffa option). For an even more in-depth look at the Inner Hebrides, head north to Skye.

GETTING AROUND THE ISLANDS
Visiting Mull and Iona

To visit Mull and ultimately Iona, you'll take a huge ferry run by Caledonian MacBrayne (CalMac) from Oban to the town of Craignure on Mull (45 minutes). From there, you'll ride a bus or drive across Mull to its westernmost ferry terminal, called Fionnphort (1.25 hours), where you can catch the ferry to Iona (10 minutes). It's a long journey, but it's all incredibly scenic; you also get about two hours of free time on Iona. There are several ways to do this.

By Tour (Easiest): If you book a tour with **West Coast Tours,**

all of the transportation is taken care of. The Cal-Mac ferry leaves from the Oban pier daily at 9:50 (as schedule can change from year to year, confirm times locally; board at least 20 minutes before departure). You can buy tickets online at www.westcoasttours.co.uk, from the West Coast

Tours office, or from the Tour Shop Oban at the ferry building (tel. 01631/562-244, tourshop@calmac.co.uk). Book as far in advance as possible for July and August (tickets can sell out). When you book their tour, you'll receive a strip of tickets—one for each leg; if you book online, you must go to the West Coast Tours office and collect tickets in person (£35; April-Oct only, no tours Nov-March).

Tour Tips: The best inside seats on the **Oban-Mull ferry**—with the biggest windows—are in the sofa lounge on the "observation deck" (level 4) at the back end of the boat. (Follow signs for the toilets, and look for the big staircase to the top floor). The ferry has a fine cafeteria with hot meals and packaged sandwiches, a small snack bar on the top floor (hot drinks and basic sandwiches), and a bookshop. If it's a clear day, ask a local or a crew member to point out Ben Nevis, the tallest mountain in Britain. Five minutes before landing on Mull, you'll see the striking 13th-century Duart Castle on the left.

Walk-on passengers disembark from deck 3, across from the bookshop (port side). Upon arrival in Mull, find your **bus** for the entertaining and informative ride across the Isle of Mull. The right (driver's) side offers better sea views during the second half of the journey to Fionnphort, while the left side has fine views of Mull's rolling wilderness. The driver spends the entire ride chattering away about life on Mull, slowing to point out wildlife, and sharing adages like, "If there's no flowers on the gorse, snogging's gone out of fashion." These hardworking locals make historical trivia fascinating—or at least fun. At Fionnphort, you'll board a small, rocking **ferry to Iona.** You'll have about two hours to roam freely around the island before returning to Oban (arrives around 18:00).

By Public Transit: If you want an early start (and want to avoid some crowds), have more time on Iona (including spending the night—see "Sleeping and Eating on Iona"), or don't get a space on the tour described earlier, you can take the early ferry and public bus across Mull, paying individually per leg (Tue-Sat only; ap-

OBAN & INNER HEBRIDES

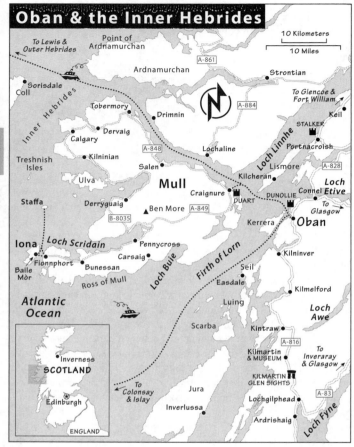

Oban & the Inner Hebrides

To Lewis &
Outer Hebrides
Point of
Ardnamurchan
Strontian
10 Kilometers
10 Miles

Sorisdale
Coll
Ardnamurchan
A-861
To Glencoe &
Fort William
Keil
Tobermory
Drimnin
STALKER
A-884
Dervaig
Calgary
Portnacroish
Kilninian
Lochaline
A-828
Treshnish
Isles
Salen
Lismore
Ulva
Kilcheran
Staffa
Mull
Craignure
DUART
DUNOLLIE
Connel
Loch
Etive
Derryguaig
▲ Ben More
A-849
Kerrera
To
Glasgow
Oban
B-8035

Iona
Loch Scridain
Pennycross
Kilninver
Fionnphort
Carsaig
Seil
Baile
Mòr
Bunessan
Ross of Mull
Easdale
Kilmelford

**Atlantic
Ocean**
Luing
Loch
Awe
Scarba
Kintraw
A-816

To
Inveraray
& Glasgow
Kilmartin
& MUSEUM
SCOTLAND
Inverness
KILMARTIN
GLEN SIGHTS
Edinburgh
To
Colonsay
& Islay
Jura
Lochgilphead
A-83
Inverlussa
Ardrishaig
Loch Fyne
ENGLAND

proximate round-trip prices: £7 for Oban-Mull ferry, £15 for public bus across Mull, £3.50 for Mull-Iona ferry).

Take the first boat of the day (departs about 7:30, buy ticket at Oban ferry terminal), then connect at Mull to bus #496 to Fionnphort (departs 8:25, 80 minutes, buy ticket from driver, no tour narration, no guarantee you'll get to sit), then hop on the Iona ferry (every 30 minutes, buy ticket from small trailer ferry office; if closed, purchase ticket from ferry worker at the dock; cash or credit/debit cards accepted; leaving Iona, do the same, as there's no ferry office). You'll have about four hours on Iona and will need to return to Fionnphort in time for the bus back (15:15). It's important to confirm all of these times locally (just pop in to the West Coast Tours office or the ferry terminal Tour Shop).

By Car: You can do this trip on your own by driving your car onto the ferry to Mull, but space is limited so book way in advance.

Because of tight ferry timings, you'll wind up basically following the tour buses anyway, you'll miss all of the commentary, and no visitor cars are allowed on Iona (£26 round-trip for the car, plus passengers, www.calmac.co.uk).

Visiting Staffa

With two extra hours, you can add a side-trip to Staffa along with your Mull/Iona visit. You'll ferry from Oban to Mull, take a bus across Mull to Fionnphort, then board a **Staffa Tours** boat (35-minute trip, about an hour of free time on Staffa). From Staffa you'll head to Iona for about two hours before returning to Mull for the bus then ferry back to Oban. You can either depart on the 9:50 ferry, returning around 20:05 (£60) or do the "early bird" tour (£55, Tue-Sat only, depart at 7:30, return 18:00; book through West Coast Tours or Staffa Tours—mobile 07831-885-985, www.staffatours.com).

For a bit more relaxed schedule, **Staffa Trips** offers a guided tour with the same route as the one above, but with more time on Staffa and Iona (£60, Tue-Sat only, depart at 7:30, return 19:10, tel. 01681/700-358, www.staffatrips.co.uk).

Turus Mara offers nature/wildlife tours to just Staffa or Staffa and the small island of Ulva, departing from Oban (book at Tour Shop at Oban ferry terminal or contact Turus Mara—tel. 01688/400-242, www.turusmara.com).

Mull

The Isle of Mull, the second largest of the Inner Hebrides (after Skye), has nearly 300 scenic miles of coastline and castles and a 3,169-foot-high mountain, one of Scotland's Munros. Called Ben More ("Big Mountain" in Gaelic), it was once much bigger. At 10,000 feet tall, it made up the entire island of Mull—until a volcano erupted. Things are calmer now, and, similarly, Mull has a  noticeably laidback population. My bus driver reported that there are no deaths from stress, and only a few from boredom.

With steep, fog-covered hillsides topped by cairns (piles of stones, sometimes indicating graves) and ancient stone circles, Mull has a gloomy, otherworldly charm. Bring plenty of rain protection and wear layers in case the sun peeks through the clouds.

As my driver said, Mull is a place of cold, wet, windy winters and mild, wet, windy summers.

On the far side of Mull, the caravan of tour buses unloads at Fionnphort, a tiny ferry town. The ferry to the island of Iona takes about 200 walk-on passengers. Confirm the return time with your bus driver, then hustle to the dock to make the first trip over (otherwise, it's a 30-minute wait; on very busy days, those who dillydally may not fit on the first ferry). At the dock, there's a small ferry-passenger building with a meager snack bar and a pay WC; a more enticing seafood bar is across the street. After the 10-minute ride, you wash ashore on sleepy Iona (free WC on this side), and the ferry mobs that crowded you on the boat seem to disappear up the main road and into Iona's back lanes.

The **About Mull Tours and Taxi** service can get you around Mull (tel. 01681/700-507 or mobile 0788-777-4550, www. aboutmull.co.uk). They also do day tours of Mull, focusing on local history and wildlife (half-day tours also available, or ask about shorter Mull tour combined with drop-off and pick-up at Fionnphort ferry dock for quick Iona trip, minimum 2 people, must book ahead).

Iona

The tiny island of Iona, just 3 miles by 1.5 miles, is famous as the birthplace of Christianity in Scotland. If you're on a day trip, you'll have about two hours here on your own before you retrace your steps (your bus driver will tell you which return ferry to take back to Mull).

A pristine quality of light and a thoughtful peace pervades the stark, (nearly) car-free island and its tiny community. With buoyant clouds bouncing playfully off distant bluffs, sparkling-white crescents of sand, and lone tourists camped thoughtfully atop huge rocks just looking out to sea, Iona is a place that's perfect for meditation. To experience Iona, it's important to get out and take a little hike; you can follow some or all of my self-guided walk outlined later. And you can easily climb a peak—nothing's higher than 300 feet above the sea.

History of Iona

St. Columba (521-597), an Irish scholar, soldier, priest, and founder of monasteries, got into a small war over the posses-

sion of an illegally copied psalm book. Victorious but sickened by the bloodshed, Columba left Ireland, vowing never to return. According to legend, the first bit of land out of sight of his homeland was Iona. He stopped here in 563 and established an abbey.

Columba's monastic community flourished, and Iona became the center of Celtic Christianity. Missionaries from Iona spread the gospel throughout Scotland and northern England, while scholarly monks established Iona as a center of art and learning. The *Book of Kells*—perhaps the finest piece of art from Dark Ages Europe—was probably made on Iona in the eighth century.

The island was so important that it was the legendary burial place for ancient Scottish clan chieftains and kings (including Macbeth, of Shakespeare fame) and even some Scandinavian monarchs.

Slowly, the importance of Iona ebbed. Vikings massacred 68 monks in 806. Fearing more raids, the monks evacuated most of Iona's treasures to Ireland (including the *Book of Kells*, which is now in Dublin). Much later, with the Reformation, the abbey was abandoned, and most of its finely carved crosses were destroyed. In the 17th century, locals used the abbey only as a handy quarry for other building projects.

Iona's population peaked at about 500 in the 1830s. In the 1840s, a potato famine hit, and in the 1850s, a third of the islanders emigrated to Canada or Australia. By 1900, the population was down to 210, and today it's only around 200.

But in our generation, a new religious community has given the abbey fresh life. The Iona Community is an ecumenical gathering of men and women who seek new ways of living the Gospel in today's world, with a focus on worship, peace and justice issues, and reconciliation (http://iona.org.uk).

Orientation to Iona

The ferry arrives at the island's only real village, Baile Mòr, with shops, a restaurant/pub, a few accommodations, and no bank (get cash back with a purchase at the grocery store). The only taxi on Iona is **Iona Taxi** (mobile 07810-325-990, www.ionataxi.co.uk). Up the road from the ferry dock is a little **Spar** grocery with free island maps. Iona's official website (www.isle-of-iona.net) has good information about the island.

Iona Walk

Here's a basic self-guided route for exploring Iona on foot (since no private cars are permitted unless you're a resident or have a permit). With the standard two hours on Iona that a day trip allows, you will have time for a visit to the abbey (with a guided tour and/or audioguide) and then a light stroll; or do the entire walk described below, but skip the abbey (unless you have time for a quick visit on your way back).

Nunnery Ruins: From the ferry dock, head directly up the single paved road that passes through the village and up a small hill to visit one of Britain's best-preserved medieval nunneries (free).

Immediately after the nunnery, turn right on North Road. You'll curve up through the fields—passing the parish church.

Heritage Center: This little museum, tucked behind the church (watch for signs), is small but well done, with displays on local and natural history and a tiny tearoom (free but donation requested, closed Sun and in off-season, tel. 01681/700-576, www.ionaheritage.co.uk).

St. Oran's Chapel and Iona Abbey: Continue on North Road. After the road swings right, you'll soon see **St. Oran's Chapel,** in the graveyard of the Iona Abbey. This chapel is the oldest church building on the island. Inside you'll find a few grave slabs carved in the distinctive Iona School style, which was developed by local stone-carvers in the 14th century. On these tall, skinny headstones, look for the depictions of medieval warrior aristocrats with huge swords. Many more of these carvings have been moved to the abbey, where you can see them in its cloister and museum.

It's free to see the graveyard and chapel; the ▲Iona Abbey itself has an admission fee, but it's worth the cost just to sit in the stillness of its lovely, peaceful interior courtyard (£7.50, tel. 01681/700-512, www.historicenvironment.scot—search for "Iona Abbey").

The abbey marks the site of Christianity's arrival in Scotland.

You'll see Celtic crosses, the original shrine of St. Columba, a big church slathered with medieval carvings, a tranquil cloister, and an excellent museum with surviving fragments of this site's fascinating layers of history. While the present abbey, nunnery, and graveyard go back to the 13th century, much of what you'll see was rebuilt in the 20th century. Be sure to read the "History of Iona" sidebar to prepare for your visit.

At the entrance building, pick up your included audioguide, and ask about the good 30-minute guided tours (4/day and worthwhile). Then head toward the church. You'll pass two faded **Celtic crosses** (and the base of a third); the originals are in the museum at the end of your visit. Some experts believe that Celtic crosses—with their distinctive shape so tied to Christianity on the British Isles—originated right here on Iona.

Facing the entrance to the church, you'll see the original **shrine to St. Columba** on your left—a magnet for pilgrims.

Head inside the **church.** It feels like an active church—with hymnals neatly stacked in the pews—because it is, thanks to the Iona Community. While much of this space has been rebuilt, take a moment to look around. Plenty of original medieval stone carving (especially the capitals of many columns) still survives. To see a particularly striking example, stand near the pulpit in the middle of the church and look back to the entrance. Partway up the left span of the pointed arch framing the transept, look for the eternally screaming face. While interpretations vary, this may have been a reminder for the priest not to leave out the fire-and-brimstone parts of his message. Some of the newer features of the church—including the base of the baptismal font near the entrance, and the main altar—are carved from locally quarried Iona marble: white with green streaks. In the right/south transept is the tomb of George Campbell—the Eighth Duke of Argyll, who donated this property in 1900, allowing it to be restored.

When you're ready to continue, find the poorly marked door into the **cloister.** (As you face the altar, it's about halfway down the nave on the left, before the transept.) This space is filled with harmonious light, additional finely carved capitals (these are modern re-creations), and—displayed along the walls—several more of the tall, narrow tombstones  like the ones displayed in St. Oran's Chapel. On these, look for a couple of favorite motifs: the long, intimidating sword (indicating a warrior of the Highland clans) and the ship with billowing sails (a powerful symbol of this seafaring culture).

Around the far side of the cloister is the shop. But before leaving, don't overlook the easy-to-miss **museum.** (To find it, head outside and walk around the left side of the abbey complex, toward the sea.) This modern, well-presented space exhibits a remarkable collection of original stonework from the abbey—including what's left of the three Celtic crosses out front—all eloquently described.

Take some time to linger and make sure you've seen all you want to see. Then go in peace.

Iona Community's Welcome Centre: Just beyond and across the road from the abbey is the Iona Community's Welcome Centre (free WCs), which runs the abbey with Historic Scotland and hosts modern-day pilgrims who come here to experience the birthplace of Scottish Christianity. (If you're staying longer, you could attend a worship service at the abbey—check the schedule here; tel. 01681/700-404, www.iona.org.uk.) Its gift shop is packed with books on the island's important role in Christian history.

Views: A 10-minute walk on North Road past the welcome center brings you to the footpath for **Dùn Ì,** a steep but short climb with good views of the abbey looking back toward Mull.

North Beach: Returning to the main road, walk another 20-25 minutes to the end of the paved road, where you'll arrive at a gate leading through a sheep- and cow-strewn pasture to Iona's pristine white-sand beach. Dip your toes in the Atlantic and ponder what this Caribbean-like alcove is doing in Scotland. Be sure to allow at least 40 minutes to return to the ferry dock.

Sleeping and Eating on Iona

For a chance to really experience peaceful, idyllic Iona, spend a night or two (Scots bring their kids and stay on this tiny island for a week). To do so, you'll have to buy each leg of the ferry-bus-ferry (and return) trip separately (see "By Public Transit," earlier). These accommodations are listed roughly in the order you'll reach them as you climb the main road from the ferry dock. The first two hotels listed have **$$$** restaurants that are open to the public for lunch, tea, and dinner and closed in winter. For more accommodation options, see www.isle-of-iona.net/accommodation.

$$ Argyll Hotel, built in 1867, proudly overlooks the waterfront, with 17 cottage-like rooms and pleasingly creaky hallways lined with bookshelves. Of the two hotels, this one feels classier (reserve far in advance for summer, comfortable lounge and sunroom, tel. 01681/700-334, www.argyllhoteliona.co.uk, reception@argyllhoteliona.co.uk).

$$$$ St. Columba Hotel, a bit higher up in town and situated in the middle of a peaceful garden with picnic tables, has 27 institutional rooms and spacious lodge-like common spaces—such as a big, cushy seaview lounge (closed Nov-March, next door to abbey on road up from dock, tel. 01681/700-304, www.stcolumba-hotel.co.uk, info@stcolumba-hotel.co.uk).

$ Calva B&B, a five-minute walk past the abbey, has three spacious rooms (second house on left past the abbey, look for sign in window and gnomes on porch, tel. 01681/700-340; friendly Janetta and Ken).

Staffa

Those more interested in nature than in church history will enjoy the trip to the wildly scenic Isle of Staffa. Completely uninhabited (except for seabirds), Staffa is a knob of rock draped with a vibrant green carpet of turf. Remote and quiet, it feels like a Hebrides nature preserve.

Most day trips give you an hour on Staffa—barely enough time to see its two claims to fame: The basalt columns of Fingal's

Cave, and (in summer) a colony of puffins. To squeeze in both, be ready to hop off the boat and climb the staircase. Partway up to the left, you can walk around to the cave (about 7 minutes). Or continue up to the top, then turn right and walk across the spine of the grassy island (about 10-15 minutes) to the cove where the puffins gather. (Your captain should point out both options and let you know how active the puffins have been.)

▲▲Fingal's Cave

Staffa's shore is covered with bizarre, mostly hexagonal basalt columns that stick up at various heights. It's as if the earth were

offering God his choice of thousands of six-sided cigarettes. (The island's name likely came from the Old Norse word for "stave"—the building timbers these columns resemble.) This is the other end of Northern Ireland's popular Giant's Causeway. You'll walk along the uneven surface of these columns, curling around the far side of the island, until you can actually step inside the gaping mouth of a cave—where floor-to-ceiling columns and crashing waves combine to create a powerful experience. Listening to

Puffins

The Atlantic puffin (Fratercula arctica) is an adorably stout, tuxedo-clad seabird with a too-big orange beak and beady black eyes. Puffins live most of their lives on the open Atlantic, coming to land only to breed. They fly north to Scotland between mid-May and early June, raise their brood, then take off again late in August. Puffins mate for life and typically lay just one egg each year, which the male and female take turns caring for. A baby puffin is called—wait for it—a puffling.

To feed their pufflings, puffins plunge as deep as 200 feet below the sea's surface to catch sand eels, herring, and other small fish. Their compact bodies, stubby wings, oil-sealed plumage, and webbed feet are ideal for navigating underwater. Famously, puffins can stuff several small fish into their beaks at once, thanks to their agile tongues and uniquely hinged beaks. This evolutionary trick lets puffins stock up before returning to the nest.

Stocky, tiny-winged puffins have a distinctive way of flying. To take off, they either beat their wings like crazy (on sea) or essentially hurl themselves off a cliff (on land). Once aloft, they beat their wings furiously—up to 400 times per minute—to stay airborne. Coming in for a smooth landing on a rocky cliff is a challenge (and highly entertaining to watch): They choose a spot, swoop in at top speed on prevailing currents, then flutter their wings madly to brake as they try to touch down. At the moment of truth, the puffin decides whether to attempt to stick the landing; more often than not, he bails out and does another big circle on the currents...and tries again... and again...and again.

the water and air flowing through this otherworldly space inspired Felix Mendelssohn to compose his overture, *The Hebrides.*

While you're ogling the cave, consider this: Geologists claim these unique formations were created by volcanic eruptions more than 60 million years ago. As the surface of the lava flow quickly cooled, it contracted and crystallized into columns (resembling the caked mud at the bottom of a dried-up lakebed, but with deeper cracks). As the rock later settled and eroded, the columns broke off into the many stair-like steps that now honeycomb Staffa.

Of course, in actuality, these

formations resulted from a heated rivalry between a Scottish giant named Fingal, who lived on Staffa, and an Ulster warrior named Finn MacCool, who lived across the sea on Ireland's Antrim Coast. Knowing that the giant was coming to spy on him, Finn had his wife dress him as a sleeping infant. The giant, shocked at the infant's size, fled back to Scotland in terror of whomever had sired this giant baby. Breathing a sigh of relief, Finn tore off the baby clothes and prudently knocked down the bridge.

▲▲Puffin Watching

A large colony of Atlantic puffins settles on Staffa each spring and summer during mating season (generally early May through early August). The puffins tend to scatter when the boat arrives. But after the boat pulls out and its passengers hike across the island, the very tame puffins' curiosity gets the better of them. First you'll see them flutter up from the offshore rocks, with their distinctive, bobbing flight. They'll zip and whirl around, and finally they'll start  to land on the lip of the cove. Sit quietly, move slowly, and be patient, and soon they'll get close. (If any seagulls are nearby, shoo them away—puffins are undaunted by humans, who do them no harm, but they're terrified of predator seagulls.)

In the waters around Staffa—on your way to and from the other islands—also keep an eye out for a variety of **marine life,** including seals, dolphins, porpoises, and the occasional minke whale, fin whale, or basking shark (a gigantic fish that hinges open its enormous jaw to drift-net plankton).

Near Oban

The following sights are worth considering for drivers. The first section outlines the best driving route from Glasgow to Oban, including the appealing pit stop at Inveraray. And the second section covers a longer route through one of Scotland's most important prehistoric sites, Kilmartin Glen.

GLASGOW TO OBAN DRIVE

The drive from Glasgow (or Edinburgh) to Oban via Inveraray provides dreamy vistas and your first look at the dramatic landscapes of the Highlands, as well as historic sites and ample opportunity to stop for a picnic.

• *Leaving Glasgow on the A-82, you'll soon be driving along the west bank of...*

Loch Lomond

The first picnic turnout has the best views of this famous lake, benches, a park, and a playground. You're driving over an isthmus between Loch Lomond and a sea inlet. Halfway up the loch, you'll find the town of Tarbet—the Viking word for isthmus, a common name on Scottish maps. Imagine, a thousand years ago, Vikings dragging their ships across this narrow stretch of land to reach Loch Lomond.

• *At Tarbet, the road forks. The signs for Oban keep you on the direct route along A-82. For the scenic option that takes you past Loch Fyne to Inveraray (about 30 minutes longer to drive), keep left for the A-83 (toward Campbeltown).*

Highland Boundary Fault

You'll pass the village of **Arrochar,** then drive along the banks of Loch Long. The scenery crescendos as you pull away from the loch and twist up over the mountains and through a pine forest, getting your first glimpse of bald Highlands mountains—it's clear that you've just crossed the **Highland Boundary Fault.** Enjoy the waterfalls, and notice that the road signs are now in English as well as Gaelic. As you climb into more rugged territory—up the valley called Glen Croe—be mindful that the roads connecting the Lowlands with the Highlands (like the one down in the glen below) were originally a military project designed to facilitate government quelling of the Highland clans.

• *At the summit, watch for the large parking lot with picnic tables on your left (signed for Argyll Forest Park). Stretch your legs at what's aptly named...*

Rest-and-Be-Thankful Pass

The colorful name comes from the 19th century, when just reach-

ing this summit was exhausting. At the top of the military road, just past the last picnic table, there's actually a stone dated 1814, put there by the military with that phrase.

As you drive on, enjoy the dramatic green hills. You may see little bits of hillside highlighted by sunbeams. Each of

The Irish Connection

The Romans called the people living in what is now Ireland the "Scoti" (meaning pirates). When the Scoti crossed the narrow Irish Sea and invaded the land of the Picts 1,500 years ago, that region became known as Scoti-land. Ireland and Scotland were never fully conquered by the Romans, and they retained similar clannish Celtic traits. Both share the same Gaelic branch of the linguistic tree.

On clear summer days, you can actually see Ireland—just 17 miles away—from the Scottish coastline. The closest bit to Scotland is the boomerang-shaped Rathlin Island, part of Northern Ireland. Rathlin is where Scottish leader Robert the Bruce retreated in 1307 after defeat at the hands of the English. Legend has it that he hid in a cave on the island, where he observed a spider patiently rebuilding its web each time a breeze knocked it down. Inspired by the spider's perseverance, Bruce gathered his Scottish forces once more and finally defeated the English at the decisive battle of Bannockburn (see page 62).

Flush with confidence from his victory, Robert the Bruce decided to open a second front against the English...in Ireland. In 1315, he sent his brother Edward over to enlist their Celtic Irish cousins in an effort to thwart the English. After securing Ireland, Edward hoped to move on and enlist the Welsh, thus cornering England with their pan-Celtic nation. But Edward's timing was bad: Ireland was in the midst of famine. His Scottish troops had to live off the land and began to take food and supplies from the starving Irish. Some of Ireland's crops may have been intentionally destroyed to keep it from being used as a colonial "breadbasket" to feed English troops. The Scots quickly wore out their welcome, and Edward the Bruce was eventually killed in battle near Dundalk in 1318.

It's interesting to imagine how things might be different today if Scotland and Ireland had been permanently welded together as a nation 700 years ago. You'll notice the strong Scottish influence in Northern Ireland when you ask a local a question and he answers, "Aye, a wee bit." And in Glasgow—on Scotland's west coast, closest to Ireland—an Ireland-like division between royalist Protestants and republican Catholics survives today in the form of soccer team allegiances. In big Scottish cities (like Glasgow and Edinburgh), you'll even see "orange parades" of protesters marching in solidarity with their Protestant Northern Irish cousins. The Irish—always quick to defuse tension with humor—joke that the Scots are just Irish people who couldn't swim home.

these is a "soot" (Sun's Out Over There). Look for soots as you drive further north into the Highlands.

• *Continue twisting down the far side of the pass. You'll drive through Glen Kinglas and soon reach...*

Loch Fyne

This saltwater "sea loch" is famous for its shellfish (keep an eye out for oyster farms and seafood restaurants). In fact, Loch Fyne is the namesake of a popular UK restaurant chain with 40 locations across the UK. While a chain restaurant is a chain restaurant, this is different: **$$$$ Loch Fyne Seafood Restaurant and Deli** in the big white building at the end of the loch is the original. It's a famous stop for locals—an elegant seafood restaurant and oyster bar worth traveling for (open daily from noon, last order 18:45, no reservations, tel. 01499/600-482, www.lochfyne.com). Even if you're not eating, it's fun to peruse their salty deli (tasty treats to go, picnic tables outside, good coffee).

• *Looping around Loch Fyne, you approach Inveraray. As you get close, keep an eye on the right (when crossing the bridge, have your camera ready) for the dramatic...*

▲Inveraray Castle

This residence of the Duke of Argyll comes with a dramatic, turreted exterior (one of Scotland's most striking) and a lavishly decorated interior that feels spacious, neatly tended, and lived in. Historically a stronghold of one of the more notorious branches of the Campbell clan, it's filled with precious-if-you're-a-Campbell artifacts and fun to tour.

Roam from room to room, reading the laminated descriptions and asking questions of the gregarious docents. The highlight is the Armory Hall that fills the main atrium, where swords and rifles are painstakingly arrayed in starburst patterns. The rifles were actually used when the Campbells fought with the British at the Battle of Culloden in 1746.

Upstairs is a room dedicated to *Downton Abbey*. Public television fans may recognize this as "Duneagle Castle" (a.k.a. Uncle Shrimpy's pad) from one of the *Downton Abbey* Christmas specials—big photos of the Grantham and MacClare clans decorate the genteel rooms.

As with many such castles, the aristocratic clan still lives here (*private* signs mark rooms where the family resides). Another upstairs room is like an Argyll family scrapbook; for example, see photos of the duke playing elephant polo—the ultimate aristocratic sport. The kids attend school in London, but spend a few months here each year; in the winter, the castle is closed to the public and they have the run of the place. After touring the interior, do a loop through the finely manicured gardens (£11, April-Oct daily 10:00-17:45, closed Nov-March, last entry 45 minutes before closing, nice café in the basement, buy tickets at the car park booth, tel. 01499/302-203, www.inveraray-castle.com).

• *After visiting the castle, spend some time exploring...*

▲Inveraray Town

Nearly everybody stops at this lovely, seemingly made-for-tourists town on Loch Fyne. Browse the main street—lined with touristy shops and cafés all the way to the church at its top. As this is the geological and demographic border between the Highlands and the Lowlands, traditionally church services here were held in both Scots and Gaelic. Just before the church is Loch Fyne Whiskies with historic bottles on its ceiling.

There's free parking on the main street and plenty of pay-and-display parking near the pier (TI open daily, on Front Street, tel. 01499/302-063; public WCs at end of nearby pier).

The **Inveraray Jail** is the main site in town—an overpriced, corny, but mildly educational former jail converted into a museum. This "living 19th-century prison" includes a courtroom where mannequins argue the fate of the accused. Then you'll head outside and explore the various cells of the outer courtyard. The playful guards may lock you up for a photo op, while they explain how Scotland reformed its prison system in 1839—you'll see both "before" and "after" cells in this complex (£11.50, includes 75-minute audioguide, open daily, tel. 01499/302-381, www.inverarayjail.co.uk).

• *To continue directly to Oban from Inveraray (about an hour), leave town through the gate at the woolen mill and get on the A-819, which takes you through Glen Aray and along Loch Awe. A left turn on the A-85 takes you into Oban.*

But if you have a healthy interest in prehistoric sites, you can go to Oban by way of Kilmartin Glen (described next, adds about 45 minutes of driving).

KILMARTIN GLEN

Except for the Orkney Islands, Scotland isn't as rich with prehistoric sites as South England is, but the ones in Kilmartin Glen, while faint, are some of Scotland's most accessible—and most important. This wide valley, clearly imbued with spiritual and/or strategic power, contains reminders of several millennia worth of inhabitants. Today it's a playground for those who enjoy tromping through grassy fields while daydreaming about who moved these giant stones here so many centuries ago. This isn't worth a long detour, unless you're fascinated by prehistoric sites.

Four to five thousand years ago, Kilmartin Glen was inhabited by Neolithic people who left behind fragments of their giant, stony monuments. And 1,500 years ago, this was the seat of the kings of the Scoti, who migrated here from Ireland around A.D. 500, giving rise to Scotland's own branch of Celtic culture. From this grassy valley, the Scoti kings ruled their empire, called Dalriada (also sometimes written Dál Riata), which encompassed much of Scotland's west coast, the Inner Hebrides, and the northern part of Ireland. The Scoti spoke Gaelic and were Christian; as they overtook the rest of the Highlands—eventually absorbing their rival Picts—theirs became a dominant culture, which is still evident in pockets of present-day Scotland. Today, Kilmartin Glen is scattered with burial cairns, standing stones, and a hill called Dunadd—the fortress of the Scoti kings.

• *To get here from Inveraray, head straight up Inveraray's main street and get on the waterfront A-83 (marked for Campbeltown); after a half-hour, in Lochgilphead, turn right onto the A-816, which takes you through Kilmartin Glen and all the way up to Oban. (To avoid backtracking, be ready to stop at the prehistoric sites lining the A-816 between Lochgilphead and Kilmartin village.)*

Visiting Kilmartin Glen

Sites are scattered throughout the valley, including some key locations along or just off the A-816 south of Kilmartin village. If you're coming from Inveraray, you'll pass these *before* you reach the village and museum itself. Each one is explained by good informational signs.

Dunadd: This bulbous hill sits just west of the A-816, about four miles north of Lochgilphead and four miles south of Kilmartin village (watch for blue, low-profile *Dunadd Fort* signs). A fort had stood here since the time of Christ, but it was the Scoti kings—who made it their primary castle from the sixth to ninth centuries—that put Dunadd on the map. Park in the big lot at its base and hike through the faint outlines of terraces to the top, where you can enjoy sweeping views over all of Kilmartin Glen; this southern stretch is a marshland called "The Great Moss" (Moine Mhor). Look for carvings in the rock: early Celtic writing, the image of a boar, and a footprint (carved into a stone crisscrossed with fissures). This "footprint of fealty" (a replica) recalls the inauguration ceremony in which the king would place his foot into the footprint, symbolizing the marriage between the ruler and the land.

Dunchraigaig Cairn: About two miles farther north on the A-816, brown *Dunchraigaig* signs mark a parking lot where you can cross the road to the 4,000-year-old, 100-foot-in-diameter Dunchraigaig Cairn—the burial place for 10 Neolithic VIPs. Circle around to find the opening, where you can still crawl into a small recess. This is one of at least five such cairns that together created a mile-and-a-half-long "linear cemetery" up the middle of Kilmartin Glen.

From this cairn, you can walk five minutes to several more prehistoric structures: Follow signs through the gate, and walk to a farm field with **Ballymeanoch**—an avenue of two stone rows (with six surviving stones), a disheveled old cairn, and a stone circle.

Sites near Kilmartin Burn: About one more mile north on the A-816, just off the intersection with the B-8025 (toward *Tayvallich*), is the small Kilmartin Burn parking lot. From here, cross the stream to a field where the five **Nether Largie Standing Stones** have stood in a neat north-south line for 3,200 years. Were these stones designed as an astronomical observatory? Burial rituals or other religious ceremonies? Sporting events? Or just a handy place for sheep to scratch themselves? From here, you can hike the rest of the way through the field (about 10 minutes) to the **Nether Largie South Cairn** and the **Temple Wood Stone Circles** (which don't have their own parking). The larger, older of these circles dates to more than 5,000 years ago, and both were added onto and modified over the millennia.

Kilmartin Museum: To get the big picture, head for the Kilmartin Museum, in the center of Kilmartin village. The cute stone house has a ticket desk, bookshop, and café; the museum—with exhibits explaining this area's powerful history—fills the basement of the adjacent building (though a new home for the exhibit is in the works). The modest but modern museum features handy explanations, a few original artifacts, and lots of re-creations (£6.50, daily except closed Christmas-Feb, tel. 01546/510-278, www.kilmartin.org).

From the museum, you can look out across the fields to see **Glebe Cairn,** one of the five cairns of the "linear cemetery."

Another one, the **Nether Largie North Cairn,** was reconstructed in the 1970s and can actually be entered (a half-mile south of the museum; ask for directions at museum).

Many more prehistoric sites fill Kilmartin Glen (more than 800 within a six-mile radius); the museum sells in-depth guidebooks for the curious, and can point you in the right direction for what you're interested in.

OBAN & INNER HEBRIDES

GLENCOE & FORT WILLIAM

Glencoe • Fort William • The Road to the Isles

Scotland is a land of great natural wonders. And some of the most spectacular—and most accessible—are in the valley called Glencoe, just an hour north of Oban and on the way to Fort William, Loch Ness, Inverness, or the Isle of Skye. The evocative "Weeping Glen" of Glencoe aches with both history and natural beauty. Beyond that, Fort William anchors the southern end of the Caledonian Canal, offering a springboard to more Highlands scenery. This is where Britain's highest peak, Ben Nevis, keeps its head in the clouds, and where you'll find a valley made famous by a bonnie prince...and (later) by a steam train carrying a young wizard named Harry.

PLANNING YOUR TIME

On a quick visit, this area warrants just a few hours between Oban and either Inverness or Skye: Wander through Glencoe village, tour its modest museum, then drive up Glencoe valley for views before continuing on your way north. But if you have only a day or two to linger in the Highlands, Glencoe is an ideal place to do it. Settle in for a night (or more) to make time for a more leisurely drive and to squeeze in a hike or two—I give an overview of the best options, from easy strolls to challenging ascents.

Beyond Glencoe, Fort William—a touristy and overrated transportation hub—is skippable, but can be a handy lunch stop. The Road to the Isles, stretching west from Fort William to the coast, isn't worth a detour, but it's very handy for those connecting to the Isle of Skye. Along the way, the only stop worth more than a quick photo is Glenfinnan, with its powerful ties to Bonnie Prince Charlie and Jacobite history.

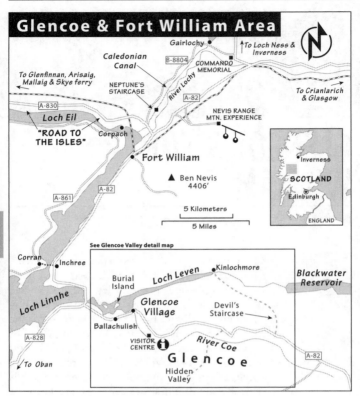

Glencoe & Fort William Area

Gairlochy

↑To Loch Ness &
Inverness

Caledonian
Canal

B-8804

COMMANDO
MEMORIAL

To Glenfinnan, Arisaig,
Mallaig & Skye ferry

NEPTUNE'S
STAIRCASE

River Lochy

A-82

To Crianlarich
& Glasgow

A-830

Loch Eil

"ROAD TO
THE ISLES"

Corpach

NEVIS RANGE
MTN. EXPERIENCE

Fort William

▲ Ben Nevis
4406'

A-861

A-82

5 Kilometers

5 Miles

SCOTLAND

Inverness

Edinburgh

ENGLAND

See Glencoe Valley detail map

Corran

Inchree

Burial
Island

Loch Leven

Kinlochmore

Blackwater
Reservoir

Glencoe
Village

Devil's
Staircase

Loch Linnhe

Ballachulish

A-828

VISITOR
CENTRE ℹ

River Coe

G l e n c o e

A-82

To Oban

Hidden
Valley

Glencoe

This valley is the essence of the wild, powerful, and stark beauty of the Highlands. Along with its scenery, Glencoe offers a good dose of bloody clan history: In 1692, government Redcoats (led by a local Campbell commander) came to the valley, and they were sheltered and fed for 12 days by the MacDonalds— whose leader had been late in swearing an oath to the British monarch. Then, on the morning of February 13, the soldiers were ordered to rise

up early and kill their sleeping hosts, violating the rules of Highland hospitality and earning the valley the nickname "The Weeping Glen." Thirty-eight men were killed outright; hundreds more fled through a blizzard, and some 40 additional villagers (mostly women and children) died from exposure. It's fitting that such an epic, dramatic incident should be set in this equally epic, dramatic

Harry Potter Sights

Harry Potter's story is set in a magical, largely fictional Britain, but you can visit real locations used in the film series. **Glencoe** was the main location for outdoor filming in *The Prisoner of Azkaban* and *The Half-Blood Prince,* and many shots of the Hogwarts grounds were filmed in the Fort William and Glencoe areas. The Hogwarts Express that carries Harry, Ron, and Hermione to school each year runs along the actual **Jacobite Steam Train** line (between Fort William and Mallaig).

In *The Prisoner of Azkaban* and *The Goblet of Fire,* **Loch Shiel, Loch Eilt,** and **Loch Morar** (near Fort William) were the stand-ins for the Great Lake. **Steal Falls,** at the base of Ben Nevis, is the locale for the Triwizard Tournament in *The Goblet of Fire.*

valley, where the cliffsides seem to weep (with running streams) when it rains.

Aside from its tragic history, this place has captured the imaginations of both hikers and artists. Movies filmed here include everything from *Monty Python and the Holy Grail* and *Highlander* to *Harry Potter and the Prisoner of Azkaban* and the James Bond film *Skyfall.* When filmmakers want a stunning, rugged backdrop; when hikers want a scenic challenge; and when Scots want to remember their hard-fought past...they all think of Glencoe.

Orientation to Glencoe

The valley of Glencoe is an easy side-trip just off the main A-828/A-82 road between Oban and points north (such as Fort William and Inverness). If you're coming from the north, the signage can be tricky—at the roundabout south of Fort William, follow signs to *Crianlarich* and *A-82.* The most appealing town here is the sleepy one-street village of Glencoe, worth a stop for its folk museum and its status as the gateway to the valley. The town's hub of activity is its grocery store, which has an ATM (daily 8:00-19:30). The slightly larger and more modern town of Ballachulish (a half-mile away) has more services, including a Co-op grocery store (daily 7:00-22:00).

In the loch just outside Glencoe (near Ballachulish), notice the burial island—where the souls of those who "take the low road" are piped home. The next island was the Island of Discussion—where those in dispute went until they found agreement.

TOURIST INFORMATION

Your best source of information (especially for walks and hikes) is the **Glencoe Visitor Centre,** described later. The nearest **TI** is in the next town, Ballachulish (buried inside a huge gift shop, daily 9:00-17:00, Nov-Easter 10:00-16:00, tel. 01855/811-866, www.glencoetourism.co.uk). For more information on the area, see www.discoverglencoe.com.

Bike Rental: At **Crank It Up Gear,** Davy rents road and mountain bikes, and can offer plenty of suggestions for where to pedal in the area (£15/half-day, £25/all day, just off the main street to the left near the start of town, 20 Lorn Drive, mobile 07746-860-023, www.crankitupgear.com, best to book ahead in summer).

Sights in Glencoe

Glencoe Village

Glencoe village is just a line of houses sitting beneath the brooding mountains. The only real sight in town is the folk museum (de-

scribed later). But walking the main street gives a good glimpse of village Scotland. From the free parking lot at the entrance to town, go for a stroll. You'll pass lots of little B&Bs renting two or three rooms, the stony Episcopal church, the folk museum, the town's grocery store, and the village hall.

At the far end of the village, on the left just before the bridge, a Celtic cross **World War I** memorial stands on a little hill. Even this

wee village lost 11 souls during that war—a reminder of Scotland's disproportionate contribution to Britain's war effort. You'll see memorials like this (usually either a Celtic cross or a soldier with bowed head) in virtually every town in Scotland.

If you were to cross the little bridge, you'd head up into Glencoe's wooded parklands, with some easy hikes (described later). But for one more landmark, turn right just before the bridge and walk about five minutes. Standing on a craggy bluff on your right is another memorial—this one to the **Glencoe Massacre,** which still haunts the memories of people here and throughout Scotland.

Glencoe and North Lorn Folk Museum

This gathering of thatched-roof, early 18th-century croft houses is a volunteer-run community effort. It's jammed with local his-

tory, creating a huggable museum filled with humble exhibits gleaned from the town's old closets and attics. When one house was being rethatched, its owner found a cache of 200-year-old swords and pistols hidden there from the government Redcoats after the disastrous Battle of Culloden. You'll also see an-

tique toys, boxes from old food products, sports paraphernalia, a cabinet of curiosities, evocative old black-and-white photos, and plenty of information on the MacDonald clan. Be sure to look for the museum's little door that leads out back, where additional, smaller buildings are filled with everyday items (furniture, farm tools, and so on) and exhibits on the Glencoe Massacre and a beloved Highland doctor. You can listen to an interview with the late Arthur Smith, a local historian, about the valley and its story in the "Scottish Highlands" program available on my Rick Steves Audio Europe app—for details, see page 203 (£3, Easter-Sept Mon-Sat 10:00-16:30, closed Sun and off-season, tel. 01855/811-664, www. glencoemuseum.com).

Glencoe Visitor Centre

This modern facility, a mile past Glencoe village up the A-82 into the dramatic valley, is designed to resemble a *clachan*, or traditional Highland settlement. The information desk inside the shop at the ranger desk is your single best resource for advice (and maps or guidebooks) about local walks and hikes (several of which are outlined later in this chapter). At the back of the complex you'll find a viewpoint with a handy 3-D model of the hills for orientation. There's also a pricey exhibition about the surrounding landscape, the region's history, wildlife, mountaineering, and conservation. It's worth the time to watch the more-interesting-than-it-sounds two-minute video on geology and the 14-minute film on the Glencoe Massacre, which thoughtfully traces the events leading up to the tragedy rather than simply recycling romanticized legends (free, exhibition-£6.50; April-Oct daily 9:30-17:30; Nov-March Thu-Sun 10:00-16:00, closed Mon-Wed; free Wi-Fi, café, tel. 01855/811-307, www.glencoe-nts.org.uk).

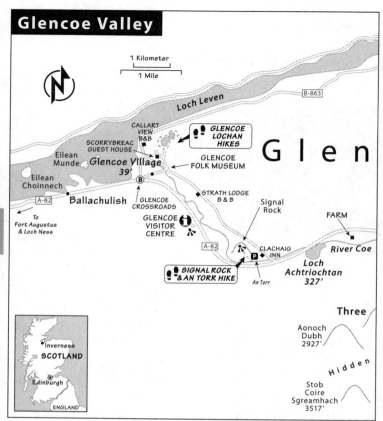

Glencoe Valley Driving Tour

If you have a car, spend an hour or so following the A-82 through the valley, past the Glencoe Visitor Centre, up into the desolate moor beyond, and back again. You'll enjoy grand views, dramatic craggy hills, and, if you're lucky, a chance to hear a bagpiper in the wind: Roadside Highland buskers often set up here on good-weather summer weekends. (If you play the recorder—and the piper's not swarmed with other tourists—ask to finger a tune while he does the hard work.)

Here's a brief explanation of the route. Along the way, I've pointed out sometimes easy-to-miss trailheads, in case you're up for a hike (hikes described in the next section).

➋ **Self-Guided Driving Tour:** Leaving Glencoe village on the A-82, it's just a mile to the **Glencoe Visitor Centre** (on the right, described earlier). Soon after, the road pulls out of the forested hills and gives you unobstructed views of the U-shaped valley.

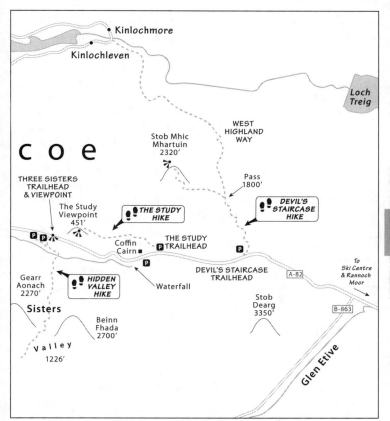

About a mile after the visitors center, on the left, is a parking lot for **Signal Rock and An Torr,** a popular place for low-impact forested hikes. Just beyond, also on the left, is a single-track road leading to the recommended **Clachaig Inn,** a classic hikers' pub. The hillsides above the inn were the setting for Hagrid's hut in the third Harry Potter movie (though nothing remains from filming).

Continuing along the A-82, you'll hit a straight stretch, passing a lake (Loch Achtriochtan), and then a small farm, both on the

right. After the farm, the valley narrows a bit as you cut through Glencoe Pass. On the right, you'll pass two small parking lots. Pull into the second one for perhaps the best viewpoint of the entire valley, with point-blank views (directly ahead) of the steep ridge-like mountains known as the **Three Sisters.** Hike about 100 feet away from the pullout to your own private bluff to enjoy the view alone—it makes a big difference. This is also the starting point for the challenging **Hidden Valley hike,** which leads between the first and second sisters.

As you continue, you'll pass a raging waterfall in a canyon—the Tears of the MacDonalds—on the right. After another mile or so—through more glorious waterfall scenery—watch on the left for the **Coffin Cairn,** which looks like a stone igloo (parking is just across the road if you want a photo op). Just after the cairn, look on the left for pullout parking for the **hike to The Study,** a viewpoint overlooking the road you just drove down (described later).

After this pullout, you'll hit a straightaway for about a mile, followed by an S-curve. At the end of the curve, look for the pullout parking on the left, just before the stand of pine trees. This is the trailhead for the **Devil's Staircase** hike, high into the hills.

Continuing past here, you're nearing the end of the valley. The intimidating peak called the Great Shepherd of Etive (on the right) looms like a dour watchman, guarding the far end of the valley. Soon you'll pass the turnoff (on the right) for **Glen Etive,** an even more remote-feeling valley. (This was the setting for the final scenes of *Skyfall.* Yes, this is where James Bond grew up.) Continuing past that, the last sign of civilization (on the right) is the Glencoe Ski Centre. And from here, the terrain flattens out as you enter the vast **Rannoch Moor**—50 bleak square miles of heather, boulders, and barely enough decent land to graze a sheep. Robert Louis Stevenson called it the "Highland Desert."

You could keep driving as far as you like—but the moor looks pretty much the same from here on out. Turn around and head back through Glencoe...it's scenery you'll hardly mind seeing twice.

Hiking in Glencoe

Glencoe is made for hiking. Many routes are not particularly well marked, so it's essential to get very specific instructions (from the rangers at the Glencoe Visitor Centre, or other knowledgeable locals) and equip yourself with a good map (the Ordnance Survey Explorer Map #384, sold at the center). Next, I've suggested a few of the most enticing walks and hikes. These vary from easy, level strolls to challenging climbs. Either way, equip yourself with proper footwear (even the easy trails can get swamped in wet weather) and rain gear—you never know when a storm will blow in.

I've listed these roughly in order of how close they are to Glencoe village, and given a rough sense of difficulty for each. Some of them (including the first two) are more forested, but the ones out in the open—which really let you feel immersed in the wonders of Glencoe—are even better.

While you can walk to the first two areas from Glencoe village, the rest are best for drivers. Some of these trailheads are tricky to find; remember, I've designed the driving commentary in the previous section to help you find the hikes off the A-82.

Glencoe Lochan (Easy)

Perched on the forested hill above Glencoe village is an improbable slice of the Canadian Rockies. A century ago, this was the personal playground of Lord Strathcona, a local boy done good when he moved to Canada and eventually became a big Canadian Pacific Railway magnate. In 1894, he returned home with his Canadian wife and built the Glencoe House (which was recently restored into an exclusive, top-of-the-top hotel, with suites starting around £500 a night). His wife was homesick for the Rockies, so he had the grounds landscaped to represent the lakes, trees, and mountains of her home country. They even carved out a man-made lake (Glencoe Lochan), which looks like a slice of Canada tucked under a craggy Scottish backdrop. (She was still homesick—they eventually returned to Canada.)

Today, the house and immediate surroundings are off-limits, but the rest of the area is open for exploration. Head to the end of Glencoe village, cross the bridge, and continue straight up (following signs for *Glencoe Lochan*)—it's a 20-minute uphill walk, or 5-minute drive, from the village center. Once there, a helpful orientation panel in the parking lot suggests three different, color-coded, one-mile walking loops—mostly around that beautiful lake, which reflects the hillsides of Glencoe.

From this area, a good trail network called the **Orbital Recreational Track** follows the river through the forest up the valley, all the way to the Clachaig Inn (about 45 minutes one-way). This links you to the Signal Rock and An Torr areas (described next). Eventually they hope to extend this trail system across the valley and back to the Glencoe Visitor Centre, which would allow a handy loop hike around the valley floor.

Signal Rock and An Torr (Easy to Moderate)

This forested area has nicely tended trails and gives you a better chance of spotting wildlife than the more desolate hikes described later. To explore this area, park at the well-marked lot just off of the A-82 and go for a walk. A well-described panel at the trailhead narrates three options: easy yellow route to the Clachaig Inn; longer blue route to Signal Rock; and strenuous black route along the hillsides of An Torr. The Signal Rock route brings you to a panoramic point overlooking the valley—so named because a fire could be lit here to alert others in case of danger.

Hidden Valley (Challenging)

Three miles east of Glencoe village, this aptly named glen is tucked between two of the dramatic Three Sisters mountains. Also called the Lost Valley (Coire Gabhail in Gaelic), this was supposedly where the MacDonalds hid stolen cattle from their rivals, the Campbells (who later massacred them). This is the most challenging of the hikes I describe—it's strenuous and has stretches with uneven footing. Expect to scramble a bit over rocks, and to cross a river on stepping stones (which may be underwater after a heavy rain). As the rocks can be slippery when wet, skip this hike in bad weather. Figure about two-and-a-half to three hours round-trip (with an ascent of more than 1,000 feet).

Begin at the second parking lot at Glencoe Pass (on the right when coming from Glencoe), with views of the Three Sisters. You're aiming to head between the first and second Sisters (counting from the left). Hike down into the valley between the road and the mountains. Bear left, head down a metal staircase, and cross the bridge over the river. (Don't cross the bridge to the right of the parking lots—a common mistake.) Once across, you'll start the treacherous ascent up a narrow gorge. Some scrambling is required, and at one point a railing helps you find your way. The next tricky part is where you cross the river. You're looking for a pebbly beach and a large boulder; stepping stones lead across the river, and you'll see the path resume on the other side. But if the water level is high, the stones may be covered—though still passable with good shoes and steady footing. (Don't attempt to scramble over the treacherous slopes on the side of the river with the loose rocks called scree.) Once across the stepping stones, keep on the trail, hiking further up into the valley.

Much Easier Alternative: If you'd simply enjoy the feeling of walking deep in Glencoe valley—with peaks and waterfalls overhead—you can start down from the parking lot toward the Hidden Valley trail, and then simply stroll the old road along the valley floor as far as you want in either direction.

The Study (Easy to Moderate)

For a relatively easy, mostly level hike through the valley with a nice viewpoint at the end, consider walking to the flat rock called "The Study" and back. It

takes about 45-60 minutes round-trip. The walk essentially parallels the main highway, but on the old road a bit higher up. You'll
park just beyond the Three Sisters and the Coffin Cairn. From
there, cut through the field of stone and marshy turf to the old
road—basically two gravel tire ruts—and follow them to your left.
You'll hike above the modern road, passing several modest waterfalls, until you reach a big, flat rock with stunning views of the
Three Sisters and the valley beyond. (Fellow hikers have marked
the spot with a pile of stones.)

The Devil's Staircase (Strenuous but Straightforward)

About eight miles east of Glencoe village, near the end of the valley, you can hike this brief stretch of the West Highland Way. It
was built by General Wade, the British strategist who came to
Scotland after the 1715 Jacobite rebellion to help secure government rule here. Designed to connect Glencoe valley to the lochside
town of Kinlochmore, to the north, it's named for its challenging
switchbacks. Most hikers simply ascend to the pass at the top (an
800-foot gain), then come back down to Glencoe. It's challenging,
but easier to follow and with more comfortable footing than the
Hidden Valley hike. Figure about 45-60 minutes up, and 30 minutes back down (add 45-60 minutes for the optional ascent to the
summit of 2,320-foot Stob Mhic Mhartuin).

From the parking lot, a green sign points the way. It's a steep
but straightforward hike up, on switchback trails, until you reach
the pass—marked by a cairn (pile of stones). From here, you can
return back down into the valley. Or, if you have stamina left, consider continuing higher—head up to the peak on the left, called
Stob Mhic Mhartuin. The 30-40-minute hike to the top (an additional gain of 500 feet) earns you even grander views over the
entire valley.

For an even longer hike, it is possible to carry on down the
other side of the staircase to **Kinlochmore** (about 2 hours descent)—but your car will still be in Glencoe. Consider this: Leave
your car in Glencoe village. Take a taxi to the trailhead. Hike
across to Kinlochmore. Then take the hourly Stagecoach bus #44
back to Glencoe and your car (see "Glencoe Connections," later).

Sleeping in Glencoe

Glencoe is an extremely low-key place to spend the night between
Oban or Glasgow and the northern destinations. You'll join two
kinds of guests: one-nighters just passing through and outdoorsy
types settling in for several days of hiking.

B&BS IN GLENCOE VILLAGE

The following B&Bs are along or just off the main road through the middle of the village.

$$ Beechwood Cottage B&B is a shoes-off, slippers-on, whisky-honor-bar kind of place where Jackie rents three lovely rooms and Ian pursues his rock-garden dreams in the yard (look for the sign at the church on Main Street, tel. 01855/811-062, www.beechwoodcottage.scot, stay@beechwoodcottage.scot).

$$ Heatherlea B&B is at the far end of the village, with a relaxed atmosphere, hotel-meets-country-home rooms, and a serene grassy garden with berry bushes (which they harvest for homemade jam). Hosts Jo and Helen are fun, outdoorsy types who opened a guesthouse because they "wanted to get out of the rat race" (four rooms—one a single with private bath down the hall, sack lunches available for small fee, tel. 01855/811-519, mobile 07815-042-505, www.heatherleaglencoe.com, info@heatherleaglencoe.com).

$ Ghlasdruim B&B, behind the Glencoe Café and set back from the A-82, has three large and cozy ground-floor rooms, spacious bathrooms, a homey dining room with a fireplace, and one big table for conversational breakfasts (cash only, closed in winter, tel. 01855/811-593, http://ghlasdruim.co.uk, ghlasdruim@gmail.com, Maureen and Ken).

OUTSIDE OF TOWN

These options are a bit outside of town, with good proximity to both the village and the valley. Strath Lodge and Clachaig Inn are on the back road that runs through the forest parallel to the A-82 (best-suited for drivers). Scorrybreac is on a hill above the village, and Callart View is along the flat road that winds past Loch Leven. Strathassynt Guest House is in the center of Ballachulish.

$$ Strath Lodge, energetically run by Ann and Dan (who are generous with hiking tips and maps), brings a fresh perspective to Glencoe's sometimes-stodgy accommodations scene. Their four rooms, in a modern, light-filled, lodge-like home, are partway down the road to the Clachaig Inn (2-3 night minimum preferred, no kids under 16, tel. 01855/811-337, www.strathlodgeglencoe.com, stay@strathlodgeglencoe.com). Take the road up through the middle of Glencoe village, cross the bridge, and keep right following the river for a few minutes; it's on the right.

$$ Clachaig Inn, which runs two popular pubs on site, also rents 23 rooms, all with private bath. It's a family-friendly place surrounded by a dramatic setting that works well for hikers seeking a comfy mountain inn (recommended pub, tel. 01855/811-252, 3 miles from Glencoe, www.clachaig.com, frontdesk@clachaig.com). Follow the directions for the Strath Lodge earlier, and drive another three miles past campgrounds and hostels—the Clachaig Inn is on the right.

$ Scorrybreac Guest House enjoys a secluded forest setting and privileged position next to the restored Glencoe House (now an exclusive luxury hotel). From here, walks around the Glencoe Lochan wooded lake park are easy, and it's about a 10-minute walk down into the village. Emma and Graham rent five homey rooms and serve a daily breakfast special that goes beyond the usual offerings (family room, 2-3 nights preferred in peak season, tel. 01855/811-354, www.scorrybreacglencoe.com, scorrybreac@btinternet.com). After crossing the bridge at the end of the village, head left up the hill and follow signs.

$ Callart View B&B offers four rooms, quilted-home comfort, and a peaceful spot overlooking Loch Leven, less than a mile outside the village and close to the wooded trails of the Glencoe Lochan. You'll be spoiled by Lynn's homemade shortbread (family room, self-catering cottages, pack lunches available, tel. 01855/811-259, www.callart-view.co.uk, callartview@hotmail.com, Lynn and Geoff). Turn off from the main road for Glencoe village but instead of turning right into the village, keep left and drive less than a mile along the loch.

$ Strathassynt Guest House sits in the center of Ballachulish, across from the recommended Laroch Bar & Bistro. Some parts of the house may feel dated (it's a work in progress—they call it "modern vintage"), but the six bedrooms are all fresh and nicely modernized (family rooms, closed Nov-Feb, tel. 01855/811-261, www.strathassynt.com, info@strathassynt.com, Neil and Katya).

Eating in Glencoe

Choices around Glencoe are slim—this isn't the place for fine dining. But the following options offer decent food a short walk or drive away. For evening fun, take a walk or ask your B&B host where to find music and dancing.

In Glencoe: The only real restaurant is **$$$ The Glencoe Gathering,** with lovely dining areas and a large outdoor deck, and specializing in seafood with a Scottish twist. Choose between the quirky, fun pub or the fancier restaurant (food served daily 8:00-22:00, at junction of A-82 and Glencoe village, tel. 01855/811-265). The adjacent hotel has a more subdued and formal restaurant called **The Glencoe Inn.**

The **$ Glencoe Café,** also in the village, is just right for soups and sandwiches, and Deirdre's homemade baked goods—especially the carrot loaf—are irresistible (soup and panini lunch combo, daily 10:00-17:00, last order at 16:15, free Wi-Fi, Alan).

Near Glencoe: Set in a stunning valley a few miles from

Glencoe village, **$$ Clachaig Inn** serves solid pub grub all day long to a clientele that's half locals and half tourists. This unpretentious and very popular social hub features billiards, live music, and a wide range of whiskies and hand-pulled ales. There are two areas, sharing the same menu: The Bidean Lounge feels a bit like an upscale ski lodge while the Boots Bar has a spit-and-sawdust, pub-around-an-open-fire atmosphere (open daily for lunch and dinner, music Sat from 21:00, Sun open-mike folk music, see hotel listing earlier for driving directions, tel. 01855/811-252, no reservations).

In Ballachulish: Trying to bring some modern class to this sleepy corner of Scotland, **$$$$ The Laroch Bar & Bistro** offers a choice between the fancier bistro (pricey, more sophisticated menu, reservations smart) or the cozy bar (lighter fare, no reservations) with big-screen TVs and video games (Tue-Sun 12:00-15:00 & 18:00-21:00, closed Mon, tel. 01855/811-940, www.thelarochrestaurantandbar.co.uk). Drive three minutes from Glencoe into Ballachulish village, and you'll see it on the left. There's also a simple **$ fish-and-chips** joint next door (open until 21:30).

Glencoe Connections

Buses don't actually drive down the main road through Glencoe village, but they stop nearby at a place called **"Glencoe Crossroads"** (a short walk into the village center). They also stop in the town of **Ballachulish,** which is just a half-mile away (or a £3 taxi ride). Tell the bus driver where you're going ("Glencoe village") and ask to be let off as close as possible.

Citylink buses #914, #915, or #916 stop at Glencoe Crossroads and Ballachulish, heading north to **Fort William** (8/day, 30 minutes) or south to **Glasgow** (3 hours). Another option is Stagecoach bus #44, which runs from either Glencoe Crossroads or Ballachulish to **Fort William** (hourly, fewer on Sun). From Ballachulish, you can take Citylink bus #918 to **Oban** (2/day, 1 hour).

To reach **Inverness** or **Portree** on the Isle of Skye, transfer in Fort William. To reach **Edinburgh,** transfer in Glasgow.

Bus info: Citylink tel. 0871-266-3333, www.citylink.co.uk; Stagecoach tel. 01397/702-373, www.stagecoachbus.com.

Fort William

Fort William—after Inverness, the second biggest town in the Highlands (pop. 10,000)—is Glencoe's opposite. While Glencoe is a humble one-street village, appealing to hikers and nature-lovers, Fort William's glammed-up car-free main drag feels like one big

Scottish shopping mall (with souvenir stands and outdoor stores touting perpetual "70 percent off" sales). The town is clogged with a United Nations of tourists trying to get out of the rain. Big bus tours drive through Glencoe...but they sleep in Fort William.

While Glencoe touches the Scottish soul of the Highlands, Fort William was a steely and intimidating headquarters of the British

counter-insurgency movement—in many ways designed to crush that same Highland spirit. After the English Civil War (early 1650s), Oliver Cromwell built a fort here to control his rebellious Scottish subjects. This was beefed up (and named for King William III) in 1690. And following the Jacobite uprising in 1715, King George I dispatched General George Wade to coordinate and fortify the crown's Highland defenses against further Jacobite dissenters. Fort William was the first of a chain of intimidating bastions (along with Fort Augustus on Loch Ness, and Fort George near Inverness) stretching the length of the Great Glen. But Fort William's namesake fortress is long gone, leaving precious little tangible evidence (except a tiny bit of rampart in a park near the train station) to help today's visitors imagine its militaristic past.

With the opening of the Caledonian Canal in 1822, the first curious tourists arrived. Many more followed with the arrival of the train in 1894, and grand hotels were built. Today, sitting at the foot of Ben Nevis, the tallest peak in Britain, Fort William is considered the outdoors capital of the United Kingdom.

Orientation to Fort William

Given its strategic position—between Glencoe and Oban in the south, Inverness in the east, and the Isle of Skye in the west—you're likely to pass through Fort William at some point during your Highlands explorations. And, while "just passing through" is the perfect plan here, Fort William can provide a good opportunity to stock up on whatever you need (last supermarket before Inverness), grab lunch, and get any questions answered at the TI.

Arrival in Fort William: You'll find pay parking lots flanking the main pedestrian zone, High Street. The train and bus stations sit side by side just north of the old town center, where you'll find a handy pay parking lot.

Tourist Information: The TI is on the car-free main drag (daily July-Aug 9:30-18:30, Sept-June 9:00-17:00; free Wi-Fi,

15 High Street, tel. 01397/701-801). Free public WCs are up the street, next to the parking lot.

Sights in Fort William

Fort William's High Street

Enjoy an hour-long stroll up and down the length of Fort William's main street for lots of Scottish clichés, great people watching, and a shop at #125 (near the south end) called Aye2Aye, which favors a new referendum on Scottish independence.

▲West Highland Museum

Fort William's only real sight is its humble but well-presented museum. It's a fine opportunity to escape the elements, and—if you take the time to linger over the exhibits—genuinely insightful about local history and Highland life (free, £3 suggested donation, guidebook-£1.50, Mon-Sat 10:00-17:00, and maybe Sun in high season; Nov-Dec and March until 16:00, closed Sun; closed Jan-Feb; midway down the main street on Cameron Square, tel. 01397/702-169, www.westhighlandmuseum.org.uk).

Follow the suggested one-way route through exhibits on two floors. You'll begin by learning about the WWII green beret commandos, who were trained in secrecy near here (see "Commando Memorial" listing, later). Then you'll see the historic Governor's Room, decorated with the original paneling from the room in which the order for the Glencoe Massacre was signed. The ground floor also holds exhibits on natural history (lots of stuffed birds and other critters), mountaineering (old equipment), and archaeology (stone and metal tools).

Upstairs, you'll see a selection of old tartans and a salacious exhibit about Queen Victoria and John Brown (her Scottish servant... and, possibly, suitor). The Jacobite exhibit gives a concise timeline of that complicated history, from Charles I to Bonnie Prince Charlie, and displays a selection of items emblazoned with the prince's bonnie face—including a clandestine portrait that you can only see by looking in a cylindrical mirror. Finally, the Highland Life exhibit collects a hodgepodge of tools, musical instruments (some fine old harps that were later replaced by the much louder bagpipes as the battlefield instrument of choice), and other bric-a-brac.

NEAR FORT WILLIAM

Ben Nevis

From Fort William, take a peek at Britain's highest peak, Ben Nevis (4,406 feet). Thousands walk to its summit each year. On a clear day, you can admire it from a distance. Scotland's only mountain cable cars—at the **Nevis Range Mountain Experience**—can take you to a not-very-lofty 2,150-foot perch on the slopes of Aonach Mòr for a closer look (£14, 15-minute ride, generally open daily but closed in high winds and winter—call ahead, signposted on the A-82 north of Fort William, tel. 01397/705-825, www.nevisrange.co.uk).

▲Commando Memorial

This powerful bronze ensemble of three stoic WWII commandos, standing in an evocative mountain setting, is one of Britain's most

beloved war memorials. During World War II, Winston Churchill decided that Britain needed an elite military corps. He created the British Commandos, famous for wearing green berets (an accessory—and name—later borrowed by elite fighting forces in the US and other countries). The British Commandos trained in the Lochaber region near Fort William, in the windy shadow of Ben Nevis. Many later died in combat, and this memorial—built in 1952—remembers those fallen British heroes.

Nearby is the Garden of Remembrance, honoring British Commandos who died in more recent conflicts, from the Falkland Islands to Afghanistan. It's also a popular place to spread Scottish military ashes. Taken together, these sights are a touching reminder that the US is not alone in its distant wars. Every nation has its share of honored heroes willing to sacrifice for what they believe to be the greater good.

Getting There: The memorial is about nine miles outside of Fort William, on the way to Inverness (just outside Spean Bridge); see "Route Tips for Drivers" on page 74.

Sleeping and Eating in Fort William

Sleeping: The Hobbit-cute **$ Gowan Brae B&B** ("Hill of the Big Daisy") has an antique-filled dining room and three rooms with loch or garden views (one room has private bath down the hall, cash only, 2-night minimum July-Aug, on Union Road—a 5-minute walk up the hill above High Street, tel. 01397/704-399, www.gowanbrae.co.uk, gowan_brae@btinternet.com, Jim and Ann Clark).

Eating: These places are on traffic-free High Street, near the start of town. For lunch and picnics, try **$ Deli Craft,** with good, made-to-order deli sandwiches and other prepared foods (61 High Street, tel. 01397/698-100), or **$ Hot Roast Company,** which sells beef, turkey, ham, or pork sandwiches topped with some tasty extras, along with soup, salad, and coleslaw (127 High Street, tel. 01397/700-606).

For lunch or dinner, **$$ The Grog & Gruel** serves real ales, good pub grub, and Tex-Mex and Cajun dishes, with some unusual choices such as burgers made from boar and haggis or Highland venison. There's also a variety of "grog dogs" (66 High Street, tel. 01397/705-078).

Fort William Connections

Fort William is a major transit hub for the Highlands, so you'll likely change buses here at some point during your trip.

From Fort William by Bus to: Glencoe or **Ballachulish** (all Glasgow-bound buses—#914, #915, and #916; 8/day, 30 minutes; also Stagecoach bus #44, hourly, fewer on Sun), **Oban** (bus #918, 2/day, 1.5 hours), **Portree** on the Isle of Skye (buses #914, #915, and #916, 3/day, 3 hours), **Inverness** (buses #19 and #919, 7/day, 2 hours), **Glasgow** (buses #914, #915, and #916; 8/day, 3 hours). To reach **Edinburgh,** take the bus to Glasgow, then transfer to a train or bus (figure 5 hours total). Citylink: tel. 0871-266-3333, www.citylink.co.uk. Stagecoach: tel. 01397/702-373, www.stagecoachbus.com.

From Fort William by Train to: Glasgow (3/day, 4 hours), **Mallaig** and ferry to Isle of Skye (4/day, 1.5 hours). Also see the listing for the Jacobite Steam Train on page 78.

ROUTE TIPS FOR DRIVERS

From Fort William to Loch Ness and Inverness: Head north out of Fort William on the A-82. After about eight miles, in the village of Spean Bridge, take the left fork (staying on the A-82). About a mile later, on the left, keep an eye out for the **Commando Memorial** (described earlier and worth a quick stop). From here, the A-82 sweeps north and follows the Caledonian Canal, passing through **Fort Augustus** (a good lunch stop, with its worthwhile Caledonian Canal Visitor Centre), and then follows the north side of Loch Ness on its way to Inverness. Along the way, the A-82 passes **Urquhart Castle** and two **Loch Ness Monster exhibits** in Drumnadrochit (described in the Inverness & Loch Ness chapter).

From Oban to Fort William via Glencoe: See page 38 in the Oban chapter.

From Fort William to the Isle of Skye: You have two options: Head west on the A-830 through **Glenfinnan,** then catch the ferry from Mallaig to Armadale on the Isle of Skye (this "Road to the Isles" area is described in the next section). Or, head north on the A-82 to Invergarry, and turn left (west) on the A-87, which you'll follow (past **Eilean Donan Castle**) to Kyle of Lochalsh and the

Skye Bridge to the island. Consider using one route one way, and the other on the return trip.

The Road to the Isles

Between Fort William and the Isle of Skye lies a rugged landscape with close ties to the Jacobite rebellions. It was here that Bonnie Prince Charlie first set foot on Scottish soil in 1745, in his attempt to regain the British throne for his father. The village of Glenfinnan, about 30 minutes west of Fort William, is where he first raised the Stuart family standard—and an army of Highlanders. Farther west, the landscape grows even more rugged, offering off-shore glimpses of the Hebrides. It's all tied together by a pretty, meandering road—laid out by the great Scottish civil engineer Thomas Telford—that's evocatively (and aptly) named "The Road to the Isles." While these sights aren't worth going out of your way to see, they're ideal for those heading to the Isle of Skye (via the Mallaig-Armadale ferry), or for those who'd enjoy taking the so-called "Harry Potter train" through a Hogwartian landscape.

If you're driving, be sure you allow enough time to make it to Mallaig at least 20 minutes before the Skye ferry departs (figure at least 90 minutes of driving time from Fort William to the ferry, not including stops). In summer it's smart to reserve a spot on the ferry the day before, either online or by phone. For more tips on the Mallaig-Armadale ferry, see "Getting to the Isle of Skye" on page 136.

Sights on the Road to the Isles

I've connected these sights with some commentary for those driving from Fort William to Mallaig for the Skye ferry. (If you're interested in the Jacobite Steam Train instead, see the end of this chapter.) In addition to the sights at Glenfinnan, this route is graced with plenty of loch-and-mountain views and, near the end, passes along a beautiful stretch of coast with some fine sandy beaches.

• *From Fort William, head north on the A-82 (signed Inverness and Mallaig). At the big roundabout (where you'll see the tempting Ben Nevis Whisky Distillery with a visitors center), turn left onto the A-830 (marked for Mallaig and Glenfinnan). You'll pass a big sign listing the next Skye ferry departure. Just after, you'll cross a bridge; look up and to the right to see Neptune's Staircase. There's a park-like viewing zone on the right.*

Neptune's Staircase

This network of eight stair-step locks, designed by Thomas Telford in the early 19th century, offers a handy look at the ingenious locks of the Caledonian Canal.

For more on this remarkable engineering accomplishment—which combined natural lochs with man-made locks and canals to connect Scotland's east and west coasts—see the sidebar on page 107. Engineers might want to pull over just after the bridge (well marked) to stroll around the locks for a closer look, but the rest of us can pretty much get the gist from the road.

• *Continue west on the A-830 for another 14 miles, much of it along Loch Eil. Soon you'll reach a big parking lot and visitors center at...*

▲Glenfinnan

In the summer of 1745, Bonnie Prince Charlie—grandson of James VII of Scotland (and II of England), who was kicked off the British throne in 1688—arrived at Glenfinnan...and waited. He had journeyed a long way to this point, sailing from France by way of the Scottish Isle of Eriskay, and finally making landfall at Loch nan Uamh (just west of here). For the first time in his life, he set foot on his ancestral homeland...the land he hoped that, with his help, his father would soon rule. But to reclaim the thrones of England and Scotland for the Stuart line, the fresh-faced, 24-year-old prince would need the support of the Highlanders. And here at Glenfinnan, he held his breath at the moment of truth. Would the Highland clans come to his aid?

As Charlie waited, gradually he began to hear the drone of bagpipes filtering through the forest. And then, the clan chiefs appeared: MacDonalds. Camerons. MacDonnells. McPhees. They had been holding back—watching and waiting, to make sure they weren't the only ones. Before long, the prince felt confident that he'd reached a clan quorum. And so, here at Glenfinnan, on August 19, 1745, Bonnie Prince Charlie raised his royal standard—officially kicking off the armed Jacobite rebellion that came to be known as "The '45." Two days later, Charlie and his 1,500 clansmen compatriots headed south to fight for control of Scotland. (Sadly, Glenfinnan is also the place where Bonnie Prince Charlie retreated eight months later, after his campaign's crushing defeat at Culloden—see page 97.)

Today Glenfinnan, which still echoes with history, is a wide spot in the road with a big visitors center and two landmarks: a monument to Bonnie Prince Charlie's raising of the standard, and a railroad viaduct made famous by the Hogwarts Express.

Visiting Glenfinnan: Pay £2 to park your car, then head into the **visitors center** (free, daily July-Aug 9:30-17:30, April-June and Sept-Oct 10:00-17:00, closed Nov-March, café, WCs, tel. 0844-493-2221).

The **Jacobite Exhibit** inside the visitors center is small but enlightening, using modern exhibits to explain the story of Bonnie Prince Charlie and "The '45."

The **Glenfinnan Viaduct,** with 416 yards of raised track over 21 supporting arches, is visible from the parking lot. But if you

have time, it's worth hiking 10 minutes up the adjacent hill for much better views. Find the well-marked, steeply switchbacked path behind the visitors center and huff on up. From the viewpoint, you'll enjoy sweeping (if distant) views of the viaduct in one direction, and the monument and banks of Loch Shiel in the other. You may even catch a glimpse of the Jacobite Steam Train chugging along (described later).

The **Glenfinnan Monument,** between the visitors center and the loch, is a pillar capped with a stirring statue of a kilted "Unknown Highlander" standing below the standard. (From here you can see the viaduct and the viewpoint above the visitors center.)

• *Carrying on west along the A-830, the scenery grows more rugged. Shortly you'll begin to catch glimpses of silver sand beaches at the heads of the rocky lochs. (If catching a ferry, figure 50 minutes' drive from Glenfinnan to Mallaig.) Soon you'll reach the village of...*

Arisaig

While there's not much to see in this village, it has an interesting history. Gaelic for "safe place," Arisaig has provided shelter for many seafarers—including the real Long John Silver (Robert Louis Stevenson was inspired by tales from his father, who was an engineer who built lighthouses here). In the 20th century, remote Arisaig was a secret training ground for WWII-era spies. The "Special Operations Executive" prepared brave men and women here for clandestine operations in Nazi-occupied Europe.

• *Around Arisaig, signs for the Alternative Coastal Route direct you to the B-8008, which parallels the A-830 highway the rest of the way (7 miles) to Mallaig. If you've got ample time to kill, consider taking these* *back roads for a more scenic approach to the end of the road. Either way, you'll end up at **Mallaig** and the **Skye Ferry.***

The Jacobite Steam Train

The West Highland Railway Line chugs 42 miles from Fort William west to the ferry port at Mallaig. This train (they don't actually call it the "Hogwarts Express") offers a small taste of the Harry Potter experience...but it may be a letdown for those who take this trip only for its wizarding connections. Although one of the steam engines and some of the coaches were used in the films, don't expect a Harry Potter theme ride. However, you can expect beautiful scenery. Along the way, the train stops for 20 minutes at Glenfinnan Station (just after the Glenfinnan Viaduct), and then gives you too much time (1.75 hours) to poke around the dull port town of Mallaig before heading back to Fort William.

Cost and Hours: One-way-£30; round-trip-£35; more for first class, tickets must be purchased in advance—see details next, 1/day Mon-Fri mid-May-Oct, 2/day Mon-Fri early June-Aug, also 1/day Sat-Sun late-June-late-Sept, departs Fort William at 10:15 and returns at 16:00, afternoon service in summer departs Fort William at 14:30 and returns at 20:30, about a 2-hour ride each way, tel. 0844-850-4680, www.jacobitetrain.com. Pay lockers for storing luggage are at the Fort William train station (station open long hours daily).

Prebooking Tickets: Trains leave from Fort William's train station, but you must book ahead online or by phone—you cannot buy tickets for this train at ticket offices. A limited number of seats may be available each day on a first-come, first-served basis (cash only, buy from conductor at coach D), but in summer, trips are often sold out. Rail passes are not accepted.

Cheaper Alternative: The 84-mile round-trip from Fort William takes the better part of a day to show you the same scenery twice. Modern "Sprinter" trains follow the same line and accept rail passes. Consider taking the steam train one-way to Mallaig, then speeding back on a regular train to avoid the long Mallaig layover and slow return (£12.50 one-way between Fort William and Mallaig, 4/day, 1.5 hours, to ensure a seat in peak season book by 18:00 the day before, tel. 0845-755-0033, www.nationalrail.co.uk).

Skye Connection: Note that you can use either the steam train or the Sprinter to reach the Isle of Skye: Take the train to Mallaig, walk onto the ferry to Armadale (on Skye), then catch a bus in Armadale to your destination on Skye (bus #52, www.stagecoachbus.com).

INVERNESS & LOCH NESS

Inverness • Culloden Battlefield • Clava Cairns • Loch Ness

Inverness, the Highlands' de facto capital, is an almost-unavoidable stop on the Scottish tourist circuit. It's a pleasant town and an ideal springboard for some of the country's most famous sights. Hear the music of the Highlands in Inverness and the echo of muskets at Culloden, where government troops drove Bonnie Prince Charlie into exile and conquered his Jacobite supporters. Ponder the mysteries of Scotland's murky prehistoric past at Clava Cairns, and enjoy a peek at Highland aristocratic life at Cawdor Castle. Just to the southwest of Inverness, explore the locks and lochs of the Caledonian Canal while playing hide-and-seek with the Loch Ness monster.

PLANNING YOUR TIME

Though it has little in the way of sights, Inverness does have a workaday charm and is a handy spot to spend a night or two between other Highland destinations. With two nights, you can find a full day's worth of sightseeing nearby.

Note that Loch Ness is between Inverness and Oban, Glencoe, and the Isle of Skye. If you're heading to or from one of those places, it makes sense to see Loch Ness en route, rather than as a side-trip from Inverness.

GETTING AROUND THE HIGHLANDS

With a car, the day trips around Inverness are easy. Without a car, you can get to Inverness by train (better from Edinburgh, Stirling, Glasgow, or Pitlochry) or by bus (better from Skye, Oban, and Glencoe), then side-trip to Loch Ness, Culloden, and other nearby sights by public bus or with a package tour.

Inverness

Inverness is situated on the River Ness at the base of a castle (now

used as a courthouse, but with a public viewpoint). Inverness' charm is its normalcy—it's a nice, midsize Scottish city that gives you a palatable taste of the "urban" Highlands and a contrast to cutesy tourist towns. It has a disheveled, ruddy-cheeked grittiness and is well located for enjoying the surrounding countryside sights. Check out the bustling, pedestrianized downtown, or meander the picnic-friendly riverside paths and islands—best at sunset, when the light hits the castle and couples hold hands while strolling along the water and over its footbridges.

Orientation to Inverness

Inverness, with about 70,000 people, has been one of the fastest-growing areas of Scotland in recent years. Marked by its castle,

Inverness clusters along the River Ness. The TI is on High Street, an appealing pedestrian shopping zone a few blocks away from the river; nearby are the train and bus stations. Most of my recommended B&Bs huddle atop a gentle hill behind the castle (a 10-minute uphill walk from the city center).

TOURIST INFORMATION
At the TI, you can pick up the self-guided *City Centre Trail* walking-tour leaflet and the *What's On* weekly events sheet (June-Sept Mon-Sat 8:45-18:30, shorter hours on Sun and off-season, free Wi-Fi, 36 High Street, tel. 01463/252-401, www.inverness-scotland.com).

HELPFUL HINTS
Charity Shops: Inverness is home to several pop-up charity shops. Occupying vacant rental spaces, these are staffed by volunteers who are happy to talk about their philanthropy. You can pick

up a memorable knickknack, adjust your wardrobe for the weather, and learn about local causes.

Festivals and Events: The summer is busy with special events, which can make it tricky to find a room. Book far ahead during these times, including the Etape Loch Ness bike race (early June), Highland Games (late June), Belladrum Tartan Heart Festival (music, late July), Black Isle farm show (early Aug), and Loch Ness Marathon (late Sept). The big RockNess Music Festival has been on hiatus due to budget cuts, but may return.

For a real Highland treat, catch a **shinty match** (a combination of field hockey, hurling, and American football—but without pads). Inverness Shinty Club plays at Bught Park, along Ness Walk (the TI or your B&B can tell you if there are any matches on, or search online for the Inverness Shinty Club).

Bookstore: Leakey's Bookshop, located in a converted church built in 1649, is the place to browse through teetering towers of musty old books and vintage maps, warm up by the wood-burning stove, and climb the spiral staircase to the loft for views over the stacks (Mon-Sat 10:00-17:30, closed Sun, Church Street, tel. 01463/239-947, Charles Leakey).

Baggage Storage: The train station has lockers (open Mon-Sat 6:40-20:30, Sun from 10:40), or you can leave your bag at the bus station's ticket desk (small fee, daily until 17:30).

Laundry: New City Launderette is near the west end of the Ness Bridge (self-service or same-day full-service, Mon-Sat 8:00-18:00, until 20:00 Mon-Fri in summer, Sun 10:00-16:00 year-round, last load one hour before closing, 17 Young Street, tel. 01463/242-507). **Thirty Degrees Laundry** on Church Street is another option (full-service only, drop off before 10:00 for same-day service, Mon-Sat 8:30-17:30, closed Sun, a few blocks beyond Victorian Market at 84 Church Street, tel. 01463/710-380).

Tours in Inverness

IN TOWN
Skip the City Sightseeing hop-on, hop-off bus tour (this format doesn't work in Inverness).

Inverness Bike Tours
Hardworking Alison leads small groups on two-hour bike tours. Her six-mile route is nearly all on traffic-free paths along canals and lochs outside of the city and comes with light guiding along the way. You'll pedal through Ness Island, stop at the Botanical

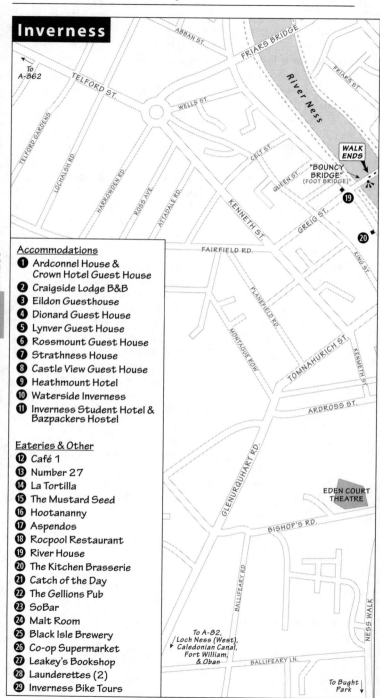

Inverness

INVERNESS & LOCH NESS

Accommodations
1. Ardconnel House & Crown Hotel Guest House
2. Craigside Lodge B&B
3. Eildon Guesthouse
4. Dionard Guest House
5. Lynver Guest House
6. Rossmount Guest House
7. Strathness House
8. Castle View Guest House
9. Heathmount Hotel
10. Waterside Inverness
11. Inverness Student Hotel & Bazpackers Hostel

Eateries & Other
12. Café 1
13. Number 27
14. La Tortilla
15. The Mustard Seed
16. Hootananny
17. Aspendos
18. Rocpool Restaurant
19. River House
20. The Kitchen Brasserie
21. Catch of the Day
22. The Gellions Pub
23. SoBar
24. Malt Room
25. Black Isle Brewery
26. Co-op Supermarket
27. Leakey's Bookshop
28. Launderettes (2)
29. Inverness Bike Tours

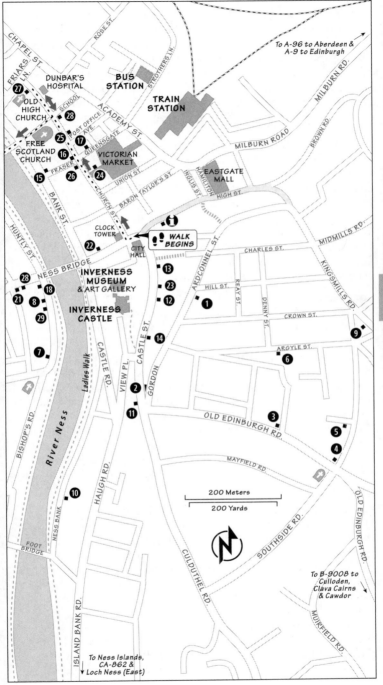

Gardens, ride along the Caledonian Canal with its system of locks (you may even catch a boat passing through the locks), and cycle through a nature preserve (£21, no kids under 14, 10-person max; daily in season at 10:00, 13:00, and 16:00; best to book a spot in advance online, goes even in light rain, meet near west end of Ness Bridge at Riva Restaurant at 5 Ness Walk, call or text mobile 07443-866-619, www.invernessbiketours.co.uk, info@invernessbiketours.co.uk). Arrive a bit early to size up your bike and helmet.

EXCURSIONS FROM INVERNESS

While thin on sights of its own, Inverness is a great home base for day trips. A variety of tour companies offer day trips—details and tickets are available at the TI. While the big sellers among Inverness day-trips are the many Loch Ness tours (because the monster is on every bucket list), I far prefer an Isle of Skye all-day joyride—which gives you a good look at Loch Ness and its famous castle along the way. Study the various websites for comparative details. For Isle of Skye and Orkney Island tours in summer, it's a good idea to book about a week in advance.

Loch Ness

The famous lake is just a 20-minute drive from Inverness. Tours will often include a short boat ride, a visit to the Urquhart Castle, and a stop at the Loch Ness monster exhibits. The lake is not particularly scenic. The castle, while scenic, is just a shell. And the monster is mostly a promotional gimmick. Still, if you have no car, this can be the most efficient way to check this off your list. **Jacobite Tours** focuses on trips that include Loch Ness, from a one-hour basic boat ride to a 6.5-hour extravaganza. Their four-hour "Sensation" tour includes a guided bus tour with live narration, a half-hour Loch Ness cruise, and visits to Urquhart Castle and the Loch Ness exhibits (£35, for more options see www.jacobite.co.uk, tel. 01463/233-999).

Isle of Skye

Several companies do good day tours to the Isle of Skye. They travel 110 miles (a 2.5-hour drive) to the heart of Skye (Portree). With about six hours of driving, and one hour for lunch in Portree, that leaves two or three hours for a handful of quick and scenic photo stops. All travel along Loch Ness so you can see Urquhart Castle and try for a monster sighting. And all stop for a view of Eilean Donan Castle. The longer rides loop around the Trotternish Peninsula. Websites explain the exact itineraries.

Wow Scotland's ambitious 12-hour itinerary goes in a big bus. They depart at 8:30 from the Inverness bus station and include short but smart and adequate stops all along the way (£77, 5/week June-Aug, fewer departures in April-May and Sept, none

Oct-March, tel. 01808/511-773, www.wowscotlandtours.com). I'd pay the extra for the £99 front row.

Highland Experience Tours runs another, shorter Isle of Skye itinerary in 24-seat buses (daily April-Oct, less off-season, 10 hours) but doesn't make it as far north as the Trotternish Peninsula (£55, tel. 01463/719-222, www.highlandexperience.com). They offer a variety of other daylong tours, including to the far north with John O'Groats, or a trip to Royal Deeside and the Speyside Whisky Trail.

Happy Tours Scotland organizes daily minibus tours on a 10-hour joy ride (getting all the way to Quiraing) with top-notch guides (£70, 8 people per minibus, daily at 8:30, leaves from 7 Ness Walk at Columba Hotel, mobile 07828-154-683, book at www.happy-tours.biz, run by Cameron). They also do other tours including itineraries focusing on Loch Ness, the *Outlander* books and TV series, a Speyside whisky tour, and private minibus tours.

Rabbie's Small Group Tours does 12-hour trips to Skye in its 16-seater buses for £52 nearly daily from Inverness. Their website explains their busy program (www.rabbies.com).

Iona Highland Tours takes eight people on several different Isle of Skye itineraries, including one that allows hiking time at the Fairy Pools (£70, 9 hours, tel. 01463/250-457, www.ionahighlandtours.com).

By Train Then Tour: To avoid a long bus ride or skip the sights along the way to Skye, take the train from Inverness to Kyle of Lochalsh, where a Skye-based tour company will pick you up and take you around. Try **Skye Tours** (tel. 01471/822-716, www.skye-tours.co.uk) or **Tour Skye** (tel. 01478/613-514, www.tourskye.com). The train leaves Inverness before 9:00 and arrives around 11:30; the return train is around 17:15 (covered by BritRail Pass).

The Orkney Islands

For a very ambitious itinerary, John O'Groats Ferries offers an all-day tour that departs Inverness at 7:15, drives you up to John O'Groats to catch the 40-minute passenger ferry, then a second bus takes you on a whistle-stop tour of Orkney's main attractions (with an hour in the town of Kirkwall) before returning you to Inverness by 21:00. While it's a long day, it's an efficient use of your time if you're determined to see Orkney (£74, daily June-Aug only, tel. 01955/611-353, www.jogferry.co.uk).

Inverness Walk

Humble Inverness has meager conventional sights, but its fun history and quirky charm become clear as you take this short self-guided walk (walk route shown on map earlier in this chapter).

• *Start at the clock tower.*

Clock Tower: Notice the **Gaelic language** on directional and street signs all around you. While nobody speaks Gaelic as a first language (and only about 60,000 Scottish people speak it fluently), this old Celtic language symbolizes the strength of Scottish Highland culture.

The clock tower looming 130 feet above you is all that remains of a tollbooth building erected in 1791. This is the highest spire in town, and for generations was a collection point for local taxes. Here, four streets—Church, Castle, Bridge, and High—come together, integrating God, defense, and trade—everything necessary for a fine city.

About 800 years ago, a castle was built on the bluff overhead and the town of Inverness coalesced right about here. For centuries, this backwater town's economy was based on cottage industries. Artisans who made things also sold them. In 1854, the train arrived, injecting energy and money from Edinburgh and Glasgow, and the Victorian boom hit. With the Industrial Age came wholesalers, distributors, mass production, and affluence. Much of the city was built during this era, in Neo-Gothic style—over-the-top and fanciful, like the City Hall (from 1882, kitty-corner to the clock tower). With the Victorian Age also came tourism.

Look for the **Bible quotes** chiseled into the wall across the street from the City Hall. A civic leader, tired of his council members being drunkards, edited these Bible verses for maximum impact, especially the bottom two.

Hiding just up the hill (behind the eyesore concrete home of the Inverness Museum and Art Gallery) is **Inverness Castle.** While the "castle" is now a courthouse, there is a small exhibition and a chance to climb to the top of the tower (£5). It's worth hiking up to the castle at some point during your visit to enjoy some of the best views of Inverness and its river. The courthouse in the castle doesn't see a lot of action. In the last few decades, there have been only two murders to prosecute. As locals like to say, "no guns, no problems." While hunters can own a gun, gun ownership in Scotland is complicated and tightly regulated.

• *Walk a few steps away from the river (toward McDonald's)...*

Mercat Cross and Old Town Center: Standing in front of the City Hall is a well-worn mercat cross, which designated the market in centuries past. This is where the townspeople gathered to hear important proclamations, share news, watch hangings, gossip, and so on. The scant remains of a prehistoric stone at the base of the cross are what's left of Inverness' "Stone of Destiny." According to tradition, whenever someone moved away from Inverness, they'd take a tiny bit of home with them in the form of a chip of this stone—so it's been chipped and pecked almost to oblivion.

The yellow **Caledonian** building faces McDonald's at the base of High Street. (Caledonia was the ancient Roman name for Scotland.) It was built in 1847, complete with Corinthian columns and a Greek-style pediment, as the leading bank in town, back when banks were designed to hold the money of the rich and powerful... and intimidate working blokes. Notice how nicely pedestrianized High Street welcomes people and seagulls...but not cars.

• *Next we'll head up Church Street, which begins between the clock tower and The Caledonian.*

Church Street: The street art you'll trip over at the start of Church Street is called *Earthquake*— a reminder of the quake that hit Inverness in 1816. As the slabs explain, the town's motto is "Open Heartedness, Insight, and Perseverance."

Stroll down Church Street. Look up above the modern storefronts to see Old World facades. **Union Street** (the second corner on the right)—stately, symmetrical, and Neoclassical—was the fanciest street in the Highlands when it was built in the 19th century. Its buildings had indoor toilets. That was big news.

Midway down the next block of Church Street (on the right), an alley marked by an ugly white canopy leads to the **Victorian**

Market. Venturing down the alley, you'll pass **The Malt Room** (a small and friendly whisky bar eager to teach you to appreciate Scotland's national tipple; see "Nightlife in Inverness") and **The Old Market Bar** (a dive bar worth a peek). Stepping into the Victorian Market, you'll find a gallery of shops under an iron-and-glass domed roof dating from 1876. The first section seems abandoned, but delve deeper to find some more active areas, where local shops mix with tacky "tartan tat" souvenir stands. If you're seriously into bagpipes, look for **Cabar Fèidh,** where American expat

Brian sells CDs and sheet music, and repairs and maintains the precious instruments of local musicians.

Go back out of the market the way you came in, and continue down Church Street. At the next corner you come to **Hootananny,** famous locally for its live music (pop in to see what's on tonight). Just past that is **Abertarff House,** the oldest house in Inverness. It was the talk of the town in 1593 for its "turnpike" (spiral staircase) connecting the floors.

Continue about a block farther along Church Street. The lane on the left leads to the **"Bouncy Bridge"** (where we'll finish this walk). Opposite that lane (on the right) is **Dunbar's Hospital,** with four-foot-thick walls. In 1668, Alexander Dunbar was a wealthy landowner who built this as a poor folks' home. You can almost read the auld script in his coat of arms above the door.

A few steps farther up Church Street, walk through the iron gate on the left and into the churchyard (we're focusing on the shorter church on the right—ignore the bigger one on the left). Looking at the WWI and WWII memorials on the church's wall, it's clear which war hit Scotland harder. While no one famous is buried here, many tombstones go back to the 1700s. Being careful not to step on a rabbit, head for the bluff overlooking the river and turn around to see...

Old High Church: There are a lot of churches in Inverness (46 Protestant, 2 Catholic, 2 Gaelic-language, and one offering a Mass in Polish), but these days, most are used for other purposes. This one, dating from the 11th century, is the most historic (but is generally closed). It was built on what was likely the site of a pagan holy ground. Early Christians called upon St. Michael to take the fire out of pagan spirits, so it only made sense that the  first Christians would build their church here and dedicate the spot as St. Michael's Mount.

In the sixth century, the Irish evangelist monk St. Columba brought Christianity to northern England, the Scottish islands (at Iona), and the Scottish Highlands (in Inverness). He stood here amongst the pagans and preached to King Brude and the Picts.

Study the bell tower from the 1600s. The small door to nowhere (one floor up) indicates that back before the castle offered protection, this tower was the place of last refuge for townsfolk under attack. They'd gather inside and pull up the ladder. The church became a prison for Jacobites after the Battle of Culloden, and executions were carried out in the churchyard.

Every night at 20:00, the bell in the tower rings 100 times. It has rung like this since 1730 to remind townsfolk that it's dangerous to be out after dinner.

• *From here, you can circle back to the lane leading to the "Bouncy Bridge" and then hike out onto the bridge. Or you can just survey the countryside from this bluff.*

The River Ness: Emptying out of Loch Ness and flowing seven miles to the sea (a mile from here), this is one of the shortest rivers in the country. While it's shallow (you can almost walk across it), there are plenty of fish in it. A 64-pound salmon was once pulled out of the river right here. In the 19th century, Inverness was smaller, and across the river stretched nothing but open fields. Then, with the Victorian boom, the suspension footbridge (a.k.a. "Bouncy Bridge") was built in 1881 to connect new construction across the river with the town.

• *Your tour is over. Inverness is yours to explore.*

Sights in Inverness

Inverness Museum and Art Gallery

This free, likable town museum is worth poking around on a rainy day to get a taste of Inverness and the Highlands. The ground-floor exhibits on geology and archaeology peel back the layers of Highland history: Bronze and Iron ages, Picts (including some carved stones), Scots, Vikings, and Normans. Upstairs you'll find the "social history" exhibit (everything from Scottish nationalism to hunting and fishing) and temporary art exhibits.

Cost and Hours: Free, April-Oct Tue-Sat 10:00-17:00, shorter hours off-season, closed Sun-Mon year-round, cheap café, in the ugly modern building on the way up to the castle, tel. 01463/237-114, www.highlifehighland.com.

Inverness Castle

Aside from nice views from the front lawn, a small exhibition on the ground floor, and a tower climb, Inverness' biggest nonsight is not open to the public. A wooden fortress that stood on this spot was replaced by a stone structure in the 15th century. In 1715, that castle was named Fort George to assert English control over the area. In 1745, it was destroyed by Bonnie Prince Charlie's Jacobite army and remained a ruin until the 1830s, when the present castle was built. The statue outside (from 1899) depicts Flora MacDonald, who helped Bonnie Prince Charlie escape from the English (see page 99). The castle was built as the courthouse, and when trials are in session, loutish-looking men hang out here, waiting for their bewigged barristers to arrive. For £5 you can climb to the top of the tower for a commanding city view. In a few years, the castle will host what promises to be a top-notch new museum.

River Walks

As with most European cities, where there's a river, there's a walk. Inverness, with both the River Ness and the Caledonian Canal, does not disappoint. Consider an early-morning stroll along the Ness Bank to capture the castle at sunrise, or a post-dinner jaunt to Bught Park for a local shinty match (see "Helpful Hints—Festivals and Events," earlier). The path is lit at night. The forested islands in the middle of the River Ness—about a 10-minute walk south of the center—are a popular escape from the otherwise busy city.

Here's a good plan for your Inverness riverside constitutional: From the Ness Bridge, head along the riverbank under the castle (along the path called "Ladies Walk"). As you work your way up the river, you'll see the architecturally bold Eden Court Theatre (across the river), pass a white pedestrian bridge, see a WWI memorial, and peek into the gardens of several fine old Victorian sandstone riverfront homes. Nearing the tree-covered islands, watch for fly-fishers in hip waders on the pebbly banks. Reaching the first, skinny little island, take the bridge with the wavy, wrought-iron railing and head down the path along the middle of the island. Notice that this is part of the Great Glen Way, a footpath that stretches from here all the way to Fort William (79 miles). Enjoy this little nature break, with gurgling rapids—and, possibly, a few midges. Reaching the bigger bridge, cross it and enjoy strolling through tall forests. Continue upriver. After two more green-railinged bridges, traverse yet another island, and find one last white-iron bridge that takes you across to the opposite bank. You'll pop out at the corner of Bught Park, the site of shinty practices and games—are any going on today?

From here, you can simply head back into town on this bank. If you'd like to explore more, you could continue farther south. It's not as idyllic or as pedestrian-friendly, but in this zone you'll find minigolf, a skate park, the Highland Archive building, the free Botanic Gardens (daily 10:00-17:00, until 16:00 Nov-March), and the huge Active Inverness leisure center, loaded with amusements including a swimming pool with adventure slides, a climbing wall, a sauna and steam area, and a gymnasium (www.invernessleisure. co.uk).

Continuing west from these leisure areas, you'll eventually hit the Caledonian Canal; to the south, this parallels the River Ness, and to the north is where it meets Beauly Firth, then Moray Firth and the North Sea. From the Tomnahurich Bridge, paths on either bank allow you to walk along the Great Glen Way until you're ready to turn around.

Nightlife in Inverness

Scottish Folk Music

While you can find traditional folk-music sessions in pubs and hotel bars anywhere in town, two places are well established as *the* music pubs. Neither charges a cover for the music, unless a bigger-name band is playing.

The Gellions has live folk and Scottish music nightly (from 21:30). It has local ales on tap and brags it's the oldest bar in town (14 Bridge Street, tel. 01463/233-648, www.gellions.co.uk).

Hootananny is an energetic place with several floors of live rock, blues, or folk music, and drinking fun nightly. It's rock (upstairs) and reel (ground floor). Music in the main bar (ground floor) usually begins about 21:30 (traditional music sessions Sun-Wed, trad bands on weekends; also a daytime session on Sat afternoon at 14:30). On Friday and Saturday nights only, upstairs is the Mad Hatter's nightclub, complete with a cocktail bar (67 Church Street, tel. 01463/233-651, www.hootananny.co.uk).

Billiards and Darts

SoBar is a sprawling pub with dart boards (free but £5 deposit), pool tables (£7.50 per hour), a museum's-worth of sports memorabilia, and the biggest TV screens in town (popular on big game nights). It's a fine place to hang out and meet locals if you'd rather not have live music (just across from the castle at 55 Castle Street, tel. 01463/229-780).

Whisky Tastings and Brew Pubs

For a whisky education, or just a fine cocktail, drop in to the intimate **Malt Room,** with whiskies ranging from £4 to £75. The whisky-plus-chocolate flight makes for a fun nightcap (just off Church Street in the alley leading to the Victorian Market, 34 Church Street, tel. 01463/221-888, Lee and Matt).

At the **Black Isle Brewery,** you can sample their local organic beers and ciders. Choose from 26 beers on tap (including some non-Black Isle brews), all listed on the TV screen over the bar (wood-fired pizzas, 68 Church Street, tel. 01463/229-920).

Sleeping in Inverness

B&BS NEAR THE TOWN CENTER

These B&Bs are popular; book ahead for June through August (and during the peak times listed in "Helpful Hints," earlier), and be aware that some require a two-night minimum during busy times. The places I list are a 10-15-minute walk from the train station and town center. To get to the B&Bs, either catch a taxi (£5) or walk: From the train and bus stations, go left on Academy Street. At the first stoplight (the second if you're coming from the bus station), veer right onto Inglis Street in the pedestrian zone. Go up the Market Brae steps. At the top, turn right onto Ardconnel Street.

On or near Ardconnel Street

These places line up above Castle Street (with several recommended restaurants).

$$ Ardconnel House is a classic, traditional place offering a nice, large guest lounge, along with six spacious and comfortable rooms (family room, two-night minimum preferred in summer, no children under 10, 21 Ardconnel Street, tel. 01463/240-455, www.ardconnel-inverness.co.uk, ardconnel@gmail.com, John and Elizabeth).

$ Craigside Lodge B&B has five large rooms with tasteful modern flair, nice tartan touches, and fun stuffed-animal doorstoppers. The breakfast room is a nice place to soak up city views (family room, no kids under 8, just above Castle Street at 4 Gordon Terrace, tel. 01463/231-576, www.craigsideguesthouse.co.uk, enquiries@craigsideguesthouse.co.uk, hospitable Paul and Mandy).

$ Crown Hotel Guest House has seven pleasant rooms (two with private bath down the hall) and is a bargain if you're willing to put up with a few quirks—some dated elements and owners who are still learning the ins and outs of running a guesthouse (family room, 19 Ardconnel Street, tel. 01463/231-135, www.crownhotel-inverness.co.uk, crownhotelguesthouse@gmail.com, Munawar and Asia).

Around Old Edinburgh Road and Southside Road

These places are just a couple of minutes farther out from Castle Street and the places on Ardconnel.

$$ Eildon Guesthouse, set on a quiet corner, offers five tranquil rooms with spacious baths. The cute-as-a-button 1890s countryside brick home exudes warmth and serenity from the moment you open the gate (family rooms, 2-night minimum in summer, no kids under 10, in-room fridges, parking, 29 Old Edinburgh Road, tel. 01463/231-969, www.eildonguesthouse.co.uk, eildonguesthouse@yahoo.co.uk, Jacqueline).

$$ Dionard Guest House, wrapped in a fine hedged-in garden, has cheerful common spaces, six lovely rooms, some fun stag art, and lively hosts Gail and Anne—best friends turned business partners (family suite, in-room fridges, they'll do guest laundry for free, 39 Old Edinburgh Road, tel. 01463/233-557, www. dionardguesthouse.co.uk, enquiries@dionardguesthouse.co.uk).

$$ **Lynver Guest House** will make you feel spoiled, with three large, boutique-y rooms (all with sitting areas), a backyard stone patio that catches the sun, and veggie and fish options at breakfast (2-night minimum preferred in summer, no kids under 10, in-room fridges, 30 Southside Road, tel. 01463/242-906, www. lynver.co.uk, info@lynver.co.uk, Michelle and Brian).

$$ **Rossmount Guest House** feels like home, with its curl-up-on-the-couch lounge space, unfussy rooms (five in all), and friendly hosts (two rooms share a bath and are cheaper, 2-night minimum in summer, Argyle Street, tel. 01463/229-749, www. rossmount.co.uk, mail@rossmount.co.uk, Ruth and Robert).

B&BS ACROSS THE RIVER

$$$ **Strathness House** has a prime spot on the river a block from Ness Bridge. Formerly a hotel, it's a bigger place, with 12 rooms and a large ground-floor lounge, but comes with the same intimate touches of a guesthouse. They cater to all diets at breakfast, including vegan, gluten-free, halal, and kosher (family room for 3, no kids under 5, street or off-site parking, 4 Ardross Terrace, tel. 01463/232-765, www.strathnesshouse.co.uk, info@ strathnesshouse.com, Joan and Javed).

$$ **Castle View Guest House** sits right along the River Ness at the Ness Bridge—and, true to its name, it owns smashing views of the castle. Its five big and comfy rooms (some with views) are colorfully furnished, and the delightful place is lovingly run by Eleanor (2A Ness Walk, tel. 01463/241-443, www.castleviewguesthouseinverness. com, enquiries@castleviewguesthouseinverness.com).

HOTELS

Inverness has a number of big chain hotels. These tend to charge a lot when Inverness is busy but may be worth a look if the B&Bs are full or if it's outside the main tourist season. Options include the Inverness Palace Hotel & Spa (a Best Western fancy splurge right on the river with a pool and gym), Premier Inn (River Ness location), and Mercure. The following hotels are smaller and more local.

$$$ **Heathmount Hotel**'s understated facade hides a chic retreat for comfort-seeking travelers. Its eight elegant rooms come with unique decoration, parking, and fancy extras (family room, no elevator, restaurant, Kingsmill Road, tel. 01463/235-877, www. heathmounthotel.com, info@heathounthotel.com,).

$$$ **Waterside Inverness,** in a nice, peaceful location along the River Ness, has 35 crisp rooms and a river-view

restaurant (parking, 19 Ness Bank, tel. 01463/233-065, www. thewatersideinverness.co.uk, info@thewatersideinverness.co.uk).

HOSTELS

For funky and cheap dorm beds near the center and the recommended Castle Street restaurants, consider these friendly side-by-side hostels, geared toward younger travelers. They're about a 12-minute walk from the train station.

¢ **Bazpackers Hostel,** a stone's throw from the castle, has a quieter, more private feel for a hostel. There are 34 beds in basic dorms (private rooms with shared bath available, reception open 7:30-23:00, no curfew, pay laundry service, 4 Culduthel Road, tel. 01463/717-663, www.bazpackershostel.co.uk, info@bazpackershostel.co.uk). They also rent a small apartment nearby (sleeps up to 4).

¢ **Inverness Student Hotel** has 57 thin-mattressed beds in nine brightly colored rooms and a laid-back lounge with a bay window overlooking the River Ness. The knowledgeable, friendly staff welcomes any traveler over 18. Dorms are a bit grungy, but each bunk has its own playful name (breakfast extra, free tea and coffee, pay laundry service, kitchen, 8 Culduthel Road, tel. 01463/236-556, www.invernessstudenthotel.com, info@invernessstudenthotel.com).

Eating in Inverness

BY THE CASTLE

The first three eateries line Castle Street, facing the back of the castle.

$$$ Café 1 serves up high-quality modern Scottish and international cuisine with trendy, chic bistro flair. Fresh meat from their own farm adds to an appealing menu (lunch and early-bird dinner specials until 18:45, open Mon-Fri 12:00-14:30 & 17:00-21:30, Sat from 13:00 & 18:00, closed Sun, reservations smart, 75 Castle Street, tel. 01463/226-200, www.cafe1.net).

$$ Number 27 has a straightforward, crowd-pleasing menu that offers something for everyone—burgers, pastas, and more. The food is surprisingly elegant for this price range (daily 12:00-15:00 & 17:00-21:00, generous portions, local ales on tap, 27 Castle Street, tel. 01463/241-999).

$$ La Tortilla has Spanish tapas, including spicy king prawns (the house specialty). It's an appealing, colorfully tiled, and vivacious dining option that feels like Spain. With the tapas format, three family-style dishes make about one meal (daily 12:00-22:00, 99 Castle Street, tel. 01463/709-809).

IN THE TOWN CENTER

$$$$ The Mustard Seed serves Scottish food with a modern twist in an old church with a river view. It's a lively place with nice outdoor tables over the river when sunny (early specials before 19:00, daily 12:00-15:00 & 17:30-22:00, reservations smart, on the corner of Bank and Fraser Streets, 16 Fraser Street, tel. 01463/220-220, www.mustardseedrestaurant.co.uk, Matthew).

$$ Hootananny is a spacious pub with a hardwood-and-candlelight vibe and a fun menu featuring dishes one step above pub grub (food served Mon-Sat 12:00-15:00 & 17:00-20:30, dinner-only on Sun). The kitchen closes early to make way for the live music scene that takes over each night after 21:30 (see "Nightlife in Inverness," earlier).

$$ Aspendos serves up freshly prepared, delicious Turkish dishes in a spacious, dressy, and exuberantly decorated dining room (daily 12:00-21:30, 26 Queensgate, tel. 01463/711-950).

Picnic: There's a **Co-op** market with plenty of cheap picnic grub at 59 Church Street (daily until 22:00).

ACROSS THE RIVER

$$$$ Rocpool Restaurant is a hit with locals, good for a splurge, and perhaps the best place in town. Owner/chef Steven Devlin serves creative modern European food to a smart clientele in a sleek, contemporary dining room (early-bird weekday special until 18:45, open Mon-Sat 12:00-14:30 & 17:45-22:00, closed Sun, reservations essential; across Ness Bridge at 1 Ness Walk, tel. 01463/717-274, www.rocpoolrestaurant.com).

$$$$ River House, a classy, sophisticated, but unstuffy riverside place, is the brainchild of Cornishman Alfie—who prides himself on melding the seafood know-how of both Cornwall and Scotland, with a bit of Mediterranean flair (Mon-Sat 15:00-21:30, closed Mon off-season and Sun year-round, reservations smart, 1 Greig Street, tel. 01463/222-033, www.riverhouseinverness.co.uk).

$$$ The Kitchen Brasserie is a modern building overlooking the river, popular for their homemade comfort food—pizza, pasta, and burgers (early-bird special until 19:00, daily 12:00-15:00 & 17:00-22:00, 15 Huntly Street, tel. 01463/259-119, www.kitchenrestaurant.co.uk, Christine).

Fish-and-Chips: Consider the **$ Catch of the Day** chippy for a nicely presented sit-down meal or to go (daily 12:00-14:00 & 16:30-22:00, closed Sun at lunch, a block over Ness Bridge on Young Street, mobile 07909-966-525).

Inverness Connections

From Inverness by Train to: Pitlochry (hourly, 1.5 hours), **Stirling** (every 1-2 hours, 3 hours, some transfer in Perth), **Kyle of Lochalsh** near Isle of Skye (4/day, 2.5 hours), **Edinburgh** (hourly, 4 hours, some with change in Perth), **Glasgow** (11/day, 3 hours, 4 direct, others change in Perth), **Thurso** (for ferries to Orkney; 4/day, 4 hours). The Caledonian Sleeper provides overnight service to **London** (www.sleeper.scot). Train info: tel. 0345-748-4950, www.nationalrail.co.uk.

By Bus: Inverness has a handy direct bus to **Portree** on the Isle of Skye (bus #917, 3/day, 3 hours), but for other destinations in western Scotland, you'll first head for **Fort William** (bus #19 or #919, 8/day, 2 hours). For connections onward to **Oban** (figure 4 hours total) or **Glencoe** (3 hours total), see "Fort William Connections" on page 74. Inverness is also connected by direct bus to **Edinburgh** (express bus #G90, 2/day, 3.5 hours; slower bus #M90, 6/day, 4 hours) and **Glasgow** (5/day on Citylink express bus #G10, 3 hours; 1/day direct on National Express #588, 4 hours). Scottish Citylink: www.citylink.co.uk.

Tickets are sold in advance online, by phone at tel. 0871-266-3333, or in person at the Inverness bus station (daily 7:45-18:15, baggage storage, 2 blocks from train station on Margaret Street, tel. 01463/233-371). For bus travel to England, check National Express (www.nationalexpress.com) or Megabus (http://uk.megabus.com).

ROUTE TIPS FOR DRIVERS

Inverness to Edinburgh (160 miles, 3.25 hours minimum): Leaving Inverness, follow signs to the A-9 (south, toward Perth). If you haven't seen the Culloden Battlefield yet (described later), it's an easy detour: Just as you leave Inverness, head four miles east off the A-9 on the B-9006. Back on the A-9, it's a wonderfully speedy, scenic highway (A-9, M-90, A-90) all the way to Edinburgh. If you have time, consider stopping en route in Pitlochry (just off the A-9; see the Eastern Scotland chapter).

Inverness to Portree, Isle of Skye (110 miles, 2.5 hours): The drive from Inverness to Skye is pretty but much less so than the valley of Glencoe or the Isle of Skye itself. You'll drive along boring Loch Ness and then follow signs to Portree and Skye on A-87 along Loch Cluanie (a loch tamed by a dam built to generate hydroelectric power). This valley was once a "drovers' route" for the cattle drive from the islands to the market—home of the original Scottish cowboys.

Inverness to Fort William (65 miles, 1.5 hours): This city, southwest of Inverness via the A-82, is a good gateway to Oban and Glencoe. See page 290.

Near Inverness

Inverness puts you in the heart of the Highlands, within easy striking distance of several famous and worthwhile sights: Commune with the Scottish soul at the historic Culloden Battlefield, where British history reached a turning point. Wonder at three mysterious Neolithic cairns, which remind visitors that Scotland's story goes back thousands of years. And enjoy a homey country castle at Cawdor. Loch Ness—with its elusive monster—is another popular and easy day trip.

In addition to the sights in this section, note that the Speyside Whisky Trail, the Leault Working Sheepdogs farm show, and the Highland Folk Museum are also within side-tripping distance of Inverness (all are covered in the Eastern Scotland chapter).

CULLODEN BATTLEFIELD

Jacobite troops under Bonnie Prince Charlie were defeated at Culloden (kuh-LAW-dehn) by supporters of the Hanover dynasty (King George II's family) in 1746.

Sort of the "Scottish Alamo," this last major land battle fought on British soil spelled the end of Jacobite resistance and the beginning of the clan chiefs' fall from power. Wandering the desolate, solemn battlefield, you sense that something terrible occurred here. Locals still bring white roses and speak of "The '45" (as Bonnie Prince Charlie's entire campaign is called) as if it just happened. The battlefield at Culloden and its high-tech visitors center together are worth ▲▲▲.

Orientation to Culloden

Cost and Hours: £11, £5 guidebook; daily April-Oct 9:00-17:30, June-Aug until 18:00, Nov-Dec and Feb-March 10:00-16:00, closed Jan, café, tel. 01463/796-090, http://www.nts.org.uk/culloden.

Tours: The included **audioguide** leads you through both the exhibition and the battlefield. There are several free tours daily along with costumed events (see schedule posted at entry).

Getting There: It's a 15-minute **drive** east of Inverness. Follow signs to *Aberdeen*, then *Culloden Moor*—the B-9006 takes you right there (well-signed on the right-hand side). Parking is £2. Public **buses** leave from Inverness' Queensgate Street and drop you off in front of the entrance (£5 round-trip ticket, bus #5, roughly hourly, 40 minutes, ask at TI for route/schedule updates). A **taxi** costs around £15 one-way.

Length of This Tour: Allow 2 hours.

Background

The Battle of Culloden (April 16, 1746) marks the steep decline of the Scottish Highland clans and the start of years of cruel repression of Highland culture by the British. It was the culmination of a year's worth of battles, and at the center of it all was the charismatic, enigmatic Bonnie Prince Charlie (1720-1788).

Charles Edward Stuart, from his first breath, was raised with a single purpose—to restore his family to the British throne. His grandfather was King James II (VII of Scotland), deposed in 1688 by the English Parliament for his tyranny and pro-Catholic bias. The Stuarts remained in exile in France and Italy, until 1745, when young Charlie crossed the Channel from France to retake the throne in the name of his father (James VIII and III to his supporters). He landed on the west coast of Scotland and rallied support for the Jacobite cause. Though Charles was not Scottish-born, he was the rightful heir directly down the line from Mary, Queen of Scots—and why so many Scots joined the rebellion out of resentment at being ruled by a "foreign" king (King George II, who was born in Germany, couldn't even speak English).

Bagpipes droned, and "Bonnie" (handsome) Charlie led an army of 2,000 tartan-wearing, Gaelic-speaking Highlanders across Scotland, seizing Edinburgh. They picked up other supporters of the Stuarts from the Lowlands and from England. Now 6,000 strong, they marched south toward London—quickly advancing as far as Derby, just 125 miles from the capital—and King George II made plans to flee the country. But anticipated support for the Jacobites failed to materialize in the numbers they were hoping for (both in England and from France). The Jacobites had so far been victorious in their battles against the Hanoverian government forces, but the odds now turned against them. Charles retreated to the Scottish Highlands, where many of his men knew the terrain and might gain an advantage when outnumbered. The English government troops followed closely on his heels.

Against the advice of his best military strategist, Charles' army faced the Hanoverian forces at Culloden Moor on flat, barren terrain that was unsuited to the Highlanders' guerrilla tactics. The Jacobites—many of them brandishing only broadswords, targes (wooden shields covered in leather and studs), and dirks (long

daggers)—were mowed down by King George's cannons and horsemen. In less than an hour, the government forces routed the Jacobite army, but that was just the start. They spent the next weeks methodically hunting down ringleaders and sympathizers (and many others in the Highlands who had nothing to do with the battle), ruthlessly killing, imprisoning, and banishing thousands.

Charles fled with a £30,000 price on his head (an equivalent of millions of today's pounds). He escaped to the Isle of Skye, hidden by a woman named Flora MacDonald (her grave is on the Isle of Skye, and her statue is outside Inverness Castle). Flora dressed Charles in women's clothes and passed him off as her maid. Later, Flora was arrested and thrown in the Tower of London before being released and treated like a celebrity.

Charles escaped to France. He spent the rest of his life wandering Europe trying to drum up support to retake the throne. He drifted through short-lived romantic affairs and alcohol, and died in obscurity, without an heir, in Rome.

Though usually depicted as a battle of the Scottish versus the English, in truth Culloden was a civil war between two opposing dynasties: Stuart (Charlie) and Hanover (George). However, as the history has faded into lore, the battle has come to be remembered as a Scottish-versus-English standoff—or, in the parlance of the Scots, the Highlanders versus the Strangers.

The Battle of Culloden was the end of 60 years of Jacobite rebellions, the last major battle fought on British soil, and the final stand of the Highlanders. From then on, clan chiefs were deposed; kilts, tartans, and bagpipes were outlawed; and farmers were cleared off their ancestral land, replaced by more-profitable sheep. Scottish culture would never fully recover from the events of the campaign called "The '45."

❍ Self-Guided Tour

Your tour takes you through two sections: the exhibit and the actual battlefield.

The Exhibit

As you pass the ticket desk, note the **family tree**: Bonnie Prince Charlie ("Charles Edward Stuart") and George II were distant cousins. Then the exhibit's shadowy-figure **touchscreens** connect you with historical figures who give you details from both the Hanoverian and Jacobite perspectives. A **map** shows the other power struggles happening in and around Europe, putting this fight for political control of Britain in a wider context. This battle was no small regional skirmish, but rather a key part of a larger struggle between Britain and its neighbors, primarily France, for control over trade and colonial power. In the display case are **medals** from the early 1700s, made by both sides as propaganda.

From here, your path through this building is cleverly designed to echo the course of the Jacobite army. Your short march

(with lots of historic artifacts) gets under way as Charlie sails from France to Scotland, then finagles the support of Highland clan chiefs. As he heads south with his army to take London, you, too, are walking south. Along the way, maps show the movement of troops, and wall panels cover the buildup to the attack, as seen from both sides. Note the clever division of information: To the left and in red is the story of the "government" (a.k.a. Hanoverians/Whigs/English, led by the Duke of Cumberland); to the right, in blue, is the Jacobites' perspective (Prince Charlie and his Highlander/French supporters).

But you, like Charlie, don't make it to London—in the dark room at the end, you can hear Jacobite commanders arguing over whether to retreat back to Scotland. Pessimistic about their chances of receiving more French support, they decide to U-turn, and so do you. Heading back up north, you'll get some insight into some of the strategizing that went on behind the scenes.

By the time you reach the end of the hall, it's the night before the battle. Round another bend into a dark passage, and listen to the voices of the anxious troops. While the English slept soundly in their tents (recovering from celebrating the Duke's 25th birthday), the scrappy and exhausted Jacobite Highlanders struggled through the night to reach the battlefield (abandoning their plan of a surprise night attack at Nairn and instead retreating back toward

Inverness).

At last the two sides meet. As you wait outside the theater for the next showing, study the chart depicting how the forces were arranged on the battlefield. Once inside the theater, you'll soon be surrounded by the views and sounds of a windswept moor. An impressive four-minute **360° movie** projects the re-enacted battle with you right in the center of the action. The movie drives home just how out-matched the Jacobites were.

The last room has **period weapons,** including ammunition and artifacts found on the battlefield, as well as **historical depictions** of the battle. You'll also find a section describing the detective work required to piece together the story from historical evidence. Be sure to tour the **aftermath corridor,** which talks about the nearly genocidal years following the battle and the cultural wake of this event to this day. Be sure to examine the **huge map,** with narration explaining the combat you've just experienced while giving you a bird's-eye view of the field through which you're about to roam.

The Battlefield

Leaving the visitors center, survey the battlefield (which you'll tour with the help of your audioguide). In the foreground is a cottage used as a makeshift hospital during the conflict. Red flags show the front line of the government army (8,000 troops). This is where most of the hand-to-hand fighting took place. The blue flags in the distance are where the Jacobite army (5,500 troops) lined up.

As you explore the battlefield, notice how uneven and boggy the ground is in parts, and imagine trying to run across this hum-mocky terrain with all your gear, toward almost-certain death.

The old stone memorial cairn, erected in 1881, commemorates

the roughly 1,500 Jacobites buried in in this field. It's known as the Graves of the Clans. As you wander the battlefield, following the audiogu-ide, you'll pass by other **mass graves,** marked by small headstones, and ponder how entire clans fought, died, and were buried here.

Heading back to the parking lot, notice the wall of **protruding bricks.** Each represents a soldier who died. The handful of Hanoverian casualties are on the left (about 50); the rest of the long wall's raised bricks represent the multitude of dead Jacobites.

CLAVA CAIRNS

Scotland is littered with reminders of prehistoric peoples—especially in Orkney and along the coast of the Moray Firth—but

the Clava Cairns, worth ▲, are among the best-preserved, most interesting, and easiest to reach. You'll find them nestled in the spooky countryside just beyond Culloden Battlefield. These "Balnauran of Clava" are Neolithic burial chambers dating from 3,000 to 4,000 years ago. Although they appear to be just some giant piles of rocks in a sparsely forested clearing, a closer look will help you appreciate the prehistoric logic behind them. (The site is explained by an information plaque near the entry.) There are three structures: a central "ring cairn" with an open space in the center but no access to it, flanked by two "passage cairns," which were once buried under turf-covered mounds. The entrance shaft in each passage cairn lines up with the setting sun at the winter solstice. Each cairn is surrounded by a stone circle, and the entire ensemble is framed by evocative trees—injecting this site with even more mystery.

Enjoy the mystery of the site: Were the stone circles part of a celestial calendar system? Or did they symbolize guardians?

Why were the clamshell-sized hollows carved into the stones facing the chambers? Was the soul of the deceased transported into the next life by the ray of sunlight on that brief moment that it filled the inner chamber? No one knows.

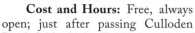

Cost and Hours: Free, always open; just after passing Culloden Battlefield on the B-9006 coming from Inverness, signs on the right point to *Clava Cairns.* Follow this twisty road a couple miles, over the "weak bridge" and to the free parking lot by the stones. Skip the cairns if you don't have a car.

CAWDOR CASTLE

Homey, intimate, and worth ▲, this castle is still the residence of the Dowager (read: widow) Countess of Cawdor, a local aristocratic branch of the Campbell family. While many associate the castle with Shakespeare's *Macbeth* (because "Cawdor" is mentioned more than a dozen times in the play), there is no actual connection with Shakespeare. *Macbeth* is set 300 years before the castle was even built. The castle is worth a visit simply because it's historic and beautiful in its own right—and because the woman who owns it flies a Buddhist flag from its tower. She is from Eastern Europe and was the Earl's second wife.

Cost and Hours: £11, good £5 guidebook explains the family and the rooms, May-Sept daily 10:00-17:30, closed Oct-April, tel. 01667/404-401, www.cawdorcastle.com.

Getting There: It's on the B-9090, just off the A-96, about 15 miles east of Inverness (6 miles beyond Culloden and Clava Cairns). In recent years, public transportation to the castle has been nonexistent—but ask at the Inverness TI just in case it has resumed.

Visiting the Castle: You'll follow a one-way circuit around the castle with each room explained with posted explanations written by the countess' late husband, the sixth Earl of Cawdor. His notes bring the castle to life and make you wish you'd known the old

chap. Cawdor feels very lived-in because it is. While the Dowager Countess moves out during the tourist season, for the rest of the year this is her home. You can imagine her stretching out in front of the fireplace with a good book. Notice her geraniums in every room.

The drawing room (for "with-drawing" after dinner) is lined with a family tree of portraits looking down. In the Tapestry Bedroom you'll see the actual marriage bed of Sir Hugh Campbell from 1662 and 17th-century tapestries warming the walls. In the Yellow Room, a flat-screen TV hides inside an 18th-century cabinet (ask a docent to show you). In the Tartan Passage, lined with modern paintings, find today's dowager—Lady Angelika—in a beautiful 1970 pastel portrait, staring at her late husband's predecessors. Notice how their eyes follow you creepily down the hall—but hers do not.

A spiral stone staircase near the end of the tour leads down to the castle's proud symbol: a holly tree dating from 1372. According to the beloved legend, a donkey leaned against this tree to mark the spot where the castle was to be built...and it was, around the tree.

The **gardens,** included with the ticket, are worth exploring, with some 18th-century linden trees and several surprising species (including sequoia and redwood). Note the hedge maze crowned by a minotaur (not open to the public) and surrounded by a laburnum arbor (dripping with yellow blossoms in May and June).

The nine-hole **golf course** on the castle grounds provides a quick and affordable way to have a Scottish golfing experience. The course is bigger than pitch-and-putt and fun even for non-golfers (£18/person with clubs). You're welcome to try the putting green for £4.

Nearby: The close but remote-feeling **village of Cawdor**—with a few houses, a village shop, and a tavern—is also worth a look if you've got time to kill.

Loch Ness

I'll admit it: I had my zoom lens out and my eyes on the water. The local tourist industry thrives on the legend of the Loch Ness monster. It's a thrilling thought, and there have been several seemingly reliable "sightings" (by monks, police officers, and sonar imaging). But even if you ignore the monster stories, the loch is impressive: 23 miles long, less than a mile wide, 754 feet deep, and containing more water than all of the freshwater bodies of England and Wales combined. It's essentially the vast chasm of a fault line, filled with water.

Getting There: The Loch Ness sights are a 20-minute drive southwest of Inverness. To drive the full length of Loch Ness takes about 45 minutes. Fort William-bound buses #19 and #919 make stops at Urquhart Castle and Drumnadrochit (8/day, 40 minutes).

Sights on Loch Ness

In July 1933, a couple swore they saw a giant sea monster shimmy across the road in front of their car by Loch Ness. Within days, ancient legends about giant monsters in the lake (dating as far back as the sixth century) were revived—and suddenly everyone was spotting "Nessie" poke its head above the waters of Loch Ness. Further sightings and photographic "evidence" have bolstered the claim that there's something mysterious living in this unthinkably deep and murky lake. (Most sightings take place in the deepest part of the loch, near Urquhart Castle.) Most witnesses describe a waterbound dinosaur (resembling the real, but extinct, plesiosaur). Others cling to the slightly more plausible theory of a gigantic eel. And skeptics figure the sightings can be explained by a combination of reflections, boat wakes, and mass hysteria. The most famous photo

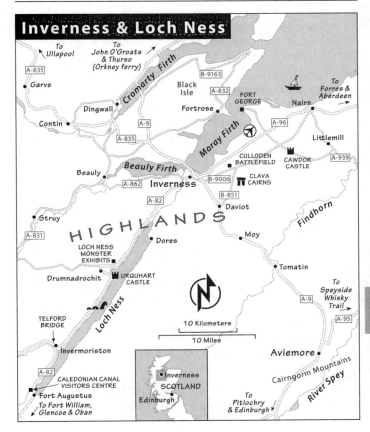

Inverness & Loch Ness

To Ullapool

To John O'Groats & Thurso (Orkney ferry)

Cromarty Firth

A-835

Garve

B-9163

Black Isle

A-832

FORT GEORGE

To Forres & Aberdeen

Nairn

Dingwall

Fortrose

Contin

A-9

Moray Firth

A-835

A-96

Littlemill

A-939

Beauly Firth

CULLODEN BATTLEFIELD

CAWDOR CASTLE

Beauly

A-862

Inverness

B-9006

CLAVA CAIRNS

B-851

A-82

Daviot

Struy

HIGHLANDS

Moy

Findhorn

A-831

Dores

LOCH NESS MONSTER EXHIBITS

Tomatin

Drumnadrochit

URQUHART CASTLE

To Speyside Whisky Trail

A-9

A-95

10 Kilometers

TELFORD BRIDGE

Loch Ness

10 Miles

Invermoriston

Aviemore

A-82

CALEDONIAN CANAL VISITORS CENTRE

Cairngorm Mountains

Fort Augustus

To Fort William, Glencoe & Oban

Inverness

SCOTLAND

Edinburgh

To Pitlochry & Edinburgh

River Spey

of the beast (dubbed the "Surgeon's Photo") was later discredited—the "monster's" head was actually attached to a toy submarine. But

that hasn't stopped various cryptozoologists from seeking photographic, sonar, and other proof.

And that suits the thriving local tourist industry just fine. The Nessie commercialization is so tacky that there are two different monster exhibits within 100 yards of each other, both in the town of Drumnadrochit. Of the two competing sites, Nessieland is pretty cheesy while the Loch Ness Centre and Exhibition (described next) is surprisingly thoughtful. Each has a tour-bus parking lot and more square footage devoted to their kitschy shops than to the exhibits. While Nessieland is a tourist trap, the Loch Ness Centre may appease that small part of you that knows the *real* reason you wanted to see Loch Ness.

▲Loch Ness Centre & Exhibition

This exhibit has two parts: First you make six stops in a series of video rooms, and then you enter the exhibition explaining the history of the Great Glen and Loch Ness. It's spearheaded by Adrian Shine, a naturalist fond of saying "I like mud," who has spent many years researching lake ecology and scientific phenomena. With video presentations and special effects, this exhibit explains the geological and historical environment that bred the monster story, as well as the various searches that have been conducted. Refreshingly, it retains an air of healthy skepticism instead of breathless monster-chasing. It also has some artifacts related to the search, such as a hippo-foot ashtray used to fake monster footprints and the *Viperfish*—a harpoon-equipped submarine used in a 1969 Nessie search. You'll also learn how in 1952 record-seeker John Cobb died going 200 mph in his speedboat on the loch.

Cost and Hours: £8, ask about RS%, daily Easter-Oct 9:30-17:45, July-Aug until 18:45, Nov-Easter 10:00-16:15, last entry 45 minutes before closing, in the big stone mansion right on the main road to Inverness, tel. 01456/450-573, www.lochness.com.

▲Urquhart Castle

The ruins at Urquhart (UR-kurt), just up the loch from the Nessie exhibits, are gloriously situated with a view of virtually the entire lake and create a traffic jam of tourism on busy days.

The visitors center has a tiny exhibit with interesting castle artifacts and an eight-minute film taking you on a sweep through a thousand years of tumultuous history—from St. Columba's visit to the castle's final destruction in 1689. The castle itself, while dramatically situated and fun to climb through, is an empty shell. After its owners (who supported the crown) blew it up to keep the Jacobites from taking it, the largest medieval castle in Scotland (and the most important in the Highlands) wasn't considered worth rebuilding or defending, and was abandoned. Well-placed, descriptive signs help you piece together this once-mighty fortress. As you walk toward the ruins, take a close look at the trebuchet (a working replica of one of the most destructive weapons of English King Edward I),

The Caledonian Canal

Two hundred million years ago, two tectonic plates collided, creating the landmass we know as Scotland and leaving a crevice of thin lakes slashing diagonally across the country. This Great Glen Fault, from Inverness to Oban, is easily visible on any map.

British engineer Thomas Telford connected the lakes 200 years ago with a series of canals so ships could avoid the long trip around the north of the country. The Caledonian Canal runs 62 miles from Scotland's east to west coasts; 22 miles of it is man-made. Telford's great feat of engineering took 19 years to complete, opening in 1822 at a cost of one million pounds.

But bad timing made the canal a disaster commercially. Napoleon's defeat in 1815 meant that ships could sail the open seas more freely. And by the time the canal opened, commercial ships were too big for its 15-foot depths. Just a couple of decades after the Caledonian Canal opened, trains made the canal almost useless...except for Romantic Age tourism. From the time of Queen Victoria (who cruised the canal in 1873), the canal has been a popular tourist attraction. To this day the canal is a hit with vacationers, recreational boaters, and lock-keepers who compete for the best-kept lock.

The scenic drive from Inverness along the canal is entertaining, with Drumnadrochit (Nessie centers), Urquhart Castle, Fort Augustus (five locks), and Fort William (under Ben Nevis, with the eight-lock "Neptune's Staircase"). As you cross Scotland, you'll follow Telford's work—22 miles of canals and locks between three lochs, raising ships from sea level to 51 feet (Ness), 93 feet (Lochy), and 106 feet (Oich).

While Neptune's Staircase, a series of eight locks near Fort William, has been cleverly named to sound intriguing (see page 76), the best lock stop is midway, at Fort Augustus, where the canal hits the south end of Loch Ness. In Fort Augustus, the **Caledonian Canal Visitor Centre,** overlooking the canal just off the main road, gives a good rundown on Telford's work (described next). Stroll past several shops and eateries to the top for a fine view.

Seven miles north, in the town of **Invermoriston,** is another Telford structure: a stone bridge, dating from 1805, that spans the Morriston Falls as part of the original road. Look for a small parking lot just before the junction at A-82 and A-887, on your right as you drive from Fort Augustus. Carefully cross the A-82 and walk three minutes back the way you came. The bridge, which took eight years to build and is still in use, is on your right.

and ponder how this giant catapult helped Edward grab almost every castle in the country away from the native Scots.

Cost and Hours: £9, guidebook-£5, daily April-Sept 9:30-18:00, Oct until 17:00, Nov-March until 16:30, last entry 45 minutes before closing, café, tel. 01456/450-551, www.historic-scotland.gov.uk.

Loch Ness Cruises

Cruises on Loch Ness are as popular as they are pointless. The lake is scenic, but far from Scotland's prettiest—and the time-consuming boat trips show you little more than what you'll see from the road. As it seems that Loch Ness cruises are a mandatory part of every "Highlands Highlights" day tour, there are several options, leaving from the top, bottom, and middle of the loch. The basic one-hour loop costs around £14 and includes views of Urquhart Castle and lots of legends and romantic history (Jacobite is the dominant outfit of the many cruise companies, www.jacobite.co.uk). I'd rather spend my time and money at Fort Augustus or Urquhart Castle.

▲Fort Augustus

Perhaps the most idyllic stop along the Caledonian Canal is the little lochside town of Fort Augustus. It was founded in the 1700s—before there was a canal here—as part of a series of garrisons and military roads built by the English to quell the Highland clansmen, even as the Jacobites kept trying to take the throne in London. Before then, there were no developed roads in the Highlands—and without roads, it's hard to keep indigenous people down.

From 1725 to 1733, the English built 250 miles of hard roads and 40 bridges to open up the region; Fort Augustus was a central Highlands garrison at the southern tip of Loch Ness, designed to awe clansmen. It was named for William Augustus, Duke of Cumberland—notorious for his role in destroying the clan way of life in the Highlands. (When there's no media and no photographs to get in the way, ethnic cleansing has little effect on one's reputation.)

Fort Augustus makes for a delightful stop if you're driving through the area. Parking is easy. There are plenty of B&Bs, charming eateries, and an inviting park along the town's five locks. You can still see the capstans, surviving from the days when the locks were cranked open by hand.

The fine little **Caledonian Canal Visitor Centre** tells the story of the canal's construction (free, daily Easter-Oct, tel. 01320/366-493). Also, consider the pleasant little canalside stroll out to the head of the loch.

Eating in Fort Augustus: You can eat reasonably at a string of eateries all lining the same side of the canal. Consider **The Little Neuk,** a good café serving filled rolls and homemade soups; **The**

Lock Inn, cozy and pub-like with great canalside tables, ideal if it's sunny; **The Bothy,** another pub with decent food; and the **Canalside Chip Shop** offering fish-and-chips to go (no seating, but plenty of nice spots on the canal). A small grocery store is at the gas station, next to the TI, which is a few steps from the canal just after crossing the River Oich (also housing the post office, a WC, and an ATM).

EASTERN SCOTLAND

*Pitlochry • Sights West of the Cairngorms • Loch Tay
• Speyside Whisky Trail • Balmoral Castle & the Royal
Deeside • Dunnottar Castle*

Between Edinburgh and Inverness, the eastern expanse of Scotland bulges out into the North Sea. The main geological landmark is Cairngorms National Park, with gently rugged Highland scenery and great hiking terrain. If your time is limited, Scotland is more satisfying elsewhere. But this region is easily accessible—you'll likely pass through at some point—and has a lot to offer, especially for those with special interests.

This chapter is organized geographically: sights west and east of the Cairngorms. Those in a hurry should focus on the west, where the A-9 highway links up some fun choices. Pitlochry has a green-hills-and-sandstone charm, a warm welcome, and a pair of great distilleries linked by a nice hike, making it the region's best overnight stop. Nearby you'll find a fascinating trip back to prehistory (at the Scottish Crannog Centre on Loch Tay), a fun sheepdog show, and an open-air folk museum.

East of the Cairngorms, the attractions require more of a detour (most convenient for those connecting Inverness and St. Andrews), but an even better look at rural Scotland. Whisky connoisseurs flock to Speyside, royalists visit Balmoral Castle and the nearby home-base village of Ballater, and ruined-castle fans head to Dunnottar.

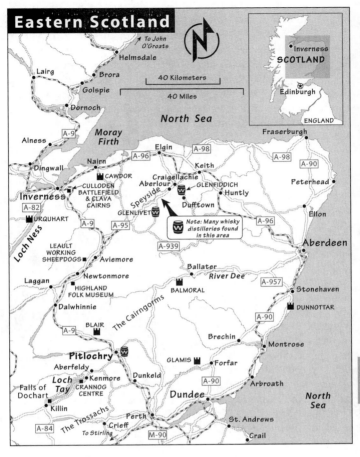

Eastern Scotland

Note: Many whisky distilleries found in this area

West of the Cairngorms

The A-9 highway, connecting Inverness, Stirling, and Edinburgh, may be Scotland's most touristy road. Heading south on the A-9, soon after leaving Inverness, the highway begins to skirt around the curved west edge of Cairngorms National Park, which it follows almost all the way to Pitlochry. These bald, heather-covered hills are what many people picture when they imagine Highland scenery. The best look at the Cairngorms is on the east side of the park, around the village of Ballater and Balmoral Castle (see page 129); the A-939, connecting the valley of the River Spey to Ballater, is particularly dramatic. But you'll get a decent glimpse of scenery along the A-9.

As you follow the A-9, it seems every exit is stacked with

brown "tourist attraction" signs. For the most part, the options along here are more convenient than good; they tend to pale in comparison to alternatives elsewhere in the country. But if your trip to Scotland isn't taking you beyond this Highland corridor, some of these may be worth a stop. Pitlochry, described next, is the top town (particularly for those seeking a handy overnight); after that, I've listed more options in the order you'll reach them traveling from Inverness to Edinburgh.

Pitlochry

This likable tourist town, famous for its whisky and its hillwalking (both beloved by Scots), makes an enjoyable overnight stop. Just outside the craggy Highlands, Pitlochry is set amid pastoral rolling hills that offer plenty of forest hikes. It seems that tourism is the town's only industry—with perhaps Scotland's highest concentration of woolens shops and outdoor outfitters. (The name "Pitlochry" comes from the old Pictish word for "tourist

trap.") But Pitlochry also has the feel of a real community. People here are friendly and bursting with town pride: They love to chat about everything from the high-quality local theater to the salmon ladder at the hydroelectric dam. It's also a restful place, where—after the last tour bus pulls out—you can feel your pulse slow as you listen to gurgling streams.

Orientation to Pitlochry

Plucky little Pitlochry (pop. 2,500) lines up along its tidy, tourist-minded main street, Atholl Road, which runs parallel to the River Tummel. The train station is on Station Road, off the main street. Its two distilleries are a walk—or short drive—out of town (see my self-guided whisky walk). Navigate by following the black directional signs to Pitlochry's handful of sights.

TOURIST INFORMATION

The helpful TI, at one end of town, has free Wi-Fi and sells maps for local hill walks and scenic drives. Their good £1 *Pitlochry Path Network* brochure is handy (Mon-Sat 9:30-17:30, Sun 10:00-16:00, longer hours in summer, shorter hours and closed Sun Nov-March; 22 Atholl Road, tel. 01796/472-215).

HELPFUL HINTS

Special Events: In summer, a pipe band marches through town every Monday evening. In May and June, the salmon ladder at the dam comes to life (described later, under "Sights in Pitlochry"). Pitlochry's Highland Games are in early September (www.pitlochryhighlandgames.co.uk). And in October, the Enchanted Forest light-and-water show set to music illuminates Faskally Wood, just outside of town (www.enchantedforest.org.uk).

Bike Rental: Escape Route Bikes, located across the street and a block from the TI (away from town), rents a variety of bikes (£16/5 hours, £24/24 hours, includes helmet and lock if you ask, Mon-Sat 9:00-17:30, Sun 10:00-17:00, 3 Atholl Road, tel. 01796/473-859, www.escape-route.co.uk).

Parking: Drivers who aren't spending the night can park in the large pay-and-display lot next to the TI, in the center of town.

Sights in Pitlochry

DISTILLERIES

Pitlochry's two distilleries can be linked by a relaxing two-hour hike (described later, under "Pitlochry Whisky Walk").

▲▲Edradour Distillery

This cute distillery (pronounced ED-rah-dower)—the smallest historic distillery in Scotland (est. 1825)—takes pride in making its whisky with a minimum of machinery, and maintains a proud

emphasis on tradition. Small white-and-red buildings are nestled in a delightfully green Scottish hillside. ("Edradour"—also the name of the stream that gurgles through the complex—means "land between two rivers.") With its idyllic setting and gregarious spirit, it's one of the most enjoyable distillery tours in Scotland. Unlike the bigger distilleries, they allow you to take photos of the equipment. If you like the whisky, buy some here and support the Pitlochry economy—this is one of the few independently owned distilleries left in Scotland.

Cost and Hours: £7.50 for a one-hour tour, departs 3/hour, April-Oct Mon-Sat 10:00-17:00, closed Sun and off-season, last

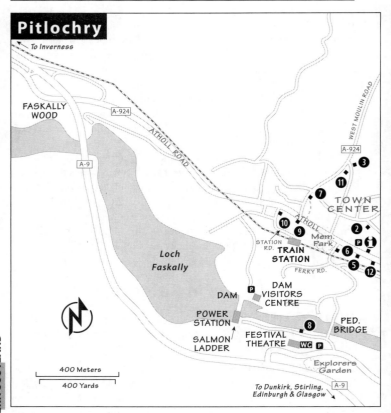

Pitlochry

To Inverness

FASKALLY WOOD

A-924

ATHOLL ROAD

A-9

WEST MOULIN ROAD

A-924

❸

❶❶

❼

T O W N
C E N T E R

Loch Faskally

❶⓪
❾

ATHOLL

STATION RD.

Mem. Park

TRAIN STATION

FERRY RD.

❷

P ❶

❻

❺

⓬

DAM

P

DAM VISITORS CENTRE

POWER STATION

SALMON LADDER

FESTIVAL THEATRE

WC P

❽

PED. BRIDGE

Explorers Garden

To Dunkirk, Stirling, Edinburgh & Glasgow
A-9

400 Meters
400 Yards

EASTERN SCOTLAND

tour departs one hour before closing, tel. 01796/472-095, www.edradour.com.

Getting There: Most come to the distillery by car (follow signs from the main road, 2.5 miles into the countryside), but you can also get there on a peaceful hiking trail that you'll have all to yourself (follow my "Pitlochry Whisky Walk," next page).

Visiting the Distillery: You'll watch a 10-minute orientation film, then enjoy a sit-down education while tasting two different drams. Then the guided tour proceeds through the facility: from the malt barn (where the barley is germinated and dried) to the still (where giant copper stills turn distiller's beer into whisky) to the warehouse (where 6,000 casks age in the darkness). Take a deep whiff of the rich aroma—you're smelling the so-called "angels' share," the tiny percentage of each cask that's lost to evaporation.

Bell's Blair Athol Distillery
This big, ivy-covered facility is conveniently located (about a half-mile from the town center) and more corporate-feeling, offering hour-long tours with a wee taste at the end. I'd tour this only if

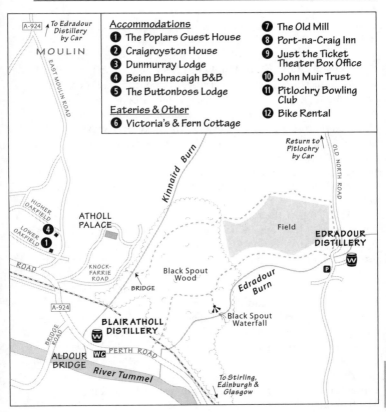

Accommodations
1. The Poplars Guest House
2. Craigroyston House
3. Dunmurray Lodge
4. Beinn Bhracaigh B&B
5. The Buttonboss Lodge

Eateries & Other
6. Victoria's & Fern Cottage
7. The Old Mill
8. Port-na-Craig Inn
9. Just the Ticket Theater Box Office
10. John Muir Trust
11. Pitlochry Bowling Club
12. Bike Rental

you're a whisky completist, or if you lack the wheels or hiking stamina to reach Edradour.

Cost and Hours: £7.50, Easter-Oct tours depart 2/hour daily 10:00-17:00, July-Aug until 17:30, last tour departs one hour before closing; shorter hours, fewer tours, and closed Sat-Sun off-season; tel. 01796/482-003, www.discovering-distilleries.com/blairathol.

Pitlochry Whisky Walk

A fun way to visit the distilleries is to hill-walk from downtown Pitlochry. The entire loop trip takes 2-3 hours, depending on how long you linger in the distilleries (at least an hour of walking each way). You'll see lush fern forests and a pretty decent waterfall. The walk is largely uphill on the way to the Edradour Distillery; wear good shoes, bring a rain jacket just in case, and be happy that you'll stroll easily downhill *after* you've had your whisky samples.

At the TI, pick up the *Pitlochry Path Network* brochure and follow along with its map. You'll be taking the **Edradour Walk** (marked on directional signs with yellow hiker icons; on the map it's a series of yellow dots). Leave the TI and head left along the busy A-924. The walk can be done in either direction, but I'll describe it counterclockwise.

Within 10 minutes, you'll walk under the railroad tracks and then come to **Bell's Blair Athol Distillery** on your left. If you're a whisky buff, stop in here. Otherwise, hold out for the much more atmospheric Edradour. You'll pass a few B&Bs and suburban homes, then a sign marked *Black Spout* on a lamppost. Just after this, you'll cross a bridge, then take the next left, walking under another stone rail overpass and away from the road. Following this path, you'll come to a clearing, and as the road gets steeper, you'll see signs directing you 50 yards off the main path to see the "Black Spout"—a wonderful waterfall well worth the few extra steps on your right.

At the top of the hill, you'll arrive in another clearing, where a narrow path hugs a huge field on your left. Low rolling hills surround you in all directions. It seems like there's not another person around for miles, with just the thistles to keep you company. From here it's an easy 20 minutes to the **Edradour Distillery.**

Leaving the distillery, to complete the loop, head right, following the paved road (Old North Road). In about 50 yards, a sign points left into the field. Take the small footpath that runs along the left side of the road. (If you see the driveway with stone lions on both sides, you've gone a few steps too far.) You'll walk parallel to the route you took getting to the distillery, hugging the far side of the same huge field. The trail then swoops back downhill through the forest, until you cross the footbridge and make a left. You'll soon reach Knockfarrie Road—take this downhill; you'll pass a B&B and hear traffic noises as you emerge from the forest. The trail leads back to the highway, with the TI a few blocks ahead on the right.

TOWN CENTER
Strolling the High Street

Pitlochry's main street is a pleasant place to wander and window-shop. As you stroll, consider this: The town exists thanks to the arrival of the train, which conveniently brought Romantic Age tourists from the big cities in the south to this lovely bit of Scotland. Queen Victoria herself visited three times in the 1860s, putting Pitlochry on the tourist map. The postcard-perfect Victorian sandstone architecture on the main street makes it clear that this was a delightful escape for city folks back in the 19th century.

Here are some things to look for, listed in order of how you'll reach them from the TI. The **memorial park** with the Celtic cross honors men from the local parish whose lives were lost fighting in World War I—a reminder of Scotland's disproportionate sacrifices in that conflict. Throughout Scotland, even many tiny villages have similar monuments.

Ferry Road, next to the park, branches off under the rail bridge and leads to a footbridge that takes you to the other side of the river—home to Pitlochry's spunky Festival Theatre, as well as a power station with a salmon ladder (a fun excuse for a lazy walk—described later).

Peek inside **The Hardware Centre.** In small towns like Pitlochry—without a Wal-Mart (I mean, Tesco)—shops like this serve

as catch-all general stores for the community. In addition to hardware, it carries a full range of kitchenware.

The **Love Your Sweets** shop, with a purple awning, stocks a staggering variety of uniquely Scottish candies in bulk. Step in to buy a mixed bag of some unusual flavors of hard candies, such as clove, rhubarb, or Irn-Bru. At the next little park on the right, a surging stream angles away from the main road and to the recommended Old Mill restaurant.

On the corner with Station Road is the headquarters of the **John Muir Trust.** John Muir (1838-1914) was born in Scotland, moved to the US when he was 10, and later helped establish the world's first national park system in the US. Inside is a free tiny exhibit called Wild Land, with a feel-good nature video and a small art gallery. They also sell books, maps, and other conservation-themed souvenirs (Mon-Sat 10:00-17:00, Sun 11:00-16:00, shorter hours and closed Tue off-season, tel. 01796/470-080, www. jmt.org).

Lawn Bowls
The **Pitlochry Bowling Club** lets outsiders rent shoes and balls and try their hand at the game (£3, generally Mon-Fri 10:00-12:00 & 14:00-16:00, 24 West Moulin Road, tel. 01796/473-459).

ACROSS THE RIVER
These sights lie along the largely undeveloped riverbank opposite Pitlochry's town center. While neither are knockouts, they're a fine excuse for a pretty stroll or drive. Walkers can reach this area easily in about 15 minutes: Head down Ferry Road (near the memorial park), cross the footbridge, and turn right.

EASTERN SCOTLAND

Pitlochry Dam Visitors Centre and Salmon Ladder

Pitlochry's dam on the River Tummel provides a nice place to go for a stroll, and comes with a salmon ladder—a series of chambers that allow salmon to "step" their way upstream next to the dam (salmon generally run May-June).

The well-designed and family-friendly Visitors Centre celebrates hydroelectric power in the Highlands. Its fine nine-minute video, "Power from the Glens," explains the epic vision of generating clean power from—and for—the Highlands. You can also walk all the way across the top of the dam, pausing to read informational plaques and to peer through windows into the hydroelectric plant (free, daily 9:30-17:30). Their cafeteria is delightful with a nice river view.

Pitlochry Festival Theatre

This theater company rotates its productions, putting on a different play every few nights. Most are classics, with a few musicals and new shows mixed in (£15-35; plays generally run May-Oct Mon-Sat). The theater hosts concerts on Sunday evenings—usually tribute acts—and a variety of other performances in winter (purchase tickets online or by phone; in person at Just the Ticket—Mon-Sat 9:00-17:00, closed Sun, 89 Atholl Road; or at the theater—same price, box office open daily 10:00-20:00, tel. 01796/484-626, www.pitlochryfestivaltheatre.com).

Nearby: Just above the theater's parking lot, the six-acre **Explorers Garden** features plants and wildflowers from around the world (£4, daily 10:00-17:00, closed Nov-March, last entry 45 minutes before closing, tel. 01796/484-626, www.explorersgarden.com).

Sleeping in Pitlochry

All of these have free parking.

$$ The Poplars Guest House, perched regally on a meticulously landscaped hill high above the main road, has been stylishly renovated by Jason and Nathalie. The huge home has a spacious lounge with views, and six rooms that combine modern comforts with a respect for tradition. Start the day off right with their whisky porridge (family room, closed in winter, at the end of Lower Oakfield at #27, tel. 01796/472-129, www.poplars-pitlochry.com, info@poplars-pitlochry.com).

$$ Craigroyston House, my sentimental favorite in Pitlochry, is a quaint, large Victorian country house with eight large and luxe bedrooms. Their terraced yard is a great place to sip some wine or play croquet. Vaughan and Susan, originally from Orkney, are welcoming and generous (family rooms, right above the TI parking lot at 2 Lower Oakfield, tel. 01796/472-053, www.craigroyston.co.uk, reservations@craigroyston.co.uk). Drivers can reach it on Lower Oakfield Road; walkers can walk up from the huge parking lot next to the TI on Atholl Road (find the small gate at the back of the lot).

$$ Dunmurray Lodge is a calming place to call home, with four springtime-colored rooms, and friendly hosts (family room, no kids under 5; breakfast includes gluten-free, vegetarian, and other options; 5-minute walk from town at 72 Bonnethill Road, mobile 0778-346-2625, www.dunmurray.co.uk, lorraine@dunmurray. co.uk, Lorraine and Mike).

$$ Beinn Bhracaigh (pronounced "benny vrackie," meaning "speckled mountain") is a guesthouse with a hotel feel. The 13 rooms are modern and tasteful, and they have a sitting room where you can serve yourself at the well-stocked honesty bar. Of my listings, it sits the highest above the main road—still within a (longish, steep) walk, but easier by car. The location comes with fine views across the town center and river to the hills beyond (minimum two-night stay in peak season and on weekends, no kids under 8, no elevator, 14 Higher Oakfield, tel. 01796/470-355, www.beinnbhracaigh. com, info@beinnbhracaigh.com, James and Kirsty).

$ The Buttonboss Lodge has a less idyllic setting, right along the busy main road across from the TI (expect some traffic noise). But it's affordable and convenient for train travelers. The eight rooms, managed by Cristian, are straightforward and a bit old-fashioned (25 Atholl Road, tel. 01796/472-065, mobile 0790-247-2065, www.buttonbosslodge.co.uk, info@buttonbosslodge.co.uk).

Eating in Pitlochry

Plenty of options line the main drag, including several bakeries selling picnic supplies.

$$ Victoria's restaurant and coffee shop, a local favorite, feels like a down-home diner, serving up an eclectic menu of comfort food (daily 10:00-21:00, patio seating, free Wi-Fi, at corner of memorial park, 45 Atholl Road, tel. 01796/472-670).

$$$ The Old Mill, tucked a block behind the main drag in an actual old mill, has good Scottish food, plus some pastas and salads. Sit in their popular, high-energy pub, calmer restaurant in back, or at picnic tables outside (food served daily 12:00-21:00, tel. 01796/474-020).

$$$ Fern Cottage, just behind Victoria's, has a darker, candlelit, dressier ambience and a Mediterranean spin on their menu (daily 12:00-15:00 & 17:00-20:30, Ferry Road, tel. 01796/473-840).

$$$ Port-na-Craig Inn, on the river just downhill from the theater, is a fancier option catering to theatergoers. For a calmer experience, go at 20:00, after the show has started (lunch specials, daily 11:00-21:00, tel. 01796/472-777).

Pitlochry Connections

The train station is open Monday to Saturday 8:00-18:30 and Sunday 10:30-18:00.

From Pitlochry by Train to: Inverness (almost hourly, 2 hours), **Stirling** (5/day direct, 1 hour, more with transfer in Perth), **Edinburgh** (8/day direct, 2 hours), **Glasgow** (9/day, 2 hours, some transfer in Perth). Train info: Tel. 0845-748-4950, www.nationalrail.co.uk.

By Bus to: Glasgow (1/day direct on National Express #588; 5/day on Citylink to Perth, then change to Megabus to Glasgow, 2.5 hours—train is faster), **Edinburgh** (3/day on Citylink #M90, 2.5 hours).

Sights West of the Cairngorms

ALONG THE A-9 HIGHWAY
▲▲Leault Working Sheepdogs

Each afternoon, Neil Ross presents a 45-minute demonstration of his well-trained sheepdogs. The experience is vividly real and fascinating. You'll hunker down in a natural little amphitheater in the turf while Neil describes his work. He'll demonstrate why shepherds have used a crook for thousands of years, and explain why farmers get frustrated when "fancy people with numbers after their names" try to tell them how to manage their land. Then the dogs get to work: With shouts and whistles, each dog follows individual commands, demonstrating an impressive mastery over the sheep. (Watching in awe, you can't help but think: Sheepdogs are smart... and sheep are idiots.) After the presentation, you'll meet (and pet) the border collie stars of the show, and may have the

chance to feed some lambs or to try your hand at shearing sheep. If they happen to have a litter of border collie puppies, even those who dislike dogs may find it hard to resist smuggling one home.

Cost and Hours: £5, demonstration only once per day, May-Oct Sun-Fri at 16:00, closed to the public at other times, no demonstrations Sat or Nov-April, tel. 01540/651-402, www. leaultworkingsheepdogs.co.uk.

Getting There: The entrance to the farm is a gravel road that literally runs across the A-9. But since the little road sneaks up on you, it's safer to exit for Kincraig, then follow the brown signs around to a driveway that takes you (carefully) back across the A-9 and up to the farm.

▲Highland Folk Museum

Scotland doesn't have a top-notch open-air folk museum—but this is close enough. Just off the highway on the outskirts of Newtonmore, the museum features re-creations of traditional buildings from the surrounding area from the 1700s through the 1930s. The buildings are a bit spread out, and it's quiet outside of frequent "activity days" (check the schedule online).

Cost and Hours: Free but donations welcome, daily April-Aug 10:30-17:30, Sept-Oct 11:00-16:30, closed Nov-March, helpful £5 guidebook, tel. 01540/673-551, www.highlifehighland. co.uk.

Getting There: Exit the A-9 in Newtonmore, then follow brown signs for about five minutes through the village to the museum (free parking).

Visiting the Museum: The highlight of the museum is a circa-1700, thatched-roof Highland township called **Baile Gean,** a gathering of four primitive stone homes and three barns, each furnished as it would have been in the Jacobite era (it's a 15-minute walk from the entry—go to the right through a pine forest and up a small hill). Although built for the museum, the township was closely based on an actual  settlement a few miles away that was populated until the 1830s. Costumed docents can explain traditional Highland lifestyles, and you'll likely see—and smell—a peat fire filling one of the homes with its rich smoke. (Because peat doesn't spit or spark, it was much safer to burn than wood—which was too valuable to feed fires anyway, as most tools were made of wood.) This area provided an ideal backdrop for some of the rural-life scenes in the TV production of *Outlander.*

With more time, visit the other structures in the rest of the open-air museum, such as the tweed shop; the schoolhouse, where you'll learn about early-20th-century classrooms; or the Lochanhully House (look for the house with red eaves, past the playground), which depicts a 1950s Scottish home. At the far end of the complex you may see some hairy "coos."

▲Blair Castle

If you like Scottish history, heritage, and antlers, you'll like Blair Castle. It's a convenient stop for those zipping past on the A-9. In Gaelic, a "blàr" or "blair" is a flat bit of land surrounded by hills. And sure enough, this stately, white palace rises up from a broad clearing. A stout fortress during the Jacobite wars, it was later renovated and expanded as a mansion in the Scottish Baronial style.

The former residence of the Dukes of Atholl (a.k.a. Clan Murray) is now owned and run as a business by a trust. It's filled with paintings, historic artifacts, Clan Murray mementoes, and grand, creaky staircases. Following the self-guided, one-way route, you'll enjoy a fine look at 19th-century aristocratic life. The WWI room recalls how the house was used as a hospital during that conflict. A highlight is the wood-paneled ballroom at the end, draped in tartan and bristling with antlers.

If time allows, explore the grounds—especially the walled Hercules Garden, where rugged plantings surround a lily-padded pond, overlooked by a statue of Hercules (accessed via the trail near the parking lot).

Cost and Hours: £11, April-Oct daily 9:30-17:30, closed Nov-March, last entry one hour before closing, tel. 01796/481-207, www.blair-castle.co.uk.

Getting There: From the town of Blair Atholl (just off of the A-9), drive down the long, tree-lined driveway to the free parking lot. From Pitlochry, you can take the more scenic B-8019/B-8079 instead of the A-9. Bus #87 runs from Pitlochry (5/day in summer, fewer off-season, 15 minutes, www.elizabethyulecoaches.co.uk).

Nearby: The **Atholl Country Life Museum** is a humble, volunteer-run museum literally across the street from Blair Castle. A local teacher created these exhibits, filling an old school to show the other side of the social and economic coin. Chatting with the volunteers makes a visit extra fun (£4, generally daily 13:30-17:00, July-Aug from 10:00, tel. 01796/481-232, www. athollcountrylifemuseum.org.uk).

▲Dunkeld

This charming wee town, just off the A-9, is worth a stretch-your-legs break. While the town center is pleasant—with flower boxes and cleverly named shops—its claim to fame is its partially ruined cathedral, which sits on the banks of the River Tay.

Pay-and-display parking is at both ends of town (the north end has a WC). The TI and cathedral are just down High Street from the main drag, Atholl Street.

The **Cathedral of St. Columba** was actually Scotland's leading church for a brief time in the ninth century, when that im-

portant saint's relics were being stored here during Viking raids. Later it blossomed into a large cathedral complex in a secluded, riverside setting. But it was devastated by the one-two punch of Reformation iconoclasts (who tore down most of the building) and Jacobites (who fought the Battle of Dunkeld near here).

Duck inside to see the stony interior and its one-room museum (pick up the free info sheet or consider borrowing the good audioguide for a £1 donation). Outside, as you circle the entire complex, you'll discover that the current church is merely the choir of the original structure—a huge, ruined nave (currently undergoing restoration) stretches behind it.

The **$ Scottish Deli** is nice for a drop in, with soups, sandwiches, and salads (a few tables inside, corner of High Street and Atholl Street, tel. 01350/728-028).

ON LOCH TAY

A 30-minute drive west of the A-9, Loch Tay is worth visiting mostly for its excellent Scottish Crannog Centre—the best place in Scotland to learn about early Iron-Age life. You can also drive along Loch Tay (and past the thundering Falls of Dochart) to connect Pitlochry and the A-9 corridor with the Trossachs and Loch Lomond.

▲▲Scottish Crannog Centre

Across Scotland, archaeologists know that little round islands on the lochs are evidence of crannogs—circular houses on stilts, dating to 500 years before Christ. Iron-Age Scots built on the water because in an age before roads, people traveled by

EASTERN SCOTLAND

boat, and because waterways were easily defended against rampaging animals (or people). Scientists have found evidence of 18 such crannogs on Loch Tay alone. One has been rebuilt, using mostly traditional methods, and now welcomes visitors. Guided by a passionate and well-versed expert, you'll spend about an hour visiting the crannog and learning about how its residents lived.

Cost and Hours: £10, family tickets available, daily 10:00-17:30, closed Nov-March, well-marked just outside Kenmore on the south bank of Loch Tay, tel. 01887/830-583, www.crannog.co.uk.

Visiting the Museum: The highlight is the two-part tour, led by guides dressed in prehistoric garb. Join whichever group is going next.

One part of the tour takes you out across the rustic wooden bridge to the crannog itself, where you'll huddle under the thatched roof and learn about Iron Age architecture. Your guide explains how families of up to 20 people lived in just one crannog—along with their livestock—and paints a vivid picture of what life was like in those rugged times.

In the other part of the tour, guides demonstrate Iron Age "technology"—turning a lathe, grinding flour, spinning yarn, and even starting a fire using nothing but wood and string. You'll then have a hands-on opportunity to try the tools yourself—and realize how easy the guides made it look.

A modest exhibit just off the gift shop explains the history of crannogs, excavation efforts, and the building of this new one.

Kenmore

Located where Loch Tay empties into the River Tay, Kenmore is a sleepy, one-street, black-and-white village with a big hotel, a

church, and a post office/general store. There's not much to do here, other than visit the nearby Scottish Crannog Centre, enjoy the Loch Tay scenery, and consider hiking through the woods to the Taymouth Castle (currently being renovated). With its classic old hotel, Kenmore can be a handy home base for this area.

Sleeping and Eating in Kenmore: $$ Kenmore Hotel,

EASTERN SCOTLAND

dominating the village center, feels like a classic Scottish country hotel—it claims to be the oldest inn in Scotland (dating from 1572). The 39 rooms are old-fashioned but cozy, and welcoming lounges, terraces, and other public spaces sprawl through the building. Look for the Robert Burns poem above the fireplace in one of the bars (elevator, The Square, Kenmore, tel. 01887/830-205, www.kenmorehotel.com, reception@kenmorehotel.com). The **$$$** pub, dining room, and various outdoor dining areas all share the same menu.

Falls of Dochart

At the far end of Loch Tay from Kenmore, in the village of Killin, the road passes on a stone bridge over a churning waterfall where the peat-brown waters of the River Dochart tumble dramatically into the loch. The romantic bridge is busy with passing motorists enjoying a photo op; eateries and gift shops surround the scene. You can clamber down onto the flat stones for a closer look. From the bridge, notice the stone archway marking the burial ground of the Clan Macnab.

East of the Cairngorms

While the A-9 corridor to the west is studded with touristy amusements, the area east of the Cairngorms (while hardly undiscovered) feels more rugged and lets you dig deeper into the countryside. In this area, I've focused on two river valleys with very different claims to fame: Speyside, curling along the top of the Cairngorms, is famous for its many distilleries; Royal Deeside, cutting through the middle of the Cairngorms, is the home of the Queen's country retreat at Balmoral and the neighboring village of Ballater. Overnighting in Ballater is an ideal way to linger in this region and sleep immersed in Cairngorms splendor.

Speyside Whisky Trail

Of the hundred or so distilleries in Scotland, half lie near the valley of the River Spey—a small area called Speyside. The ample waters of the river, along with generous peat deposits, have attracted distillers here for centuries. While I prefer some of the smaller, more intimate distillery tours elsewhere (including Oban Distillery in Oban, Talisker on the Isle of Skye, and Edradour near Pitlochry), Speyside is convenient to Inverness and practically a pilgrimage for aficionados. The distilleries here feel bigger and more corporate, but they also include some famous names (including the world's two best-selling brands of single malts, Glenfiddich and Glenlivet). And for whisky lovers, it's simply enjoyable to spend time in a region steeped in such reverence for your favorite drink.

PLANNING YOUR TIME

A quick car tour of Speyside takes about a half-day, and is a scenic way to connect Inverness to Royal Deeside (it also works as a side-trip from Inverness). Whisky aficionados will have their own list of distilleries they want to hit. But, for the typical traveler, here is an easy plan for the day:

Enjoy the scenic drive to Aberlour, tour the Speyside Cooperage, tour the Glenfiddich distillery, and finally have a short stop in Dufftown. These four stops are within about five miles of each other.

If driving south from Inverness, you could easily do these stops and then drive down to Balmoral Castle to tour it and sleep nearby in Ballater.

Orientation to Speyside

The A-95, which parallels the River Spey, is the region's artery (to reach it, take the A-9 south from Inverness and turn off toward Grantown-on-Spey). Brown *Malt Whisky Trail* signs help connect the dots. While several distilleries lie along the main road, even more are a short side-trip away. Three humdrum villages form the nucleus of Speyside: Aberlour (the biggest), Craigellachie (a wide spot in the road), and Dufftown (with a clock tower and a good dose of stony charm).

Because public transit connections aren't ideal, Speyside works best for drivers—though if you're determined, you could take the train from Inverness to Elgin and catch the "whisky bus" from there (Stagecoach bus #38, stops in Craigellachie and Aberlour on the way to Dufftown, about hourly, none Sun).

A word of caution: In Scotland, DUI standards are very low (0.05 percent) and strictly enforced. Go easy on the tastings, or bring a designated driver. Distilleries are often happy to give drivers their dram "to go" so they can enjoy it safely later.

Sights in Speyside

I've listed these roughly west to east, as you'll reach them approaching Speyside on the A-95.

Aberlour

Officially named "Charlestown of Aberlour" for its founder, this attractive sandstone town lines up along the A-95. It's famous both for its namesake whisky distillery (www.aberlour.com) and as the home of Walkers Shortbread, which you'll see sold in red-tartan boxes all over Scotland (you can get some at the factory store in town, but no tours). **$$ The Mash Tun,** just off the main road (next to a welcoming little visitors center), is an atmospheric whisky bar that serves lunch and rents rooms upstairs (tel. 01340/881-771, www.mashtun-aberlour.com).

Craigellachie

The blink-and-you'll-miss-it village of Craigellachie (craig-ELL-a-kee) is home to the landmark **$$ Craigellachie Hotel.** This classic, grand old hotel, a handy home base for whisky pilgrims, is famous for its whisky bar—stocking more than 800 bottles (opens daily at 17:00, the receptionist may let you in for a peek at other times, 26 rooms, tel. 01340/881-204 www.craigellachiehotel.co.uk). Just past the hotel on the A-941, keep an eye out on the left for the picturesque **Craigellachie Bridge,** built by the great Scottish industrial architect Thomas Telford.

Note that the A-95 takes a sharp turn to the right in Craigellachie (just before the hotel), leading to the cooperage described next, and beyond that, to the Glenfiddich Distillery and Dufftown; the main road (past the hotel and the bridge) becomes A-941.

▲Speyside Cooperage

Perhaps the single biggest factor in defining whisky's unique flavor is the barrel it's aged in. At this busy workshop on the outskirts

of Craigellachie, you can watch master coopers build or refurbish casks for distilleries throughout Scotland. The 14 coopers who work here—and who must first complete a four-year apprenticeship to get the gig—are some of the last of a dying breed; while just about everything used to be transported in barrels, today it's only booze. First you'll view an engaging, almost tear-jerking 15-minute film, then you'll follow your guide up to an observation deck peering down over the factory floor. Oak timber is shaped into staves, which are gathered into metal hoops, then steamed to make them more pliable. Finally the inside is charred with a gas flame, creating a carbonized coating that helps give whisky its golden hue and flavor. Because the vast majority of casks used in Scotland are hand-me-downs from the US (where bourbon laws only allow one use per barrel), you're more likely to see reassembly of old casks (with new ends) rather than from-scratch creation of new ones. But the process is equally fascinating. Apart from observing the barrel-making, it's also interesting to see the intensity of the workers—who are paid by the piece.

Cost and Hours: £3.50, tours depart every 30 minutes, Mon-Fri 9:00-15:30, closed Sat-Sun, Dufftown Road, Craigellachie, tel. 01340/871-108, www.speysidecooperage.co.uk.

Glenfiddich Distillery

As you enter Dufftown, keep an eye out on the left for the home of Scotland's top-selling single malt whisky. This sprawling but charming factory—with a name that means "Valley of the Deer" (hence the logo)—offers excellent tours and tastings. After a 15-minute promotional video, your kilted guide will walk you through the impressive plant, which includes a busy bottling hall. Your tour finishes with an extensive tasting session.

Cost and Hours: Basic £10 "Explorers" visit includes 1.5-hour tour and 4 tastings (departs every 30 minutes), more expensive options available, daily 9:30-16:00 (last tour), tel. 01340/822-373, www.glenfiddich.com.

Glenfiddich or Glenlivet? The two big distilleries of Speyside each offer £10 tours and tastings. Both tours are excellent, and they handle their crowds very well. I prefer Glenfiddich as it feels more historic and less corporate, and it's closer to other sights.

Dufftown

This charming, sleepy town has a characteristic crossroads street plan radiating from its clock-tower-topped main square. A few steps up Conval Street from the tower, the humble, one-room **Whisky Museum** doubles as the TI. You'll see a small selection of historical displays and tools from the whisky trade. Most importantly, you'll have a chance to chat with the fun retirees who run the place (free, daily 10:00-16:00 in summer, tel. 01340/821-591). **The Whisky Shop,** directly behind the  tower, is a serious place selling 650 different types of whisky (daily

EASTERN SCOTLAND

10:00-18:00, closed Sun in winter, 1 Fife Street, tel. 01340/821-097, www.whiskyshopdufftown.com).

Glenlivet Distillery

Sitting five miles south of the A-95 (turn off at Bridge of Avon), this is one of the area's most famous and popular distilleries to

tour. Their 75-minute tour spares you the gauzy video intro that comes with most tours and takes you right through the sprawling production facility—perched on a ridge overlooking Cairngorms National Park. The tour finishes with three tastings. If you're not taking the tour, you're welcome to enjoy their history exhibit room. Note: This is just a short detour for those connecting Speyside to Ballater on the scenic route through the mountains (B-9008/A-939).

Cost and Hours: £10, daily mid-March-mid-Nov 9:30-18:00, tours depart every 30 minutes 10:00-16:30, closed in winter, head to the village of Glenlivet and follow signs from there, tel. 01340/821-720, www.theglenlivet.com.

Balmoral Castle and Royal Deeside

Royal Deeside—the forested valley of the River Dee—is two sights in one: the Scottish home of the British royal family, wrapped in some of the most gorgeous scenery of Cairngorms National Park. Driving through the park you'll see pockets of Scots pine (Scotland's national tree). While no longer widespread, these once blanketed the Scottish countryside. In fact, 2,000 years ago the Romans must have been impressed. They called this land "Caledonia Silva," meaning "wooded land." Driving on, closer to Balmoral, you'll enter a high, treeless moorland with lots of broom plants (what we'd call Scotch broom) and wild thistles (Scotland's national flower). As you drive, cresting hills to meet vast views, you can imagine royals out on the hunt. (In fact, you'll see tiny huts used by hunters to hide out while they await the stag of their dreams.) The only game you'll likely see is hairy cows and lots of roadkill—mostly rabbit. (Hare today...)

▲Balmoral Castle

The Queen stays at her 50,000-acre private estate, located within Cairngorms National Park, from August through early October. But in the months leading up to Her Royal Highness' arrival, the grounds and the castle's ballroom are open to visitors. While royal-

ists will enjoy this glimpse into the place where Liz, Chuck, Billy, and Katie unwind, cynics are disappointed that only one room (the ballroom) is open to the public. Some find the visit overrated and overpriced. Because this is a vacation palace (rather than a state residence), it lacks the sumptuous staterooms you'll see at Holyroodhouse in Edinburgh; this visit is about the grounds and the setting rather than the interior.

Cost and Hours: £11.50, includes audioguide, April-July daily 10:00-17:00, closed Aug-March, arrive at least an hour before closing, tel. 013397/42534, www.balmoralcastle.com.

Safaris: If you're caught up in the beauty of Balmoral, consider booking a ranger-led Land Rover safari through the grounds (£60, 3 hours, 2/day during the open season).

Background: Queen Victoria and Prince Albert purchased Balmoral in 1848. The thickly forested hills all around reminded Albert of his Thuringian homeland, but Victoria adored it as well—calling it her "Highland paradise." They remodeled the castle extensively in the Scottish Baronial style—a romantic, faux-antique look resembling turreted Scottish Renaissance castles from the 16th century—helping to further popularize that look. Ever since, each British monarch has enjoyed retreating to this sprawling property, designed for hunting (red deer) and fishing (salmon). The royal family was here when news broke of Princess Diana's death. (Their initial decision not to return to London or to mourn publicly was highly criticized, as depicted in the film *The Queen*.) Today Balmoral has a huge staff, 80 miles of roads, a herd of Highland cattle, and a flock of Highland ponies (stout little miniature horses useful for hauling deer carcasses over the hills).

Visiting the Castle: From the parking lot (with a TI/gift shop, WCs, and the royal church across the street—described later), walk

across the River Dee to reach the ticket booth. From here, you can either hike 10 minutes to the palace, or hop on the free trolley.

Once at the stables, pick up your included audioguide and peruse a few exhibits, including an 8-minute orientation film. In the main exhibit, you'll see a video of the kilts-

and-bagpipes welcome parade, plus a diorama of local wildlife, and lots and lots of historical photos of royals enjoying Balmoral—including about 60 years of royal family Christmas cards. Peek into the Queen's garage to see her custom Bentley.

Then follow your audioguide on a short loop through the grounds and gardens before arriving at the palace. (To cut to the chase, or if the weather is bad, you can shortcut from the exhibit directly to the palace and the one room open to the public.) As you walk through the produce and flower gardens, ponder the unenviable challenge of trying to time all of the flowers to bloom and the produce to ripen at the same time, coinciding with the royal family's arrival the first week of August (especially difficult given Scotland's notoriously uncooperative climate).

Finally you'll reach the single room in the palace open to the public: the palace ballroom. Display cases show off memorabilia (children's games played by royal tots, and a fully operational mini-Citroën that future kings and queens have enjoyed driving around). Near the exit, a touchscreen offers you a virtual glimpse at the tartaned private quarters that are off-limits to us commoners.

Nearby: For a free peek at another royal landmark, stop at **Crathie Kirk,** the small, stony, charming parish church where the royal family worships when they are at Balmoral, and where Queen Victoria's beloved servant John Brown is buried (£1 donation requested, daily 10:00-12:30 & 13:00-16:00, closed Nov-March). The church is just across the highway from the Balmoral parking lot.

The next town past Balmoral Castle (in the opposite direction from Ballater) is **Braemar** (bray-MAR). This tiny village hosts the most famous Highland Games in Scotland, as the Queen is almost always in attendance (first Sun in Sept, www.braemargathering.org). If you swing through town, you can take a look at its big games grandstand and its picturesque castle (not worth touring).

▲▲Ballater

Ballater (BAH-lah-tur) is the place where you'll feel as much royalist sentiment as anywhere in Scotland. For the people of Ballater (many of whom work, either directly or indirectly, with Balmoral Castle), the Windsors are, simply, their neighbors. Royal connections aside, Ballater is a pleasant, unpretentious, extremely tidy little town. Just big enough to have all the essential tourist services—but neatly nestled in the

wooded hills of the Cairngorms, and a bit more "away from it all" than Pitlochry—Ballater is an ideal home base for those wanting to spend a night in this part of Scotland.

It was local springs—which bubbled up supposedly healing waters—that first put Ballater on the map. But there's no question the town is what it is today thanks to Queen Victoria and Prince Albert, who bought the nearby Balmoral Castle in 1848, then built a train station in Ballater to access it. Today, the town's best attraction may be its residents, who revel in telling tales of royal encounters. Prince Charles, who lives not at Balmoral but at Birkhall (not open to the public), has a particular affection for this part of the Cairngorms. He supports Ballater charities and has been known to show up unannounced at town events...and locals love him for it. ("Prince Charles is a really nice guy," one of them told me. "Not at all like the chap you see on TV.")

Sights in Ballater: The town's only real sight—the old **train station** built by Queen Victoria to more easily commute to her new summer home at Balmoral Castle—suffered a fire in 2015. The artifacts housed in its minimuseum were saved, and the station should be reopened by the time of your visit. (It will have the TI, library, and an exhibit of how Queen Victoria relied on trains to get to Balmoral.)

The town is also fun for a wander. Facing the station are two stately sandstone buildings honoring the couple that put this little village on the map: the Prince Albert Hall and the Victoria Hall. Exploring the streets nearby, with their characteristic little shops, you'll notice several boasting the coveted seals announcing "By Appointment of her Majesty the Queen" or "By Appointment of H.R.H. the Prince of Wales"—meaning that they're authorized to sell their wares directly to the gang at Balmoral.

A block from the station—past the Balmoral Bar, with its turrets that echo its namesake castle—the unusually fine parish church is surrounded by an inviting green, with benches, flower gardens, and royal flourishes...like everything in Ballater.

Sleeping in Ballater: The town has several fine B&Bs; given the royal proximity and generally touristy nature of Ballater, prices are high...but so is quality.

$$ Osborne House is a big and cozy home, with spacious rooms, a walled garden, and delightful hosts Heather and Neil (4 Dundarroch Road, tel. 013397/55320, www.osbornehousebedandbreakfast.

com, osbornehousebedandbreakfast@gmail.com). Just down the road past the Osborne House garden, look for the white fence surrounding the Victoria barracks—where soldiers tasked with guarding the Queen reside.

$$ Gordon Guest House, right in the center of town facing the historic train station, has five richly furnished rooms (Station Square, tel. 013397/55996, www.thegordonguesthouse.com, info@ thegordonguesthouse.com, Martin and Amanda).

Eating in Ballater: If you're just passing through, consider grabbing lunch at the old-school café **$ The Bothy.** Farther along the main street (toward Aberdeen), near the end of the strip of shops, **$$ Rocksalt & Snails** is a hipper choice. There's also a handy, long-hours **Co-op grocery store** facing the parish church, and nice tables on the green. For a more serious dinner, Ballater has two good Indian restaurants (both facing the green) and a few hotel restaurants and pubs. **$$$$ Rothesay Rooms Restaurant,** sponsored by Prince Charles in 2016 as a charity project after the town suffered from devastating floods, has a good reputation (Wed-Sat 18:00-21:00, 3 Netherley Place near the church green, tel. 013397/53816, www.rothesay-rooms.co.uk). And **$$$ Clachan Grill,** serving modern Scottish cuisine, is about the most stylish and foodie place in town (Wed-Mon 17:00-21:00, closed Tue, tel. 013397/55999, look down a side lane near the bridge at 5 Bridge Square).

Scotland's East Coast

Scotland's inlet-slashed, island-speckled west coast gets all of the attention...and should. But if you're nearby, consider taking a peek at the east coast. While St. Andrews—with its links and beaches— is probably Scotland's finest east-coast town, one uniquely hulking castle ruin rises above other coastal choices: Dunnottar Castle. For those who enjoy hiking on coastal bluffs and exploring ruins, it's worth a detour on your way south from Ballater and Balmoral.

Dunnottar Castle

The mostly ruined, empty, and otherwise underwhelming castle of Dunnottar (duh-NAW-tur) owns a privileged position: clinging to the top of a bulbous bluff, flanked by pebbly beaches and surrounded nearly 360 degrees by the North Sea. It's scenic and strategic. From the parking lot, you'll walk five min-

utes to a fork: To the right, you'll come to a ridge with a panoramic view of the castle's fine setting; to the left, you'll hike steeply down (almost all the way to the beach), then steeply back up, to the castle itself. Inside, there's not much to see. The only important thing that happened here was the Battle for the Honours of Scotland, when the Scottish crown jewels were briefly hidden away in the castle from Oliver Cromwell's army, which laid siege to Dunnottar (unsuccessfully) for three days. But don't worry too much about the history, or the scant posted descriptions—just explore the stately ruins while enjoying the panoramic views, sea spray, and cry of the gulls.

Cost and Hours: The photo-op view is free (and enough for many); entering the castle costs £7, daily 9:00-17:30, shorter hours Oct-March, tel. 01569/762-173, www.dunnottarcastle.co.uk.

Getting There: It's just off the busy A-90 expressway, which runs parallel to the coast between Aberdeen and Dundee; exit for Stonehaven, and you'll find Dunnottar well-signed just to the south.

Nearby: Dunnottar sits just beyond **Stonehaven,** a pleasant, workaday seafront town that's a handy place to stretch your legs or grab some lunch (big pay parking lot right in the town center, ringed by eateries and grocery stores).

EASTERN SCOTLAND

ISLE OF SKYE

Portree • Sights on the Isle of Skye

The rugged, remote-feeling Isle of Skye has a reputation for unpredictable weather ("Skye" comes from the Old Norse for "The Misty Isle"). But it also offers some of Scotland's best scenery, and it rarely fails to charm its many visitors. Narrow, twisty roads wind around Skye in the shadows of craggy, black, bald mountains, and the coastline is ruffled with peninsulas and sea lochs (inlets).

Skye is the largest of the Inner Hebrides, and Scotland's second-biggest island overall (over 600 square miles), but it's still manageable: You're never more than five miles from the sea. The island has only about 13,000 residents; roughly a quarter live in the main village, Portree. The mountain-like Cuillin Hills separate the northern part of the island (Portree, Trotternish, Dunvegan) from the south (Skye Bridge, Kyleakin, Sleat Peninsula).

Set up camp in Portree, Skye's charming, low-key tourism hub. Then dive into Skye's attractions. Drive around the appealing Trotternish Peninsula, enjoying Scotland's scenic beauty: sparsely populated rolling fields, stony homes, stark vistas of jagged rock formations, and the mysterious Outer Hebrides looming on the horizon. Go for a hike in (or near) the dramatic Cuillin Hills, sample a peaty dram of whisky, and walk across a desolate bluff to a lighthouse at the end of the world. Learn about the sordid clan history of Skye, and visit your choice of clan castles: the MacLeods' base at Dunvegan, the MacDonalds' ruins near Armadale, and—nearby but not on Skye—the postcard-perfect Eilean Donan fortress, previously a Mackenzie stronghold but today held by the Macraes. Or just settle in, slow down, and enjoy island life.

The most useful TI is in Portree; shops in smaller towns (including Dunvegan) host more basic "information points." At nearly every pullout you'll find an info post giving background on that stop.

PLANNING YOUR TIME

With two weeks in Scotland, Skye merits two nights, allowing a full day to hit its highlights: Trotternish Peninsula loop, Dunvegan Castle, the Fairy Pools hike (or another hike in the Cuillin Hills), and the Talisker Distillery tour. Mountaineers need extra time for hiking and hillwalking. Because it takes time to reach, Skye is skippable if you only have a few days in Scotland—instead, focus on the more accessible Highlands sights (Oban and its nearby islands, and Glencoe).

Situated between Oban/Glencoe and Loch Ness/Inverness, Skye fits neatly into a Highlands itinerary. To avoid seeing the same scenery twice, it works well to drive the "Road to the Isles" from Fort William to Mallaig, then take the ferry to Skye; later, leave Skye via the Skye Bridge and follow the A-87 east toward Loch Ness and Inverness, stopping at Eilean Donan Castle en route, or vice versa. With more time, take the very long and scenic route north from Skye, up Wester Ross and across Scotland's north coast, then down to Inverness (see the Northern Scotland chapter).

GETTING TO THE ISLE OF SKYE

By Car: Your easiest bet is the slick, free **Skye Bridge** that crosses from Kyle of Lochalsh on the mainland to Kyleakin on Skye (for more on the bridge, see page 163).

The island can also be reached by **car ferry.** The major ferry line connects the mainland town of Mallaig (west of Fort William along the "Road to the Isles"—see page 75) to Armadale on Skye (£15/car with 2 people, reservations required, April-late Oct 8/day each way, off-season very limited Sat-Sun connections, must check in at least 20 minutes before sailing or your place will be sold and you will not get on, can be canceled in rough weather, 30-minute trip, operated by Caledonian MacBrayne, toll-free tel. 0800-066-5000 or tel. 01475/650-397, www.calmac.co.uk).

By Bus: Skye is connected to the outside world by Scottish Citylink buses (www.citylink.co.uk), which use Portree as their Skye hub. From Portree, buses connect to **Inverness** (bus #917, 3/day, 3.5 hours) and **Glasgow** (buses #915 and #916, 3/day, 7 hours, also stops at **Fort William** and **Glencoe**). For **Edinburgh,** you'll transfer in either Inverness or Glasgow (4/day, 8 hours total). (For connections within the Isle of Skye, see later.)

More complicated **train-plus-bus** connections are possible for the determined: Take the train from Edinburgh or Glasgow to Fort William; transfer to the "Sprinter" train to Mallaig (4/day, 1.5

hours); take the ferry across to Armadale; then catch Stagecoach bus #52 to Portree (1 hour). Alternatively, you can take the train from Edinburgh or Glasgow to Inverness, take another train to Kyle of Lochalsh, then catch a bus to Portree.

GETTING AROUND THE ISLE OF SKYE
By Car
Once on Skye, you'll need a car to thoroughly enjoy the island. (Even if you're doing the rest of your trip by public transportation, a car rental is worthwhile here to make maximum use of your time; Portree-based car-rental options are listed on page 142.) If you're driving, the roads are simple and well signposted. But if you'll be exploring, a good map can be helpful. Sample driving times: Kyleakin and Skye Bridge to Portree—45 minutes; Portree to Dunvegan—30 minutes; Portree to the tip of Trotternish Peninsula and back again—2 hours (more with sightseeing stops); Portree to Armadale/ferry to Mallaig—1 hour; Portree to Talisker Distillery—40 minutes.

By Public Bus
Skye can be frustrating by bus (slow and limited). Portree is the hub for bus traffic. Most buses within Skye are operated by Stagecoach (www.stagecoachbus.com; buy individual tickets or, for longer journeys, consider the £8.85 all-day Dayrider ticket or the £33.30 weeklong Megarider ticket; buy tickets onboard). From Portree, you can loop around the **Trotternish Peninsula** on bus #57A (counterclockwise route) or bus #57C (clockwise route; Mon-Sat 4/day in each direction, limited on Sun). Bus #56 connects Portree and **Dunvegan Castle** (3/day, does not run on Sun, 40 minutes). From Portree to **Kyleakin,** take the Inverness-bound Citylink #917 (3/day, 1 hour) or local bus #50 (2/day, 1 hour, none on Sat-Sun); to reach **Eilean Donan Castle,** take any Citylink bus heading toward Fort William or Inverness (#915, #916, and #917; get off at Dornie and walk, 6/day, 1 hour).

By Tour
Several operations on the island take visitors to hard-to-reach spots. Figure £40-45 per person to join an all-day island tour (about 8 hours). Compare the offerings at the following companies, which use smaller 8- or 16-seat minibuses: **Skye Scenic Tours** (tel. 01478/617-006, www.skyescenictours.com), **Tour Skye** (tel. 01478/613-514, www.tourskye.com), and **SkyeBus** (tel. 01470/532-428, www.realscottishjourneys.com).

Portree-based **Michelle Rhodes** also does tours around the island (see page 142).

ISLE OF SKYE

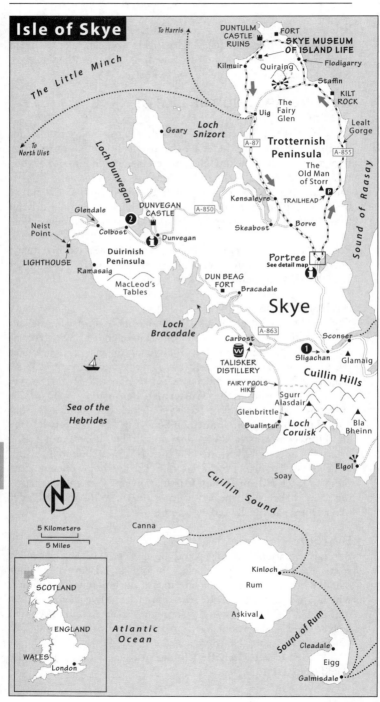

Isle of Skye

To Harris

DUNTULM CASTLE RUINS

FORT

SKYE MUSEUM OF ISLAND LIFE

Kilmuir

Quiraing

Flodigarry

Staffin

KILT ROCK

The Little Minch

The Fairy Glen

Uig

Lealt Gorge

A-87

Trotternish Peninsula

A-855

To North Uist

Geary

Loch Snizort

Loch Dunvegan

The Old Man of Storr

Kensaleyre

TRAILHEAD

Glendale

DUNVEGAN CASTLE

A-850

P

Neist Point

Colbost

Dunvegan

Skeabost

Borve

LIGHTHOUSE

Ramasaig

Duirinish Peninsula

MacLeod's Tables

DUN BEAG FORT

Bracadale

Portree

See detail map

Loch Bracadale

Skye

Carbost

A-863

Sconser

Sea of the Hebrides

TALISKER DISTILLERY

Sligachan

Glamaig

Cuillin Hills

FAIRY POOLS HIKE

Sgurr Alasdair

Glenbrittle

Bla Bheinn

Bualintur

Loch Coruisk

Elgol

Soay

Cuillin Sound

5 Kilometers

5 Miles

Canna

Kinloch

Rum

SCOTLAND

Askival

ENGLAND

Sound of Rum

Cleadale

WALES

London

Atlantic Ocean

Eigg

Galmisdale

Sound of Raasay

① Sligachan Hotel & Rest.
② Three Chimneys Restaurant
③ Broadford Hotel & Rest.

Kerrysdale

Red Point

WESTER
ROSS

Loch Torridon

Kinlochewe

Rona

Torridon

To
Inverness

Shieldaig

Sgorr Ruadh

A-890

Inner Sound

Applecross

A-896

Coulags

Arnish

APPLECROSS RD.

Strathcarron

Dun
Cann

Lochcarron

Raasay

Toscaig

Plockton

A-890

Scalpay

SKYE
BRIDGE

Kyle of
Lochalsh

A-87

Dornie

EILEAN DONAN
CASTLE

Kyleakin

Loch Alsh

A-87

Corry
Broadford

Kylerhea

Galltair

Invershiel

③

Glenelg

A-87

Sgurr
Fhuaran

Kinloch

Loch Eishort

Sleat

A-851

Loch Hourn

To
Fort Augustus,
Loch Ness
& Inverness

Teangue

GAELIC
COLLEGE

Sound of Sleat

ARMADALE CASTLE
& CLAN DONALD CENTRE

Armadale

Knoydart
Peninsula

Ardvasar

Loch Nevis

Mallaig

Loch Morar

"ROAD TO
THE ISLES"

GLENFINNAN
VIADUCT

To
Fort William,
Glencoe & Oban

Arisaig

A-830

Lochailort

Glenfinnan

ISLE OF SKYE

By Taxi or Shuttle

GoSkye offers a shuttle service to the Fairy Pools, Talisker Distillery, the Old Man of Storr, and the Quiraing (single trips or return, £8-12 one-way, tel. 01470/532-264, www.go-skye.co.uk). **Don's Taxis** is available for private rides (tel. 01478/613-100, www.donstaxis.vpweb.co.uk).

Portree

Skye's main attraction is its natural beauty, not its villages. But of those villages, the best home base is Portree (pore-TREE), Skye's largest settlement, transportation hub, and tourism center—ideally located for exploring Skye's quintessential sights on the Trotternish Peninsula loop drive.

Portree is nestled deep in its protective, pastel harbor; overlapping peninsulas just offshore guard it from battering west coast storms. Most of today's Portree dates from its early-19th-century boom time as a kelp-gathering and herring-fishing center.

As the most popular town on Scotland's most popular island, Portree is jammed with visitors in the summer. There are lots of hotels and B&Bs (which book up well in advance) and an abundance of good restaurants (the best of which merit reservations).

Orientation to Portree

Although Portree doesn't have any real sights, it does boast a gorgeous harbor area and—in the streets above—all of the necessary tourist services: a good TI, fine B&Bs, great restaurants, a grocery store, a launderette, and so on. The main business zone of this functional town of about 3,000 residents is in the tight grid of lanes on the bluff just above the harbor, anchored by Portree's tidy main square, Somerled Square. From here, buses fan out across the island and to the mainland. B&Bs line the roads leading out of town.

Tourist Information: Portree's helpful TI is a block off the main square (June-Aug Mon-Sat 9:00-18:30, Sun until 17:00; off-season Mon-Sat 9:30-16:30, closed Sun; free Wi-Fi, just below Bridge Road, tel. 01478/612-137, www.visitscotland.com).

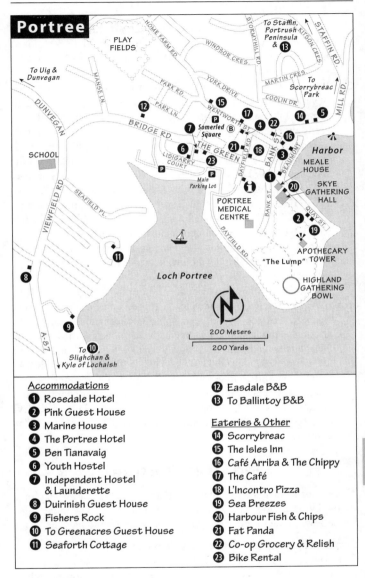

Portree

Accommodations
1. Rosedale Hotel
2. Pink Guest House
3. Marine House
4. The Portree Hotel
5. Ben Tianavaig
6. Youth Hostel
7. Independent Hostel & Launderette
8. Duirinish Guest House
9. Fishers Rock
10. To Greenacres Guest House
11. Seaforth Cottage
12. Easdale B&B
13. To Ballintoy B&B

Eateries & Other
14. Scorrybreac
15. The Isles Inn
16. Café Arriba & The Chippy
17. The Café
18. L'Incontro Pizza
19. Sea Breezes
20. Harbour Fish & Chips
21. Fat Panda
22. Co-op Grocery & Relish
23. Bike Rental

HELPFUL HINTS

WCs: Public WCs are across the street and down a block from the TI, across from the hostel.

Laundry: There's a **self-service launderette** below the Independent Hostel, just off the main square (usually 11:00-21:00, last load starts at 20:00, The Green, tel. 01478/613-737).

Bike Rental: Island Cycles rents bikes in the middle of town, just off the main square (£10/half-day, £20/24 hours, best to re-serve in advance in high season, Mon-Sat 9:00-17:00, closed Sun, shorter hours in winter, The Green, tel. 01478/613-121, www.islandcycles-skye.co.uk).

Car Rental: To make the most of your time on Skye, rent a car. Several options line up along the road to Dunvegan and charge around £40-60/day (most are closed Sun; smart to call sev-eral days ahead in peak season, but worth trying last-minute). The most user-friendly option is **M2 Motors,** which can pick you up at your B&B or the bus station (tel. 01478/613-344, www.m2-motors.co.uk). If they're booked up, try **Jansvans** (tel. 01478/612-087, www.jans.co.uk), **Highland Motors/ HM Hire** (based nearby in Borve but can pick up in Portree, tel. 01470/532-264, www.hm-hire.co.uk), or **Morrison** (tel. 01478/612-688, www.morrisoncarrental.com).

Parking: As you enter town, you'll see signs on the right directing you to a free parking lot below, at water level—after parking, just head up the stairs to the TI. You can also pay-and-display to park in the main town square (2-hour max, free after 18:00).

Town Walk: Michelle Rhodes leads guided one-hour town walks through Portree by request. While there's not a lot to say about the town, it's fun to have a local to explain things, and Michelle is a fine storyteller (£10 per person, call or email to set a time; mobile 07833-073-951, tel. 01478/611-915, www.skyehistoryandheritagetours.co.uk, michellelorrainerhodes@gmail.com). She also offers all-day guided driving tours around the island, tailored to your interests. Her specialty: clan battles, fairies, myths, and legends (£150 for two, £75/extra person).

Sights in Portree

There's not a turnstile in town, but Portree itself is fun to explore. Below I've described the village's three areas: the main square and "downtown," the harborfront, and the hill above the harbor.

Somerled Square and the Town Center

Get oriented to Portree on the broad main square, with its mercat cross, bus stops, parking lot, and highest concentration of public benches. The square is named for Somerled (Old Norse for "Sum-mer Wanderer"), the 12th-century ruler who kicked off the Mac-Donald clan dynasty and first united Scotland's western islands into the so-called Lordship of the Isles.

It seems every small Scottish town has both a mercat cross and a World War I memorial—and in Portree, they're combined into one. A mercat cross indicated the right for a town to host a market, and

was the community gathering point for celebrations, public shamings, and executions. The WWI memorial is a reminder of the disproportionate loss of life that particular conflict exacted on Scotland. In the case of wee Portree, a band of 28 Gaelic-speaking brothers went to war...and eight came back. (Ten were killed in a single night of fighting.)

Much of present-day Portree was the vision of Sir James Mac-Donald, who pushed to develop the town in the late 18th century. City leaders imported the impressive engineer Thomas Telford (famous for his many great canals, locks, and bridges) to help design the village's harbor and the roads connecting it to the rest of the island.

Wentworth Street, running from this square to the harbor, is the main shopping drag. Several English-sounding streets in Portree (Wentworth, Bosville, Douglas, Beaumont) are named for aristocratic families that the MacDonalds married into, helping to keep the clan financially afloat. Window-shop your way two blocks along Wentworth Street. Turn right on Bank Street. The **Royal Hotel,** built on the site of MacNab's Inn, where Bonnie Prince Charlie bid farewell to Flora MacDonald following his crushing defeat at Culloden, then set sail, never again to return to Scotland.

Quay Street leads down the hill to...

▲▲Portree Harbor

Portree's most pleasant space (unless you've got food the seagulls

want) is its harbor, where colorful homes look out over bobbing boats and the surrounding peninsulas. As one of the most protected natural harbors on the west coast, it's the reason that Portree emerged as Skye's leading town. Find a scenic perch at the corner of the harbor and take it all in.

While tourism is today's main industry, Portree first boomed in the mid-18th century thanks to kelp. Seaweed was gathered here, sun-dried, and burned in kilns to create an ashy-blue substance that was rich in soda, an essential ingredient in the production of glass and soap. But with the defeat of Napoleon at Waterloo, international sources of kelp opened up, causing this local industry to crash. This economic downturn coincided with a potato famine (similar to the one across the sea in Ireland), and by the mid-1800s, many locals were setting sail from this harbor to seek a better life in North America. But Portree soldiered on, bolstered by its prime location for fishing—especially for herring. By the early 20th century, a nationwide herring boom had again buoyed Portree's economy, with hundreds of fishing boats crowding its harbor.

Notice the stone building with the sealed-off door at the base of the stairs leading up into town. This was the former **ice house,** which was in operation until the 1970s. The winch at the peak of the building was used to haul big blocks of ice into an enormous subterranean cellar, to preserve Atlantic salmon throughout the summer.

Survey the harbor, enjoying the **pastel homes**—which come with lots of local gossip. Rumor has it that these used to be more uniform, until a proud gay couple decided to paint their house pink (it's now a recommended B&B). What used to be a blue-and-white house next door (now an all-blue hotel) belonged to a fan of the West Ham United soccer team. Soon the other homeowners followed suit, each choosing their own color. Speaking of bright colors, look for the traffic-cone-orange boat floating in the harbor. This belongs to the Royal National Lifeboat Institution (RNLI), Britain's charity-funded answer to the US Coast Guard.

You may notice the busy fish-and-chips joint, with its customers standing guardedly against the nearby walls and vicious seagulls perched on rooftops ready to swoop down at the first sight of battered cod.

Go for a stroll along the Telford-built pier. Along here, a couple of different companies offer 1.5-hour excursions out to the sea-eagle nests and around the bay (ask the captains at the port, or inquire at the TI). At the far end of the pier is a BP gas station with huge, underwater tanks for fueling visiting boats. When big cruise ships are in port, they drop the hook and tender their passengers in to this pier.

Ascending "The Lump" (Hill Above the Harbor)

For a different perspective on Portree—and one that gets you away from the tourists—hike up the bluff at the south end of the harbor. From the Royal Hotel, head up Bank Street.

After a few steps, you'll spot the white **Meall House** on your left—supposedly Portree's oldest surviving home (c. 1800) and once the sheriff's office and jail. Today it's a center for the Gaelic cultural organization Fèisean nan Gàidheal, which celebrates the Celtic tongue that survives about as well here on Portree as anywhere in Scotland. Hiding behind the Meall House, along the harborview path, is the stepped-gable **Skye Gathering Hall** (from 1879). This is where Portree's upper crust throws big, fancy, invitation-only balls on the days before and after Skye's Highland Games. The rest of the year, it hosts cultural events and—on most days—a fun little market with a mix of crafts and flea-market-type items.

Back on Bank Street, continue uphill. Soon you'll approach the **Portree Medical Centre**—one of just two hospitals on the entire Isle of Skye. (Is it just me, or do those parking spots each come with a graveyard cross?)

Just before the hospital's parking lot, watch on the left for the

uphill lane through the trees. Use this to hike on up to the top of the hill that locals call "The Lump" (or, for those with more local pride, "Fancy Hill"). Emerging into the clearing, you'll reach a huge, flat **bowl** that was blasted out of solid rock to hold 5,000 people during Skye's annual Highland Gathering. (For more on Highland Games, see page 20.) In addition to the typical Highland dancing, footraces, and feats of strength, Skye's games have a unique event: From this spot, runners climb downhill, swim across Loch Portree, ascend the hill on the adjacent peninsula, then swim back again.

Walk left, toward the harbor, then head left again onto a path leading away from the bowl; you'll run into a crenellated **apothecary tower.** It was built in 1834, not as a castle fortification but to alert approaching sailors that a pharmacist was open for business in Portree. This tower was literally blown over by gale-force winds in a 1991 storm, but has since been rebuilt. It's usually open if you'd like to climb to the top for views over the harbor and

the region—on a clear day, you can see all the way to the Old Man of Storr (see page 152).

Walks and Hikes near Portree

The Portree TI can offer advice about hikes in the area; if either of the below options interests you, get details there before you head out.

One popular choice, which doesn't require a car, is called the

Scorrybreac Path. To get to the trailhead—three-quarters of a mile from Somerled Square—walk north out of Portree on Mill Road, veer right onto Scorrybreac Road when you're just leaving town (following the sign for *Budhmor*), then follow the coastline to the start of the hiking trail, marked by signs. From here, you'll walk along the base of a bluff with fine views back on Portree's colorful harborfront.

Drivers can tackle the more ambitious hike up to the **Old Man of Storr:** You'll drive about 15 minutes north of town (following the start of my Trotternish Peninsula Driving Tour) and park at the Old Man of Storr trailhead. Green trail signs lead you through a gate and up along a well-trod gravel path through a felled woodland. Once you've reached the top of the first bluff, take the right fork, and continue all the way up to the pinnacle. Plan on about two hours round-trip. (If you don't mind a longer drive, a better walk is at **The Quiraing**—see page 154.)

Sleeping in Portree

Portree is crowded with hikers and tourists in July and August: Book your room well in advance. You may need to check with several places. If you're late to the game, you might have better luck with a hotel, Airbnb, or one of the B&Bs lacking websites (of the ones I list, these include Marine House, Seaforth Cottage, and Easdale B&B). Spring and fall (March-June and Sept-Oct) are also busy, but a bit more manageable (and cheaper).

If looking last-minute, try the Facebook group "Skye Rooms," where hotels, B&Bs, and short-term apartments with late cancelations and random openings list their availability for the next day. Travelers looking for accommodations can also post their desired dates.

ON THE HARBOR

$$$ Rosedale Hotel fills three former fishermen's houses with mazelike hallways and 23 rooms (some modern, some more traditional). With-it Neil, a recent business school graduate, runs the hotel with the help of his family, including his mom, who cooks (family room and a few small, no-view, cheaper doubles available; no elevator, restaurant, bar for guests only, parking lot down the road; Beaumont Crescent, tel. 01478/613-131, www.rosedalehotelskye.co.uk, reservations@rosedalehotelskye.co.uk).

$$ At **Pink Guest House,** energetic Robbie and Fiona rent 11 bright, spacious rooms (8 with sea views) on the harbor. The rates include a full Scottish breakfast and the hosts' youthful enthusiasm (large family rooms, Quay Street, tel. 01478/612-263, www.pinkguesthouse.co.uk, info@pinkguesthouse.co.uk).

$ Marine House, a cozy, welcoming, delightful time warp run by sweet Skye native Fiona Stephenson, has three simple, homey rooms (two with a private bathroom down the hall) and fabulous views of the harbor. Breakfast is conversational, as you'll eat with the other guests at one big table (cash only, reserved parking right on harbor, 2 Beaumont Crescent, tel. 01478/611-557, stephensonfiona@yahoo.com).

UP IN TOWN

$$$$ The Portree Hotel is your basic, impersonal town-center accommodation (right on the main square) with 24 modernized rooms on three floors and no elevator (family rooms, bar/restaurant, no parking—must use public lots, tel. 01478/612-511, www. theportreehotel.com, contact@theportreehotel.com).

$$ Ben Tianavaig, on the busy road through town overlooking the harbor, offers four fresh and airy rooms (all with views). Charlotte and Bill are generous with travel tips, offer a breakfast special of the day, and foster a shoes-off tidiness (2-night minimum required, cash only, street parking out front; 5 Bosville Terrace, tel. 01478/612-152, www.ben-tianavaig.co.uk, info@ben-tianavaig. co.uk).

¢ Portree Youth Hostel, run by Hostelling Scotland (SYHA), is a modern-feeling, institutional, cinderblock-and-metal building with 54 beds in 16 rooms (private and family rooms available, continental breakfast extra, kitchen, laundry, tel. 01478/612-231, www.syha.org.uk, portree@syha.org.uk).

¢ Portree Independent Hostel, in the unmissable yellow building just off the main square, has 60 beds and equally bold colors inside (one double room and several 4-person rooms, no breakfast, kitchen, laundry, tel. 01478/613-737, www.hostelskye.co.uk, skyehostel@yahoo.co.uk).

JUST OUTSIDE TOWN
South of Portree, off Viewfield Road

Viewfield Road, stretching south from Portree toward the Aros Centre, is B&B central. All offer convenient parking and are within walking distance of town (figure 10-15 minutes). Some are on smaller side lanes that stretch down toward the water, but all are well marked from the main road.

$$ Duirinish Guest House feels homey, modern, and tidy. With four rooms, it sits across the main road from the water (only a few obstructed sea views) but comes with a spacious guest lounge and a warm welcome (2-night minimum, closed Nov-March, tel. 01478/613-728, www.duirinish-bandb-skye.com, ruth.n.prior@ hotmail.co.uk, Ruth and Allan).

$$ Fishers Rock, a serene waterfront retreat with a glassy, contemporary, light-filled view breakfast room, has a soothing energy and three rooms (two-night minimum, closed in winter, tel. 01478/612-122, www.fishersrock.com, fishersrock@btinternet. com, Heather).

$$ Greenacres Guest House feels estate-like and a bit more formal, with fine china on the table, fountain and manicured hedges in the garden, and a glassed-in sunroom with views. The five rooms have different color schemes and styles, and some feature Ewen's handmade headboards, built from wood recycled from an old school (cash only, closed Oct-Easter, one of the farthest houses from town on Viewfield Road, about a 20-minute walk, tel. 01478/612-605, www.greenacres-skye.co.uk, greenacreskye@aol. com, Marie and Ewen).

$ Seaforth Cottage feels like a retired sea captain's home. Overlooking tidal flats, its garden is artfully littered with nautical flotsam and jetsam. The three simple rooms come with sea views and are a bit older, but priced accordingly (cash only, tel. 01478/612-040, ianskye48@hotmail.co.uk, gentle Ian).

$ Easdale B&B is another old-school place with three rooms, a bright breakfast room, and large, traditional lounge set just above the busy main road; it's a bit closer to town than the places listed above (cash only, no kids, Bridge Road, tel. 01478/613-244—call to reserve; spunky, plainspoken, and happily computer-free Chrissie).

North of Portree, off Staffin Road

$$ Ballintoy Bed and Breakfast, set back from the road and surrounded by a large field, has three immaculate ground-floor rooms accessorized with fun pops of color and artwork (family room, 2-night minimum preferred, includes continental breakfast, 15-minute walk from town on Staffin Road, tel. 01478/611-719, www.ballintoy-skye.co.uk, ballintoyskye@gmail.com, Gillian and Gavin).

SLEEPING BETWEEN PORTREE AND KYLEAKIN

$$$ Sligachan Hotel (pronounced SLIG-a-hin), perched at a crossroads in the scenic middle of nowhere (yet handy for road-tripping sightseers) is a compound of sleeping and eating options that is a local institution and a haven for hikers. The hotel's 21 rooms are comfortable, if a bit dated and simple for the price, while the nearby campground and bunkhouse offer a budget alternative. The setting—surrounded by the mighty Cuillin Hills—is remarkably scenic (closed Nov-Feb, on the A-87 between Kyleakin and Portree in Sligachan, hotel and campground tel. 01478/650-204, bunkhouse tel. 01478/650-458, www.sligachan.co.uk, reservations@sligachan. co.uk). For location, see the map on page 138.

Eating in Portree

Note that Portree's eateries tend to close early (21:00 or 22:00), and the popular places can merit reservations any evening in the high season.

UP IN TOWN

$$$$ Scorrybreac is Portree's best splurge, offering a delightful array of well-presented international dishes that draw from local ingredients and traditions. The cozy, modern, unpretentious dining room with eight tables fills up quickly, so reservations are a must (set multicourse menus only, Tue-Sun 17:30-22:30, closed Mon, 7 Bosville Terrace, tel. 01478/612-069, www.scorrybreac.com).

$$ The Isles Inn is a happening place, popular with hikers, with two halves serving the same menu—a brighter high-energy dining area and the darker pub—or you can sit at the bar. Offering a fun energy and warm service, they dish up simple, honest food one notch above pub grub. They have popular burgers, and their big slabs of salmon or haddock are served with fresh vegetables. While other places get stuffy, this has nice, fresh air circulation (daily 12:00-15:00 & 17:00-21:30, no reservations possible after 19:00, tel. 01478/612-129, facing the main square, Somerled Square). In summer, the Isles Inn hosts live music several nights a week from 21:30.

$$ Café Arriba is a fun and welcoming space offering refreshingly eclectic flavors in this small Scottish town. With a menu that includes local specialties, burgers, and Italian, this youthful, colorful, easygoing eatery's hit-or-miss cuisine is worth trying. Drop in to see what's on the blackboard menu today (lots of vegetarian options, daily 7:00-18:00, Quay Brae, tel. 01478/611-830).

$$ The Café, a few steps off the main square, is a busy, popular hometown diner serving good crank-'em-out food to an appreciative local crowd. It's family-friendly, with a good selection of burgers and fish-and-chips (daily 9:00-15:30 & 17:30-21:00, Wentworth Street, tel. 01478/612-553). Their homemade ice cream from the stand in front is a nice way to finish your meal.

$$ L'Incontro Pizza is Portree's favorite place for pizza. A sprawling, family-friendly place, it can merit reservations, too (open 17:00-21:00, closed Mon, The Green, tel. 01478/612-535).

DINING ON THE WATERFRONT

Portree's little harbor has a scattering of good eateries but none have actual waterfront seating. My hunch: It's because of the mean seagulls that hang out here.

$$$ Sea Breezes is a popular choice, with plain decor and a seafood-focused menu. At this basic, salty, no-nonsense eatery, you'll likely need reservations for dinner (daily 12:30-14:00 & 17:30-21:30 in summer, shorter hours off-season, closed Nov-Easter, tel. 01478/612-016, www.seabreezes-skye.co.uk).

EATING CHEAPER

Fish-and-Chips: Portree has two chippies: **$ The Harbour Fish & Chips Shop** is delightfully located on the charming harbor with good fish that's cheap and in big portions (daily 11:00-21:00, later in summer). The down side: Aggressive seagulls drive diners up against the wall. It's funny to watch. For a more relaxing meal, **$ The Chippy** sells very basic fish-and-chips and burgers, just up the harbor lane (on Bank Street) with peaceful-if-grungy tables and no seagulls.

Takeaway in Town: The **Fat Panda** Asian restaurant on Bayfield Road is satisfying, the **Co-op** grocery (daily 8:00-23:00) has a small selection of sandwiches and other prepared foods, and **Relish** is a deli serving good, fresh sandwiches (eat in or to go, end of Wentworth Street).

EATING ELSEWHERE ON THE ISLE OF SKYE

In addition to the following two destination restaurants, I've described some eateries in and near Kyleakin—where Skye meets the mainland—on page 163.

In Sligachan: The **Sligachan Hotel** (described earlier) is a grand and rustic old hotel in an extremely scenic setting, nestled in the Cuillin Hills. Its Harta Restaurant offers "casual dining with fine food" and a big and sloppy bar. Popular with campers and hikers, it's also family-friendly, with a zip-line for kids in the playground. The Seumas Bar has a Scotsman-pleasing range of whiskies. Choose between the lovely **$$$** dining room (nightly 18:30-21:00) and the big, open-feeling **$$** pub serving microbrews and mountaineer-pleasing grub (long hours daily, food served until 21:30, pub closed Oct-Feb; on the A-87 between Kyleakin and Portree in Sligachan, tel. 01478/650-204).

In Colbost, near Dunvegan: Out on a deserted road with just sheep for neighbors, the **$$$$ Three Chimneys Restaurant** is known throughout Scotland as a magnet for foodies. Its 16 tables fill an old three-chimney croft house, with a stone-and-timbers decor that artfully melds old and new—a perfect complement to the modern Scottish cuisine. It's cozy, classy, candlelit, and a bit dressy (do your best), but not stuffy. Reservations are essential (set multicourse menus only: £40 or £55 for lunch, £68 or £90 for dinner; daily 12:15-14:00 & 18:30-21:30, shorter hours off-season; tel. 01470/511-258, www.threechimneys.co.uk, Eddie and Shirley Spear). They also rent six swanky, pricey **$$$$** suites next door.

Getting There: It's in the village of Colbost, a 15-minute drive west of Dunvegan (about 45 minutes each way from Portree).

Sights on the Isle of Skye

I've organized these sights geographically, roughly from north (near Portree) to south.

PLANNING YOUR TIME

There is a well-trodden tourist path around Skye, and it's clearly the most memorable way for someone with a car to spend the day. The three big sights are Dunvegan Castle, Talisker Distillery, and Trotternish Peninsula, with its memorable Skye Museum of Island Life. It's possible—but rushed—to see all three in one day. (The challenge: The Skye Museum of Island Life closes at 17:00.) To see all three, start with the first distillery tour at 9:30, tour the castle, and get to the museum by about 16:30. This will rush the wonderful natural sights along the peninsula, but it might be worth it if time is short and you want to experience it all.

While you could drive directly from the castle to the museum and then tour the peninsula in a clockwise direction, it's far more scenic to drive it in a counterclockwise route as proposed here. Summer days are long, and the light can be wonderful in the early evening for the scenic west coast of the Trotternish Peninsula. Another option is to skip the distillery, do the castle first, and then have a leisurely tour of the peninsula as laid out in this chapter. Of course, if you have two days, do it all at your own pace.

TROTTERNISH PENINSULA

This inviting peninsula north of Portree is packed with windswept castaway views, unique geological formations, a few offbeat sights, and some of Scotland's most dramatic scenery. The following loop tour starts and ends in Portree, circling the peninsula counterclockwise (see map on page 138). Along the way, you'll explore a gaggle of old-fashioned stone homes, learn about Skye's ancient farming lifestyles, and pay homage at the grave of a brave woman who rescued a bonnie prince. In good weather, a spin around Trotternish is the best activity Skye offers and is worth ▲▲▲.

With minimal stops, the drive will take about two hours—but it deserves the better part of a day. Note that during several stretches, you'll be driving on a paved single-track road; use the occasional "passing places" to pull over and allow faster cars to go by.

ISLE OF SKYE

● Self-Guided Drive

• Head north of Portree on the A-855, following signs for Staffin. About three miles out of town, you'll begin to enjoy some impressive views of the Trotternish Ridge. You'll be passing peat bogs and may notice stretches where peat has been cut from the fields by the roadside. As you pass the small loch on your right, straight ahead is the distinctive rock tower called the...

Old Man of Storr

This 160-foot-tall tapered slab of basalt stands proudly apart from the rest of the Storr (as the mountain is called). The unusual landscape of the Trotternish Peninsula is due to massive landslides (the largest in Britain). This block slid down the cliff about 6,500 years ago and landed on its end, where it has slowly been whittled by weather into a pinnacle. An icon of Skye, the Old Man of Storr has been featured in many films—from *Flash Gordon* to *Prometheus* to *Snow White and the Huntsman*. The lochs on your right supply drinking water for the town of Portree and have been linked together to spin the turbines at a nearby hydroelectric plant that once provided all of Skye's electricity.

If you'd like to tackle the two-hour hike to the Old Man, there's a parking lot directly below the formation (for details on the hike, see page 146).

• After passing the Old Man, enjoy the scenery on your right, overlooking nearby islands and the mainland.

As you drive, you'll notice that Skye seems to have more sheep than people. During the Highland Clearances of the early 19th century, many human residents were forced to move off the island to make room for more livestock. The people who remain are some of the most ardently Gaelic Scots in Scotland. While only about one percent of all Scottish people speak Gaelic (pronounced "gallic"), one-third of Skye residents are fluent. A generation ago, it was illegal to teach Gaelic in schools; today, Skye offers its residents the opportunity to enroll in Gaelic-only education, from primary school to college (Sabhal Mòr Ostaig, on Skye's Sleat Peninsula, is the world's only college with courses taught entirely in Scottish Gaelic; see page 166).

• About four miles after the Old Man parking lot, you'll pass a sign for the River Lealt. Immediately after, the turnoff on the right is an optional stop at the...

Lealt Gorge

Where the River Lealt tumbles toward the sea, it carves out a long and scenic gorge. To stretch your legs, you can walk about five

minutes along the lip of the gorge to reach a viewpoint overlooking a protected, pebbly cove and some dramatic rock formations. The formations on the left, which look like stacked rocks, are the opposite: They've been weathered by centuries of battering storms, which have peeled back any vegetation and ground the stones to their smooth state. Peering down to the beach, you'll see a smokestack and some other ruins of a plant that once processed diatomite—a crumbly, clay-like substance made from algae fossils, which has hundreds of industrial uses. This factory, which closed in 1960, is a reminder of a time when tourism wasn't the island's main source of income. When this was functioning, no roads connected this point to Portree, so the factory's waterfront location made it possible to ship the diatomite far and wide.

• *Continue along the road. Just after the village of Valtos (about 2 miles after the Lealt Gorge viewpoint), you'll reach a loch (left), next to a parking lot (right). Park at the well-marked Kilt Rock viewpoint to check out...*

▲Kilt Rock

So named because of its resemblance to a Scotsman's tartan, this 200-foot-tall sea cliff has a layer of volcanic rock with vertical lava columns that look like pleats (known as columnar jointing), sitting atop a layer of horizontal sedimentary rock. The dramatic formations in the opposite direction are just as amazing.

• *Continuing north, as you approach the village of **Staffin**, you'll begin to see interesting rock formations high on the hill to your left.*

Staffin's name, like that of the isle of Staffa (described on page 47), comes from Old Norse and means "the place of staves or pillars"—both boast dramatic basalt rock pillars. If you need a public WC, partway through town, watch on the left for the Staffin Community Hall (marked *Talla Stafainn*, sharing a building with a grocer). Or for a coffee or lunch break, you could visit (on the right) the Columba 1400 Centre, a Christian-run retreat for struggling teens from big cities. They run a nice cafeteria and shop to support their work (Mon-Sat 10:00-20:00, closed Sun, tel. 01478/611-400).

• *Just after you leave Staffin, watch for signs on the left to turn off and head up to the quintessential Isle of Skye viewpoint—a rock formation called...*

▲▲The Quiraing

You'll get fine views of this jagged northern end of the Trotternish Ridge as you drive up. Landslides caused the dramatic scenery in this area, and each rock formation has a name, such as "The Needle" or "The Prison."

At the summit of this road, you'll reach a parking area. Even a short walk to a nearby bluff—to get away from the cars and alone with the wind and the island wonder—is rewarding. And there are several exciting longer hikes from here for a closer look at the formations. If you've got the time, energy, and weather for an unforgettable hike, here's your chance. You can follow the trail toward the bluff, and at the fork, decide to stay level (to the base of the formations) or veer off to the left and switch back up (to the top of the plateau). Both paths are faintly visible from the parking area—if it's busy, you'll see hikers on each. Once up top, your reward is a view of the secluded green plateau called "The Table," another landslide block, which isn't visible from the road.

• *You could continue on this road all the way to Uig, at the other end of the peninsula. But it's more interesting to backtrack, then turn left onto the main road (A-855, now single-track), to see the...*

Tip of Trotternish

A few miles north, after the village of Flodigarry, you'll pass the **Flodigarry Hotel,** with a cottage on the premises that was once home to Bonnie Prince Charlie's protector, Flora MacDonald (the cottage is now part of the hotel and not open to the public).

Soon after, at the top of a ridge ahead, you'll see the remains of an old **fort** from World War II, when the Atlantic was monitored for U-boats from this position.

Farther down the road, at the tip of the peninsula, you'll pass (on the right) the crumbling remains of another fort, this one much older: **Duntulm Castle** (free, roadside parking, 5-minute walk from road), which was the first stronghold on Skye of the influential MacDonald clan. It was from here that the MacDonalds fought many fierce battles against Clan MacLeod (for more on these clan battles, see the sidebar on page 165). The castle was abandoned around 1730 for Armadale Castle on the southern end of Skye (see page 164). While the castle ruins are fenced off, travelers venture in at their own risk. In the distance beyond, you can see the **Outer Hebrides**—the most rugged, remote, and Gaelic part of Scotland.

• *A mile after the castle, watch for the turnoff on the left to the excellent...*

▲▲Skye Museum of Island Life

This fine little stand of seven thatched stone huts, organized into a family-run museum, explains how a typical Skye family lived a century and a half ago.

Cost and Hours: £2.50, Easter-Sept Mon-Sat 9:30-17:00, closed Sun and Oct-Easter, tel. 01470/552-206, www.skyemuseum.co.uk, run by Margaret, Hector, and Dinah. Though there are ample posted explanations, the £1 guidebook is worth buying.

Visiting the Museum: The three huts closest to the sea are original (more than 200 years old). Most interesting is The Old Croft House, which was the residence of the Graham family until 1957. Inside you'll find three rooms: kitchen (with peat-burning fire), parents' "master bedroom," and a bedroom for the 10 kids. Nearby, The Old Barn displays farm implements, and the Ceilidh House (a gathering place for the entire community) contains dense but very informative displays about crofting (the traditional tenant-farmer lifestyle on Skye), the Gaelic language, and a fascinating wall of classic Skye postcards.

The four other huts, reconstructed here, house exhibits about weaving, the village smithy, and more. As you explore, admire the smart architecture of these humble but deceptively well-planned structures. Rocks hanging from the roof keep the thatch from blowing away, and the streamlined shape of the structure embedded in the ground encourages strong winds to deflect around the hut rather than hit it head-on.

• *After touring the museum, head out to the very end of the small road that leads past the parking lot, to a lonesome cemetery. Let yourself in through the gate to reach the tallest Celtic cross at the far end, which is the...*

ISLE OF SKYE

Monument to Flora MacDonald

This fine old cemetery, with mossy and evocative old tombs to ponder, features a tall cross dedicated to the local heroine who

rescued the beloved Jacobite hero Bonnie Prince Charlie at his darkest hour. (After the original was chipped away by 19th-century souvenir seekers, this more modern replacement was placed here.) After his loss at Culloden, and with a hefty price on his head, Charlie retreated to the Outer Hebrides. But the Hanover dynasty, which controlled the islands, was closing in. Flora MacDonald rescued the prince, disguised him as her Irish maid, Betty Burke, and sailed him to safety on Skye. (Charlie pulled off the ruse thanks to his soft, feminine features—hence the nickname "Bonnie," which means "beautiful" or "handsome.") The flight inspired a popular Scottish folk song: "Speed bonnie boat like a bird on the wing, / Onward, the sailors cry. / Carry the lad that's born to be king / Over the sea to Skye." For more on Bonnie Prince Charlie and the Battle of Culloden, see page 97.

• *Return to the main road and proceed about six miles around the peninsula. Soon after what was once a loch (now a giant depression), you'll drop down over the town of Uig ("OO-eeg"), the departure point for ferries to the Outer Hebrides (North Uist and Harris islands, 3/day) and a handy spot for services (cafés, a gas station, pottery shop, brewery, and WC).*

Continue past Uig, climbing the hill across the bay. To take a brief detour to enjoy some hidden scenery, consider a visit to the Fairy Glen. To find it, just after passing the big Uig Hotel, take a very hard left, marked for Sheadar *and* Balnaknock. *Follow this single-track road about a mile through the countryside. You'll emerge into an otherworldly little valley. Wind through the valley to just past the tiny lake and park below the towering Fairy Castle rock.*

▲The Fairy Glen

Whether or not you believe in fairies, it's easy to imagine why locals claim that they live here. With evocatively undulating terrain—ruffled, conical hills called "fairy towers" reflected in glassy ponds, rising up from an otherwise flat and dull countryside—it's a magical place. There's little to see on a quick drive-by, but hikers enjoy exploring these hills, discovering little caves, weathered stone fences, and delightful views. As you explore, keep an eye out for "Skye landmines" (sheep droppings). Hardy hikers enjoy clambering 10 minutes up to the top of the tallest rock tower, the "Fairy Castle." (By the way, the sheep are actually fairies until a human enters the valley.)

• *Head back the way you came and continue uphill on the main road (A-87), with views down over Uig's port. Looking back at Uig, you can see a good example of Skye's traditional farming system—crofting.*

Traditionally, arable land on the island was divided into plots. If you look across to the hills above Uig, you can see strips of de-

marcated land running up from the water—these are crofts. Crofts were generally owned by landlords (mostly English aristocrats or Scottish clan chiefs, and later the Scottish government) and rented to tenant farmers. The crofters lived and worked under very difficult conditions and were lucky if they could produce enough potatoes and livestock to feed their families. Historically, rights to farm the croft were passed down from father to eldest son over generations, but always under the auspices of a wealthy landlord.

• *But you live in a more affluent and equitable world, and more Scottish memories await to be created here on Skye. This tour is finished. From here, you can continue along the main road south toward Portree (and possibly continue from there to the Cuillin Hills). Or you can take the shortcut road just after Kensaleyre (B-8036) and head west on the A-850 to Dunvegan and its castle. All of your Skye options are described in the following pages.*

NORTHWEST SKYE
▲▲Dunvegan Castle

Perched on a rock overlooking a sea loch, Dunvegan Castle is the residence of the MacLeod (pronounced "McCloud") clan.

One of Skye's preeminent clans, the MacLeods often clashed with their traditional rivals, the MacDonalds, whose castle is on the southern tip of the island (see page 165). The MacLeods claim that Dunvegan is the oldest continuously inhabited castle in Scotland. The current clan chief, Hugh Magnus MacLeod, is a film producer who divides his time between London and the castle, where his noble efforts are aimed at preserving Dunvegan for future generations. Worth ▲▲▲ to people named MacLeod, the castle offers an interesting look at Scotland's antiquated clan system, provides insight into rural Scottish aristocratic lifestyles, and has fine gardens that are a delight to explore. Dunvegan feels rustic and a bit worse-for-wear compared to some of the more famous Scottish castles closer to civilization.

Cost and Hours: £13, daily 10:00-17:30, closed mid-Oct-March, café in parking lot, tel. 01470/521-206, www.dunvegancastle.com.

Getting There: It's near the small town of Dunvegan in the northwestern part of the island, well signposted from the A-850 (free parking). From Portree, bus #56 takes you right to the castle's parking lot.

Visiting the Castle: Follow the one-way route through the castle, borrowing laminated descriptions in each room—and don't hesitate to ask the helpful docents if you have any questions. You'll start upstairs and then make your way to the ground floor with its unforgettable exhibit on the people of St. Kilda.

Up the main staircase and looping left, you reach the **bedroom.** On the elegant canopy bed, look for the clan's seal and motto, carved into the headboard. The words "Hold Fast," which you'll see displayed throughout the castle, recall an incident where a MacLeod chieftain saved a man from being gored by a bull by literally taking the bull by the horns and wrestling it to the ground.

Beyond the bedroom, you'll ogle several more rooms, including the dining room. Here and throughout the castle, portraits of clan chieftains and the MacLeod family seem to be constantly looking down on you. The library's shelves are crammed with rich, leather-bound books.

Then you're routed back across the top of the stairs to the right wing, with the most interesting rooms. The 14th-century **drawing room** is the oldest part of the castle—it served as the great hall of the medieval fortress. But today it's a far cry from its gloomy, stony, Gothic-vaulted original state. In the 18th century, a clan chief's new bride requested that it be brightened up and modernized, so they added a drop ceiling and painted plaster walls. The only clue to its original bulkiness is how thick the walls are (notice that the window bays are nine feet thick). In the drawing room, look for the tattered silk remains of the Fairy Flag, a mysterious swatch with about a dozen different legends attached to it (explained by the handout).

Leaving the drawing room, notice the entrance to the **dungeon**—a holdover from that stout medieval fortress. Squeeze inside the dungeon and peer down into the deep pit. (Hey, is that a MacDonald rotting down there?)

At the end of this wing is the **north room,** a minimuseum of the clan's most prestigious artifacts. In the display case in the corner, find Rory Mor's Horn—made from a horn of the subdued bull that gave the clan its motto. Traditionally, this horn would be filled with nearly a half-gallon of claret (Bordeaux wine), which a potential heir had to drink in one gulp to prove himself fit for the role. Other artifacts include bagpipes and several relics related to Bonnie Prince Charlie (including his vest). In the center glass case, next to a lock of Charlie's hair, is a portrait of Flora MacDonald and some items that belonged to her.

From here a staircase leads to the ground floor, where you'll find some important exhibits in more utilitarian rooms. A glass case holds the Claymore Sword—one of two surviving swords made of extremely heavy Scottish iron rather than steel. Dating from the late 15th or early 16th century, this unique weapon is the bazooka of swords—designed not for dexterous fencing, but for one big kill-'em-all swing.

The MacLeods owned the rugged and remote St. Kilda islands (40 miles into the Atlantic, the most distant bit of the British Isles). They collected rent from the hardscrabble St. Kilda community of 100 or so (who were finally evacuated in 1930). The artifacts and dramatic photos of this community is a highlight of the castle visit. And, finally, you can watch a 12-minute video about the castle and the MacLeods, solemnly narrated by the 29th chief of the clan.

Between the castle and the parking lot are five acres of plush **gardens** to stroll through while pondering the fading clan system. Circling down to the sea loch, you'll enjoy grand views back up to the castle (and see a dock selling 30-minute boat rides on Loch Dunvegan to visit a seal colony on a nearby island—£6, tel. 01470/521-500). Higher up and tucked away are some of the finer,

ISLE OF SKYE

hidden parts of the gardens: the walled garden, the woodland walk up to the water garden (with a thundering waterfall and a gurgling stream), and the wide-open round garden.

The flaunting of inherited wealth and influence in some English castles rubs me the wrong way. But here, seeing the rough edges of a Scottish clan chief's castle, I had the opposite feeling: sympathy and compassion for a proud way of life that's dissolving with the rising tide of modernity. You have to admire the way they "hold fast" to this antiquated system (in the same way the Gaelic tongue is kept on life support). Paying admission here feels more like donating to charity than padding the pockets of a wealthy family. In fact, watered-down MacLeods and MacDonalds from

America, eager to reconnect with their Scottish roots, help keep the Scottish clan system alive.

The Giant Angus MacAskill Museum

This oddball museum fills a humble roadside barn in the town of Dunvegan. The pride of Peter Angus MacAskill (whose son, Danny, is a YouTube star for his extreme mountain biking on Skye) is happy to tell the story of "The Giant"—all seven feet nine inches of him—who teamed up with Tom Thumb to travel around the US in the circus and make Barnum and Bailey lots of money until he died in 1863 (£2, Apr-Oct daily 10:00-18:00, closed off-season).

▲Dun Beag Fort

If driving between the distillery and Dunvegan on A-863, you'll pass Skye's best-preserved Iron Age fort or "broch." This 2,000-year-old round stone tower caps a hill a 10-minute walk above its parking lot (just north of the village of Struan). The walk rewards you with an unforgettable chance to be alone in an ancient stone structure with a commanding view. Note all the stones scattered around Dun Beag and you can imagine it standing four times as tall—perhaps with three wood-framed floors inside protecting an entire community with their animals in times of threat—back before Julius Caesar sailed to Britannia.

▲Neist Point and Lighthouse

To get a truly edge-of-the-world feeling, consider an adventure on the back lanes of the Duirinish Peninsula, west of Dunvegan.

This trip is best for hardy drivers looking to explore the most remote corner of Skye and undertake a moderately strenuous hike to a lighthouse. Although it looks close on the map, give this trip 30 minutes each way from Dunvegan, plus at least 30 minutes to hike from the parking lot to the lighthouse (with a steep uphill return). After hiking around the cliff, the lighthouse springs into view, with the Outer Hebrides beyond.

Getting There: Head west from Dunvegan, following signs for *Glendale.* You'll cross a moor, then twist around the Dunvegan sea loch, before heading overland and passing through rugged, desolate hamlets that seem like the setting for a BBC sitcom about backwater Britain. After passing through Glendale, carefully track *Neist Point* signs until you reach an end-of-the-road parking lot.

Eating: It's efficient and fun to combine this trek with lunch or dinner at the pricey, recommended **Three Chimneys Restau-**

rant, on the road to Neist Point at Colbost (reservations essential; see page 150).

WESTERN SKYE
▲▲Talisker Distillery

Talisker, a Skye institution, has been distilling here since 1830 and takes the tours it offers seriously. This venerable whisky dis-

tillery is situated at the base of a hill with 14 springs, and at the edge of a sea loch—making it easier to ship ingredients in and whisky out. On summer days, the distillery swarms with visitors: You'll sniff both peated and unpeated grains; see the big mash tuns, washbacks, and stills; and sample a wee dram at the end. Island whisky tends to be smokier than mainland whisky due to the amount of peat smoke used during malting. Talisker workers describe theirs as "medium smoky," with peppery, floral, and vanilla notes.

Cost and Hours: £10 for one-hour tour with tasting and a £5 voucher toward a bottle; Mon-Fri 9:30-17:00, open Sat-Sun April-Oct only, Sun from 11:00, last tour one hour before closing; 30 tours/day in summer, 4/day in off-season; on the loch in Carbost village, tel. 01478/614-308, www.malts.com. Be sure to call for a reservation (and plan on a 40-minute drive from Portree). Designated drivers who need to skip the tasting can ask for a dram to go.

Nearby: Note that the **Fairy Pools Hike**—an easy walk that includes some of the best Cuillin views on the island—starts from near Talisker Distillery (see next section).

CENTRAL SKYE
▲▲Cuillin Hills

These dramatic, rocky "hills" (which look more like mountains to me) stretch along the southern coast of the island, dominating Skye's landscape. Unusually craggy and alpine for Scotland, the Cuillin ("cool-in") seem to rise directly from the deep. You'll see them from just about anywhere on the southern two-thirds of the island, but no roads actually take you through the heart of the Cuillin—that's reserved for hikers and climbers, who love this area. To get the best views with a car, consider these options.

Sligachan: The road from the Skye Bridge to Portree is the easiest way to appreciate the Cuillin (you'll almost certainly drive along here at some point during your visit). These mountains are all that's left of a long-vanished volcano. As you approach, you'll see that there are three separate ranges (from right to left): red, gray, and black. The steep and challenging Black Cuillin is the most popular for serious climbers; the granite Red Cuillin ridge is more rounded.

The crossroads of Sligachan has an old triple-arched Telford bridge—one of Skye's iconic views—and a landmark hotel (see page 150). The village is nestled at the foothills of the Cuillin, and is a popular launch pad for mountain fun. The 2,500-foot-tall cone-shaped hill looming over Sligachan, named Glamaig ("Greedy Lady"), is the site of an annual 4.5-mile hill race in July: Speed hikers begin at the door of the Sligachan Hotel, race to the summit, run around a bagpiper, and scramble back down to the hotel. The record: 44 minutes (30 minutes up, 13 minutes down, 1 minute dancing a jig up top). A Gurkha from Nepal did it in near record time...barefoot. The Sligachan Hotel feels like a virtual mountaineering museum with great old photos and artifacts throughout its ground floor (especially behind the reception desk). You're welcome to browse around.

Fairy Pools Hike: Perhaps the best easy way to get some Cuillin views—and a sturdy but manageable hike—is to follow the popular trail to the Fairy Pools. This is relatively near Talisker Distillery (in the southwestern part of the island, see page 161).

To reach the hike from the A-863 between Sligachan and Dunvegan, follow signs to *Carbost*. Just before reaching the village of Carbost, watch for signs and a turn-off on the left to *Glenbrittle*. Follow this one-track road through the rolling hills, getting closer and closer to the Cuillin peaks. The well-marked *Fairy Pools* turnoff will be on your right. Parking here, you can easily follow the well-tended trail down across the field and toward the rounded peaks. (While signs

suggest a 9.5-mile, 4- to 5-hour loop, most people simply hike 30 minutes to the pools and back; it's mostly level.)

Very soon you'll reach a gurgling river, which you'll follow toward its source in the mountains. Because the path is entirely through open fields, you enjoy scenery the entire time (and you can't get lost). Soon the river begins to pool at the base of each waterfall, creating a series of picturesque pools. Although footing can be treacherous, many hikers climb down across the rocks to swim and sunbathe. This is a fun place to linger (bring a picnic, if not a swimsuit). As I overheard one visitor say, "Despite the fact that it's so cold, it's so invitin'!"

Elgol: For the best view of the Cuillin, locals swear by the drive from Broadford (on the Portree-Kyleakin road) to Elgol, at the tip of a small peninsula that faces the Black Cuillin head-on. While it's just 12 miles as the crow flies from Sligachan, give it a half-hour each way to drive to the tip (mostly on single-track roads). For even more scenery, take a boat excursion from Elgol into Loch Coruisk, a sea loch surrounded by the Cuillin (April-Oct, departures several times a day, fewer Sun and off-season, generally 3 hours round-trip including 1.5 hours free time on the shore of the loch).

SOUTH SKYE
Kyleakin

Kyleakin (kih-LAH-kin), the last town in Skye before the Skye Bridge, used to be a big tourist hub...until the bridge connecting it to the mainland enabled easier travel to Portree and other areas deeper in the island. Today this unassuming little village, with a ruined castle (Castle Moil), a cluster of lonesome fishing boats, and a forgotten ferry slip is worth a quick look but little more.

Eating in Broadford: Up the road in Broadford is the Broadford Hotel, part of an upscale Skye hotel chain (Torrin Road at junction with Elgol, tel. 01471/822-204, www. broadfordhotel.co.uk). Its **$$$$ restaurant** is attempting to bring classy cuisine to this small town in a nice contemporary setting with harbor views (set multicourse menu only, daily from 18:00). The hotel's **$$ Gabbro Bar** is a relaxed pub-grub bistro. It was at this hotel that a secret elixir—supposedly once concocted for Bonnie Prince Charlie—was re-created by hotelier James Ross after finding the recipe in his father's belongings. Now known as Drambuie, the popular liqueur—which caught on in the 19th century—is made with Scotch whisky, heather honey, and spices. With its wide variety of Drambuie drinks, the Broadford's **Spinaker Lounge** is the place to try it.

Skye Bridge

Connecting Kyleakin on Skye with Kyle of Lochalsh on the mainland, the Skye Bridge was Europe's most expensive toll bridge per

ISLE OF SKYE

foot when it opened to great controversy in 1995 amid concerns that it would damage B&B business in the towns it connects, and disrupt native otter habitat. Here's the Skye natives' take on things: A generation ago, Lowlanders (city folk) began selling their urban homes and buying cheap property on Skye. Natives had grown to enjoy the slow-paced lifestyle that came with living life according to the whim of the ferry, but these new transplants found their commute into civilization too frustrating by boat. They demanded a bridge be built. Finally a deal was struck to privately fund the bridge, but the toll wasn't established before construction began. So when the bridge opened—and the ferry line it replaced closed—locals were shocked to be charged upward of £5 per car each way to go to the mainland. A few years ago, the bridge was bought by the Scottish government, the fare was abolished, and the Skye natives were somewhat appeased. There's no denying that the bridge has been a boon for Skye tourism, making a quick visit to the island possible without having to wait for a ferry.

SKYE'S SLEAT PENINSULA
Clan Donald Center and Armadale Castle

Facing the sea just outside Armadale is the ruined castle of Clan Donald, also known as the MacDonalds (Mac/Mc = "son of"),

at one time the most powerful clan in the Scottish Highlands and Hebrides. Today it is the "spiritual home of clan Donald," a sprawling site with woodland walks, a ruined castle, and a clan history museum.

Armadale Castle—more of a mansion than a fortress—was built in 1790, during the relatively peaceful, post-Jacobite age when life at the MacDonalds' traditional home, Duntulm Castle at the tip of the Trotternish Peninsula, had become too rugged and inconvenient. Today the Armadale Castle ruins (which you can view, but not enter) anchor a sprawling visitors center that celebrates the MacDonald way of life. You'll explore its manicured gardens, ogle the castle ruins, and visit the Museum of the Isles. This modern, well-presented museum tells the history of Scotland and Skye through the lens of its most influential clan (only a few artifacts but good descriptions, includes 1.5-hour audioguide). While fascinating for people named Mac-Donald, it's pricey and not worth a long detour for anyone else. But because it's right along the main road near the Armadale-Mallaig ferry, it can be an enjoyable place to kill some time while waiting

The Feuding Clans of Skye

Skye is one of the best places to get a taste of Scotland's colorful, violent history of clan clashes. As the largest of the Inner Hebrides Islands, with easy nautical connections to Scotland's west coast and much of northern Ireland, it's logical that Skye was home to two powerful, rival clans: the MacDonalds and the MacLeods.

The MacDonalds (a.k.a. **"Clan Donald"**), with their base at Duntulm Castle, were the dominant clan of the Hebrides. In the 12th century, the MacDonalds' ancestral ruler Somerled first unified the disparate islands and western Highlands into a "Lordship of the Isles" that lasted for centuries. Throughout this period, they struggled to maintain control against rival clans—starting with the MacLeods.

Clan MacLeod, with its castle at Dunvegan (see page 157), controlled the western half of Skye. Another branch of the MacLeods was based on the Isle of Lewis, holding down the fort in the Outer Hebrides. The MacLeods' ancestor, Olav the Black, had been defeated by Somerled, pulling their territory in to the Lordship of the Isles. But over the centuries, the MacLeods frequently challenged the authority of the MacDonalds, clashing in countless minor skirmishes as well as major clan battles in 1411, 1480, and 1578.

Adding to the volatile mix was **Clan Mackenzie,** which controlled much of the northern Highlands from their base at Eilean Donan Castle (see page 171). The Mackenzies waged battle against the MacDonalds in 1491 and again in 1497.

The epic 1578 clash featured a series of grievous offenses. First, the MacLeods invaded the MacDonald-controlled Isle of Eigg, and, upon finding the islanders huddled in a cave for protection, set a roaring fire at the mouth of the cave—killing virtually the entire population. In retaliation, the MacDonalds barred the door of a church on the MacLeod-controlled Isle of Uist and burned all of the worshippers alive. In the ensuing battle, the furious MacLeods massacred the MacDonalds and buried the dead on a turf dike—earning the conflict the name "Battle of the Spoiling Dike."

The final clan battle on Skye began with a strategic marriage designed to broker a peace between the warring clans. Donald MacDonald married Margaret MacLeod, following a tradition called a "handfast," in which the groom was allowed a "trial period" of one year and one day with his new bride. After Margaret injured her eye, Donald decided to "return" her. Adding insult to injury, he sent her back to Dunvegan Castle on a one-eyed horse, led by a one-eyed man with a one-eyed dog. And so began two years of brutal warfare between the clans (the War of the One-Eyed Woman). In 1601, the Battle of Coire Na Creiche decimated both sides, but the MacDonalds emerged victorious. It would be the last of the great clan battles between the MacDonalds and the MacLeods, and it's said to be the final battle fought in Scotland using only medieval weapons (swords and arrows), not guns.

for your ferry. At the parking lot is a big shop and café with free WCs.

Cost and Hours: £8.50, Easter-Oct daily 9:30-17:30, closed off-season, 2 minutes north of the Armadale ferry landing, tel. 01471/844-305, www.clandonald.com.

Nearby: Heading north on the A-851 from the Clan Donald Centre, keep an eye out for **Sabhal Mòr Ostaig** (a big complex of white buildings on the point). Skye is very proud to host this college, with coursework taught entirely in Scottish Gaelic. Named "the big barn" after its origins, its mission is to further the Gaelic language (spoken today by about 60,000 people).

ON THE MAINLAND, NEAR THE ISLE OF SKYE
▲Eilean Donan Castle

This postcard castle, watching over a sea loch from its island perch, is scenically (and conveniently) situated on the road between the Isle of Skye and Loch Ness. While the photo op is worth ▲▲, the interior—with cozy rooms—is worth only a peek and closer to ▲. Famous from such films as Sean Connery's *Highlander* (1986) and the James Bond movie *The World Is Not Enough* (1999), Eilean Donan (EYE-lan DOHN-an) might be  Scotland's most photogenic countryside castle (chances are good it's on that Scotland calendar you bought during your trip). Strategically situated at the confluence of three sea lochs, this was the stronghold of the Mackenzies—a powerful clan that was, like the MacLeods at Dunvegan, a serious rival to the mighty MacDonalds (see sidebar). Though it looks ancient, the current castle is actually less than a century old. The original castle on this site (dating from 800 years ago) was destroyed in battle in 1719, then rebuilt between 1912 and 1932 by the Macrae family as their residence. (The Macraes became bodyguards to the Mackenzies in the 14th century and later took over from their bosses as holders of the castle.)

Cost and Hours: £7.50, good £6 guidebook; March-Oct daily 10:00-18:00, July-Aug from 9:00, may open a few days a week Nov-Feb—call ahead, last entry one hour before closing; café, tel. 01599/555-202, www.eileandonancastle.com.

Getting There: It's not actually on the Isle of Skye, but it's quite close, in the mainland town of Dornie. Follow the A-87 about 15 minutes east of Skye Bridge, through Kyle of Lochalsh and toward Loch Ness and Inverness. The castle is on the right side of the road, just after a long bridge. Buses that run between Portree and Inverness (including #915, #916, and #917) stop at Dornie, a short walk from the castle (6/day, 1 hour from Portree).

Visiting the Castle: Buy tickets at the visitors center, then walk across the bridge and into the castle complex, and make your way into the big, blocky keep. You'll begin with some audiovisual introductory exhibits (left of main castle entry), then work through the historic rooms. While the castle is a footnote on a Scottish scale, the exhibits work hard to make its story engaging. Docents posted throughout can tell you more. First you'll see the claustrophobic, vaulted Billeting Room (where soldiers had their barracks), then head upstairs to the inviting Banqueting Room, with grand portraits of the honorable John Macrae-Gilstrap and his wife (who spearheaded the modern rebuilding of the castle). This room comes to life when you get a docent to explain the paintings and artifacts here. After the renovation, this was a sort of living room. Another flight of stairs takes you to the circa-1930 bedrooms, which feel more cozy and accessible than those in many other castles—and do a great job of evoking the lifestyles of the aristocrats who built the current version of Eilean Donan as their personal castle playset. Downstairs is a cute kitchen exhibit, with mannequins preparing a meal. Finally, you'll head through a few more humble exhibits (on old guns, bagpipes, and flags) to the exit.

NORTHERN SCOTLAND

Wester Ross • The North Coast • The Orkney Islands

Scotland's far north is its rugged and desolate "Big Sky Country"—with towering mountains, vast and moody moors, achingly desolate glens, and a jagged coastline peppered with silver-sand beaches. Far less discovered than the big destinations to the south, this is where you can escape the crowds and touristy "tartan tat" of the Edinburgh-Stirling-Oban-Inverness rut, and get a picturesque corner of Scotland all to yourself. Even on a sunny summer weekend, you may not pass another car for miles. It's just you and the Munro baggers. Beyond Orkney, there's no real "destination" in the north—it's all about the journey.

This chapter covers everything north of the Isle of Skye and Inverness, divided into three sections: the scenic west coast (called Wester Ross); the sandy north coast; and the fascinating Orkney archipelago just offshore from Britain's northernmost point.

Fully exploring northern Scotland takes some serious time. The roads are narrow, twisty, and slow, and the pockets of civilization are few and far between. With two weeks or less in Scotland, this area doesn't make the cut (except maybe Orkney). But if you have time to linger, and you appreciate desolate scenery and an end-of-the-world feeling, the untrampled north is worth considering.

Even on a shorter visit, Orkney may be alluring for adventurous travelers seeking a contrast to the rest of Scotland. The islands' claims to fame—astonishing prehistoric sites, Old Norse (Norwegian) heritage, and recent history as a WWI and WWII naval base—combine to spur travelers' imaginations.

PLANNING YOUR TIME

For a scenic loop through this area, try this four-day plan:

Day 1   From the Isle of Skye, drive up the west coast (including the Applecross detour, if time permits), overnighting in Torridon or Ullapool.

Day 2   Continue the rest of the way up the west coast, then trace the north coast from west to east, catching the late-afternoon ferry to Orkney. Overnight in tidy Kirkwall (2 nights).

Day 3   Spend all day on Orkney.

Day 4   Finish up on Orkney and take the ferry back to the mainland; with enough time and interest, squeeze in a visit to John O'Groats before driving three hours back to Inverness (on the relatively speedy A-9).

The above plan includes a borderline-unreasonable amount of driving, on twisty, challenging, often single-track roads (especially on days 1 and 2). If you don't have someone to split the time behind the wheel, or if you want to really slow down, consider adding another overnight to break up the trip.

To reach **Orkney** most efficiently—without the slow-going west coast scenery—consider zipping up on a flight (easy and frequent from Inverness, Edinburgh, or Aberdeen), or make good time on the A-9 highway from Inverness up to Thurso (figure 3 hours one-way) to catch the ferry.

It's possible (but very slow) to traverse this area by bus, but I'd skip it without a car. If you're flying to Orkney, consider renting a car for your time here.

Wester Ross

North of the Isle of Skye, Scotland's sparsely populated, ruggedly scenic west coast is a big draw for travelers seeking stunning views without the crowds. For casual visitors, the views in Glencoe and on the Isle of Skye are much more accessible and just as  good as what you'll find farther north. But diehards enjoy getting away from it all in Wester Ross. This section provides a quick outline of the most scenic route, from south to north.

This area, called Wester Ross (the western part of the region of Ross), is remote, mountainous, and slashed with jagged "sea lochs." (That's "inlets" in American English, or "fjords" in Norwegian.)

NORTHERN SCOTLAND

After seeing its towering peaks, you'll understand why George R. R. Martin named the primary setting of his *Game of Thrones* epic "Westeros."

There's a fine variety of scenery—but not many towns—on the way north. Connecting Skye or Glencoe to Ullapool (the logical halfway point up the coast) takes a full day. It may not sound like that many miles (figure 130 miles from Eilean Donan Castle to Ullapool; the Applecross detour adds another 20 slow-going miles)—but they're twisty and often single-track. If you want to just get a taste of this rugged scenery—without going farther north—you can drive the Wester Ross coastline almost as far as Ullapool, then turn off on the A-835 for a quick one-hour drive to Inverness.

Sights in Wester Ross

▲▲Wester Ross Driving Tour, from
Eilean Donan Castle to Ullapool

From the A-87, a few miles east of Kyle of Lochalsh (and the Skye Bridge), follow signs for the A-890 north toward *Lochcarron*. (Note that **Eilean Donan Castle** is just a couple of miles farther east from this turnoff; if coming from Skye, you could squeeze in a visit to that castle before backtracking to this turnoff.) From here on out, you can carefully track the brown *Wester Ross Coastal Trail* signs, which will keep you on track.

You'll follow the A-890 as it cuts across a hilly spine, then twists down and runs alongside **Loch Carron.** At the end of the loch, just after the village of Strathcarron, you'll reach a T-intersection that offers two choices. The faster route up to Ullapool—which skips much of the best scenery—takes you right on the A-890 (toward *Inverness*). But for the scenic route outlined here, instead turn left, following the A-896 (following signs for *Lochcarron*). From here, you'll follow the opposite bank of Loch Carron.

Soon after you pull away from the lochside, you'll cross over

a high meadow and see a well-marked turnoff on the left for a super-scenic—but challenging—alternate route: the **Applecross Road,** over a pass called Bealach na Bà (Gaelic for "Pass of the Cattle"). Intimidating signs suggest a much more straightforward alternate route that keeps you on the A-896 straight up to Loch Torridon (if doing this, skip down to the "Loch Torridon" section, later). But if you're relatively comfortable negotiating steep switchbacks, and have the time to spare (adding about 20 miles to the total journey), this road is drivable. You'll twist up, up, up—hearing your engine struggle up gradients of up to 20 percent—and finally over, with rugged-moonscape views over peaks and lochs. From the summit (at 2,053 feet), the jagged mountains rising from the sea are the Cuillin Hills on the Isle of Skye. Finally, you'll corkscrew back down the other side, arriving at the humble seafront town of Applecross.

Once in **Applecross,** you could either return over the same pass to pick up the A-896 (slightly faster), or, for a meandering but very scenic route, carry on all the way around the northern headland of the peninsula. This provides you with further views of Raasay and Skye, through a deserted-feeling landscape on single-track roads. Then, turning the corner at the top of the peninsula, you'll begin to drive above Loch Torridon, with some of the finest views on this drive.

Whether you take the Applecross detour or the direct route, you'll wind up at the stunning sea loch called **Loch Torridon**—

hemmed in by thickly forested pine-covered hills, it resembles the Rockies. You'll pass through an idyllic fjordside town, Shieldaig, then cross over a finger of land and plunge deeper into Upper Loch Torridon. Near the end of the loch, keep an eye out for **The Torridon**—a luxurious lochfront grand hotel with gorgeous Victorian Age architecture, a café serving afternoon tea, and expensive rooms (www.thetorridon.com).

As you loop past the far end of the loch—with the option to turn off for the village of **Torridon** (which has a good youth hostel, www.syha.org.uk)—the landscape has shifted dramatically, from pine-covered hills to a hauntingly desolate glen. You'll cut through this valley—bookended by towering peaks and popular with hikers—before reaching the town of Kinlochewe.

At Kinlochewe, take the A-832 west (following *Ullapool* signs from here on out), and soon you'll be tracing the bonnie, bonnie

banks of **Loch Maree**—considered by many connoisseurs to be one of Scotland's finest lochs. You'll see campgrounds, nature areas, and scenic pull-outs as you make good time on the speedy two-lane lochside road. (The best scenery is near the beginning, so don't put off that photo stop.)

Nearing the end of Loch Maree, the road becomes single-track again as you twist up over another saddle of scrubby land. On the other side, you'll get glimpses of Gair Loch through the trees, before finally arriving at the little harbor of **Gairloch.** Just beyond the harbor, where the road straightens out as it follows the coast, keep an eye out (on the right) for the handy Gale Center. Run as a charity, it has WCs, a small café with treats baked by locals, a fine shop of books and crafts, and comfortable tables and couches for taking a break (www. galeactionforum.co.uk).

True to its name, Gair Loch ("Short Loch") doesn't last long, and soon you'll head up a hill (keep an eye out for the pullout on the left, offering fine views over the village). The next village is Polewe, on **Loch Ewe.** Just after the village, on the left, is the

Inverewe Gardens. These beautiful gardens, run by the National Trust for Scotland, were the pet project of Osgood Mackenzie, who in 1862 began transforming 50 acres of his lochside estate into a subtropical paradise. The warming Gulf Stream and—in some places—stout stone walls help make this oasis possible. If you have time and need to stretch your legs from all that shifting, spend an hour wandering its sprawling grounds. The walled garden, near the entrance, is a highlight, with each bed thoughtfully labeled (£10.50, daily, www.nts. org.uk).

Continuing on the A-832 toward Ullapool, you'll stay above Loch Ewe, then briefly pass above the open ocean. Soon you'll find yourself following **Little Loch Broom** (with imposing mountains on your right). At the end of that loch, you'll carry on straight and work your way past a lush strip of farmland at the apex of the loch. Soon you'll meet the big A-835 highway; turn left and take this speedy road the rest of the way into Ullapool. (Or you can turn right to zip on the A-835 all the way to Inverness—just an hour away.) Whew!

Ullapool

A gorgeously set, hard-working town of about 1,500 people, Ullapool (ul-la-PEWL) is what passes for a metropolis in Wester Ross. Its most prominent feature is its big, efficient ferry dock, connecting the

mainland with Stornoway on the Isle of Lewis (Scotland's biggest, in the Outer Hebrides). Facing the dock is a strip of cute little houses, today housing restaurants, shops, B&Bs, and residences. Behind the waterfront, the town is only a few blocks deep—you can get the lay of the land in a few minutes' stroll. Curving around the back side of the town—along a big, grassy campground—is an inviting rocky beach, facing across the loch in one direction and out toward the open sea in the other.

Orientation to Ullapool: Ullapool has several handy services for travelers. An excellent **bookshop** is a block up, straight ahead from the ferry dock. Many services line Argyle Street, which runs parallel to the harbor one block up the hill: the **TI** is to the right, while a Bank of Scotland **ATM** and the **post office** are to the left. On this same street, the town runs a fine little **museum** with well-done exhibits about local history (closed Sun and Nov-March, www.ullapoolmuseum.co.uk). This street, nicknamed "Art-gyle Street," also has a smattering of local art **galleries.**

Sleeping in Ullapool: Several guesthouses line the harborfront Shore Street, including **$ Point Cottage** (2 rooms, no breakfast, www.pointcottagebandb.co.uk), **$ Waterside House** (3 rooms, minimum two-night stay in peak season, www.waterside.uk.net), and the town's official **¢ youth hostel** (www.syha.org.uk). A block up from the water on West Argyle Street, **$ West House** has three rooms and requires a two-night minimum stay (no breakfast, www.westhousebandb.co.uk).

Eating in Ullapool: The two most reliable places are the **$$ Ceilidh Place,** on West Argyle Street a block above the harbor (www.theceilidhplace.com); and **$$$ The Arch Inn,** facing the water a half-block from the ferry dock (www.thearchinn.co.uk). Both have a nice pubby vibe as well as sit-down dining rooms with a focus on locally caught seafood. Both also rent rooms and frequently host live music. For a quick meal, two different **$ chippies** (around the corner from each other, facing the ferry dock) keep the breakwater promenade busy with al fresco budget diners and happy seagulls.

▲Northwest Scotland Driving Tour, from Ullapool to the North Coast

The scenery continues as you head north from Ullapool, all the way up to Scotland's northern coast. Leaving Ullapool, follow signs that read simply *North (A-835)*. You'll pass through the cute little beachside village of **Ardmair,** then pull away from the coast.

NORTHERN SCOTLAND

About 15 minutes after leaving Ullapool, just after you exit the village of Strathcanaird and head uphill, watch on the left for a pullout with a handy orientation panel describing the panorama of **towering peaks** that line the road. It looks like a mossy Monument Valley. Enjoy the scenery for about four more miles—surrounded by wee lochs and gigantic peaks—and watch for the **Knockan Crag** visitors center, above you on the right, with exhibits on local geology, flora, and fauna and suggestions for area hikes (unmanned and open daily 24 hours, WCs, www.nnr-scotland.org.uk).

Continuing north along the A-835, you'll soon pass out of the region of Ross and Cromarty and enter Sutherland. At the T-intersection, turn left for *Kylesku* and *Lochinver* (on the A-837). From here on out, you can start following the *North & West Highlands Tourist Route;* you'll also see your first sign for John O'Groats at the northeastern corner of Scotland (152 miles away).

You'll roll through moors, surrounded on all sides by hills. Just after the barely-there village of Inchnadamph, keep an eye

out on the left for the ruins of **Ardvrech Castle,** which sits in crumbled majesty upon its own little island in Loch Assynt, connected to the world by a narrow sandy spit. Just after these ruins, you'll have another choice: For the fastest route to the north coast, turn right to follow A-894 (toward *Kylesku*

and *Durness*). If you have some time to spare, you could carry on straight to scenically follow Loch Assynt toward the sleepy fishing village of **Lochinver** (12 miles). After seeing the village, you could go back the way you came to the main road, or continue all the way around the little peninsula on the B-869, passing several appealing sandy beaches and villages.

Back on the main A-894, you'll pass through an almost lunar landscape, with peaks all around, finally emerging at the gorgeous, mountain-rimmed **Loch Glendhu,** which you'll cross on a stout modern bridge. From here, it's a serene landscape of rock, heather, and ferns, with occasional glimpses of the coast—such as at **Scourie,** with a particularly nice sandy beach. Finally (after the road becomes

A-838—keep left at the fork, toward *Durness*), you'll head up,

over, and through a vast and dramatic glen. At the end of the glen, you'll start to see sand below you on the left; this is **Kyle of Durness,** which goes on for miles. You'll see the turnoff for the ferry to Cape Wrath, then follow tidy stone walls the rest of the way into **Durness.**

The North Coast

Scotland's north coast, which stretches a hundred miles from Cape Wrath in the northwest corner to John O'Groats in the northeast, is gently scenic, but less dramatic than Wester Ross—the jagged mountains loom far to the south, and your views are dominated by an alternating array of moors and jagged coastline. This is a good place to make up the long miles. I've described the driving route along the north coast from west to east.

NORTH COAST DRIVING TOUR
Durness to Thurso

Durness is a beachy village of cow meadows perched on a bluff above sandy shores. This area has a different feel from Wester Ross—it's less rugged and more manicured, with tidy farms hemmed in by neatly stacked stone walls. There's not much to see or do in the town, but there is a 24-hour gas station (gas up now—this is your last chance for a while...trust me) and a handy TI (by the big parking lot with the "Award Winning Beach," tel. 01971/509-005).

Head east out of the village on the A-838, watching for brown signs on your right to *Durness Village Hall.* Pull over here to stroll through the small **memorial garden for John Lennon,** who enjoyed his boyhood vacations in Durness.

Just after the village hall, on the left, pull over at **Smoo Cave** (free WCs in parking lot). Its goofy-sounding name comes from the Old Norse *smúga,* for "cave." (Many places along the north coast—which had a strong Viking influence—have Norse rather than Gaelic or Anglo-Saxon place names.) It's free to hike down the well-marked stairs to a protected cove, where an underground river has carved a deep cave into the bluff. Walk inside the cave to get a free peek at the waterfall; for a longer visit, you can pay for a 20-minute boat trip and guided walk (unnecessary for most; sign up at the mouth of the cave).

Back on the road, soon after Smoo Cave, on the left, is the gorgeous **Ceannabeinne Beach** (Gaelic for "End of the Moun-

tains"). Of the many Durness-area beaches, this is the locals' favorite.

Heading east from the Durness area, you'll traverse many sparsely populated miles—long roads that cut in and out from the coast, with scrubby moorland and distant peaks on the other side. You'll emerge at the gigantic **Loch Eriboll,** which you'll circumnavigate—passing lamb farms and crumbling stone walls—to continue your way east. Leaving this fjord, you'll cut through some classic fjord scenery until you finally pop out at the scenic **Kyle of Tongue.** You'll cross over the big, modern bridge, then twist up through the village of Tongue and continue your way eastward (the A-838 becomes the A-836)—through more of the same scrubby moorland scenery. Make good time for the next 40 lonely miles. Notice how many place names along here use the term "strath"—a wide valley (as opposed to a narrower "glen"), such as where jagged mountains open up to the sea.

Finally—after going through little settlements like Bettyhill and Melvich—the moors begin to give way to working farms as you approach Thurso.

Thurso, John O'Groats, and Nearby

The main population center of northern Scotland (pop. 8,000), Thurso is a functional transit hub with a charming old core. As you face out to sea, the heavily industrialized point on the left is **Scrabster,** with the easiest ferry crossing to Orkney (for details, see "Getting to Orkney" on page 181).

• *Continuing east from Thurso (following brown* John O'Groats *signs on the A-836), it's about eight miles to the village of Dunnet. If you have time for some rugged scenery, turn off here to drive the four miles (each way) to...*

Dunnet Head

While John O'Groats is often mistakenly called "Britain's northernmost point," Dunnet Head pokes up just a bit farther. And, while it lacks the too-cute signpost marking distances to faraway landmarks, views from here are better than from John O'Groats. Out at the tip of Dunnet Head, a lonely lighthouse enjoys panoramic views across the Pentland Firth to Orkney, while a higher vantage point is just up the hill. Keep an eye out for seabirds, including puffins.

• *In the village of Dunnet, between the main road and Dunnet Head, look for the well-signed...*

Mary-Ann's Cottage

This little stone house explains traditional crofting lifestyles—left just as it was when 92-year-old Mary-Ann Calder moved out in 1990 (very limited hours).

• *Back on the main A-836, about four miles farther east is the turnoff for the...*

Castle of Mey

The Queen Mother grew up at Glamis Castle, but after her daughter became Queen Elizabeth II, she purchased and renovated this

sprawling property as an escape from the bustle of royal life... and you couldn't get much farther from civilization than this. For nearly 50 years, the Queen Mum stayed here for annual visits in August and October. Today it welcomes visitors to tour its homey interior and 30 acres of manicured gardens

(closed Oct-mid-May, www.castleofmey.org.uk).

• *From Mey, it's another six miles east to John O'Groats. About halfway there, in Gills Bay, is another ferry dock for cars heading to Orkney (see "Getting to Orkney" on page 181).*

John O'Groats

A total tourist trap that's somehow also genuinely stirring, John O'Groats marks the northeastern corner of the Isle of Britain—bookending the country with Land's End, 874 miles to the southwest in Cornwall. People enjoy traversing the length of Britain by motorcycle, by bicycle, or even by foot (it takes about eight weeks to trudge along the "E2E" trail—that's "End to End"). And upon arrival, whether they've walked for two months or just driven up for the day from Inverness, everyone wants to snap a "been there, done that" photo with the landmark

signpost. Surrounding that is a huge parking lot, a souvenir stand masquerading as a TI, and lots of tacky "first and last" shops and restaurants. Orkney looms just off the coast.

Nearby: The real target of "End to End" pilgrims isn't the signpost, but the **Duncansby Head Lighthouse**—about two miles to the east, it's the actual northeasternmost point, with an even more end-of-the-world vibe. (By car, head away from the John O'Groats area on A-99, and watch for the Duncansby Head turnoff on the left, just past the Seaview Hotel.) If you have time for a hike, about a mile south of the lighthouse are the **Duncansby Stacks**—dramatic sea stacks rising up above a sandy beach.

• *You made it! Great job. Now to complete your journey, turn around and drive (or walk) 874 miles to Land's End.*

The Orkney Islands

The Orkney Islands, perched just an hour's ferry ride north of the mainland, are uniquely remote, historic, and—for the right traveler—well worth the effort.

Crossing the 10-mile Pentland Firth separating Orkney from northern Scotland, you leave the Highlands behind and enter a

new world. With no real tradition for clans, tartans, or bagpipes, Orkney feels not "Highlander" or even "Scottish," but Orcadian (as locals are called). Though Orkney was inhabited by Picts from the sixth century B.C., during most of its formative history—from 875 all the way

until 1468—it was a prized trading hub of the Norwegian realm, giving it a feel more Scandinavian than Celtic. The Vikings (who sailed from Norway, just 170 miles away) left their mark, both literally (runes carved into prehistoric stone monuments) and culturally: Many place names are derived from Old Norse, and the Orkney flag looks like the Norwegian flag with a few yellow accents.

There are other historic connections. In later times, Canada's Hudson's Bay Company recruited many Orcadians to staff its outposts. And given its status as the Royal Navy headquarters during both World Wars, Orkney remains one of the most pro-British corners of Scotland. In the 2014 independence referendum, Orkney cast the loudest "no" vote in the entire country (67 percent against).

Orkney's landscape is also a world apart: Aside from some dramatic sea cliffs hiding along its perimeter, the main island is mostly flat and bald, with few trees, the small town of Kirkwall, and lots of tidy farms with gently mooing cows. While the blustery weather (which can change several times a day) keeps the vegetation on the scrubby side, for extra greenery each town has a sheltered community garden run by volunteers. Orkney's fine sandy beaches seem always empty—as if lying on them will give you hypothermia. Sparsely populated, the islands have no traffic lights and most roads are single lane with "passing places" politely spaced as necessary.

Today's economy is based mostly on North Sea oil, renewable energy, and fishing. The boats you'll see are creel boats with nets and cages to collect crabs, lobsters, scallops, and oysters. Unless a cruise ship drops by, tourism seems to be secondary.

For the sightseer, Orkney has two draws unmatched elsewhere in Scotland: It has some of the finest prehistoric sites in northern Europe, left behind by an advanced Stone Age civilization that flourished here. And the harbor called Scapa Flow has fascinating remnants of its important military role during the World Wars—from intentional shipwrecks designed to seal off the harbor, to muscular Churchill-built barriers to finish the job a generation later.

Orientation to Orkney

Orkney (as the entire archipelago is called) is made up of 70 islands, with a total population of 24,500. The main island—with the primary town (Kirkwall) and ferry ports connecting Orkney to northern Scotland (Stromness and St. Margaret's Hope)—is called, confusingly, Mainland. (It just goes to show you: One man's island is another man's mainland.)

PLANNING YOUR TIME

Orkney merits at least two nights and one full day. Some people (especially WWII aficionados) spend days exploring Orkney, but I've focused on the main sights to see in a short visit—all on the biggest island.

The only town of any substance, Kirkwall is your best home base. You can see its sights in a few hours (a town stroll, the fine Orkney Museum, and its striking cathedral). From there, to see the best of Orkney in a single day, plan on driving about 70 miles, looping out from Kirkwall in two directions: Spend the morning at the prehistoric sites (Maeshowe and nearby sites, Skara Brae), and the afternoon driving along the Churchill Barriers and visiting the Italian Chapel.

Cruise Crowds: Orkney is Scotland's busiest cruise port; on days when ships are in port, normally sleepy destinations can be jammed. Check the cruise schedule at www.orkneyharbours.com

and plan accordingly to avoid busy times at popular sights (such as Skara Brae, the Italian Chapel).

GETTING TO ORKNEY

By Car/Ferry: Two different car ferry options depart from near Thurso, which is about a three-hour drive from Inverness (on the A-9); for the scenic longer route, you could loop all the way up Wester Ross, and then along the north coast from Durness to Thurso (see earlier in this chapter). The two companies land at opposite corners of Orkney, at Stromness and St. Margaret's Hope; from either, it's about a 30-minute drive to Kirkwall.

Plan on about £60 one-way for a car on the Northlink ferry, or £40 on the Pentland ferry, plus £20 per passenger. For either company, reserve online at least a day in advance; check in at the ferry dock 30 minutes before departure.

For most, the best choice is the **Scrabster-Stromness** ferry, operated by NorthLink (3/day in each direction in summer, 2/day

off-season, 1.5-hour crossing, www.northlinkferries.co.uk). While it's a slightly longer crossing, it's also a bigger boat, with more services (including a good sit-down cafeteria—and famously tasty fish-and-chips), and it glides past the Old Man of Hoy, giving you an easy glimpse at one of Orkney's top landmarks. This ferry is coordinated with bus #X99, connecting Scrabster to Inverness (www.stagecoachbus.com).

The **Gills Bay-St. Margaret's Hope** route is operated by Pentland Ferries; its main advantage is the proximity of Gills Bay to John O'Groats, making it easy to visit Britain's northeasternmost point on your way to or from the ferry—but Gills Bay is also that much farther from Inverness (2-3/day in each direction, one-hour crossing, www.pentlandferries.co.uk).

There's also a **passenger-only boat** directly from John O'Groats to Burwick, which connects conveniently to an onward bus to Kirkwall (3/day July-Aug, 1/day May and Sept, none Oct-April, 40-minute crossing, www.jogferry.co.uk). While this works for those leaving their car at John O'Groats for a quick Orkney day trip, it's more weather-dependent.

By Plane: To get there fast, fly. Kirkwall's little airport has direct flights to Inverness, Edinburgh, Glasgow, and Aberdeen (www.flybe.com has good deals if you book ahead). Landing at the airport, you're four miles from Kirkwall; pick up a town map at the info desk. It's convenient to pick up a rental car at the airport. There

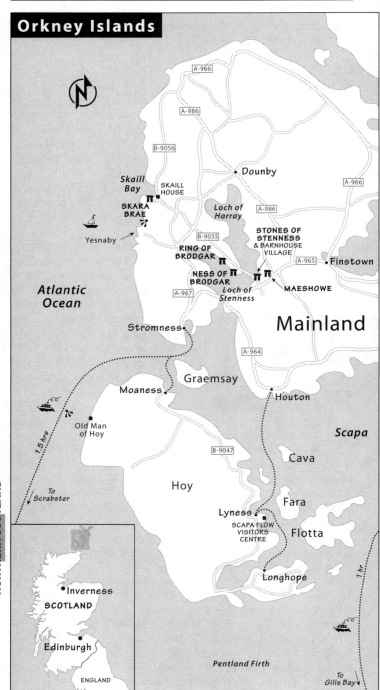

Orkney Islands

To Scrabster

To Gills Bay

NORTHERN SCOTLAND

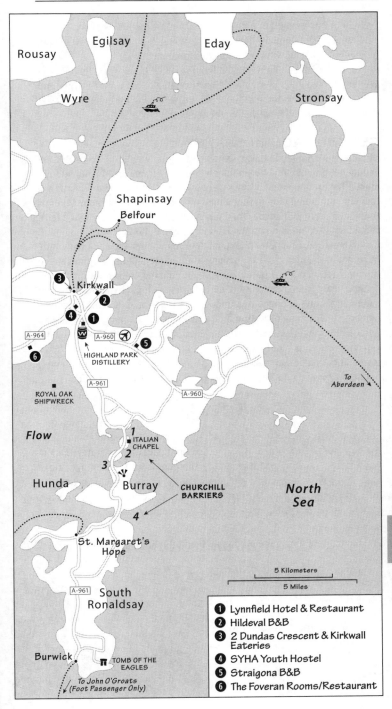

Rousay

Egilsay

Eday

Wyre

Stronsay

Shapinsay

Belfour

③ Kirkwall ②
④ ①
A-964 [W] A-960 ✈ ⑤ Straigona
HIGHLAND PARK DISTILLERY
⑥
A-961
A-960
To Aberdeen

ROYAL OAK SHIPWRECK

Flow

1 ■ ITALIAN CHAPEL
2
3
Hunda   Burray   CHURCHILL BARRIERS

North Sea

4

St. Margaret's Hope

A-961

South Ronaldsay

Burwick   TOMB OF THE EAGLES

To John O'Groats (Foot Passenger Only)

5 Kilometers
5 Miles

① Lynnfield Hotel & Restaurant
② Hildeval B&B
③ 2 Dundas Crescent & Kirkwall Eateries
④ SYHA Youth Hostel
⑤ Straigona B&B
⑥ The Foveran Rooms/Restaurant

NORTHERN SCOTLAND

are not many taxis, so without a car your best bet is the bus that runs every 30 minutes—just pay the driver (airport code: KOI, tel. 01856/872-421, www.hial.co.uk/kirkwall-airport).

By Tour from Inverness: The John O'Groats foot ferry operates a very long all-day tour from Inverness that includes bus and ferry transfers, and a guided tour around the main sights (£72, daily June-Aug only, www.jogferry.co.uk).

GETTING AROUND ORKNEY

While this chapter is designed for travelers with a car (or a driver/guide—see next), **public buses** do connect sights on Mainland (operated by Stagecoach, www.stagecoachbus.com). From Mainland, **ferries** fan out to outlying islets (www.orkneyferries.co.uk); the main ports are Kirkwall (for points north) and Houton (for Hoy). If taking a car on a ferry, it's always smart to book ahead.

Local Guide: Orkney Uncovered is run by husband-and-wife team Kinlay (who guides) and Kirsty (who manages the office). Energetic and passionate about sharing their adopted home with visitors, their standard itinerary hits both prehistoric and wartime highlights (everything in this chapter—which Kinlay helped research). But they're happy to tailor an itinerary to your interests and offer a special price for Rick Steves readers (£300 for a full-day, 9-hour tour in a comfy van, more for 5 or more people, multiday tours and cruise excursions possible, tel. 01856/878-822, www. orkneyuncovered.co.uk, enquiries@orkneyuncovered.co.uk).

Kirkwall

Kirkwall (pop. 9,000) is tidy and functional. Like the rest of the island, most of its buildings are more practical than pretty. But it has an entertaining and interesting old center and is a smart home base from which to explore the island. Whether sleeping here or not, you'll likely pass through at some point (to gas up, change buses, use the airport, or stock up on groceries).

Orientation to Kirkwall

Historic Kirkwall's shop-lined, pedestrian-only main drag leads from the cathedral down to the harbor, changing names several times as it curls through town. It's a workaday strip, lined with a combination of humble local shops and places trying to be trendy. You'll pop out at the

little harbor, where fishing boats bob and ferries fan out to the northern islets.

The handy **TI,** with free Wi-Fi, is at the bus station (on West Castle Street, daily 9:00-18:00, shorter hours off-season, tel. 01856/872-856, www.visitorkney.com). They produce a handy "breakfast bulletin" with the day's events and tourist news. The bus station stores bags for free (but not overnight). If you don't have a car, **Craigies Taxi** is reliable and responds quickly to a call (tel. 01856/878-787).

You're likely to find live music somewhere most nights. The **Reel Coffee Shop,** next to the cathedral, is passionate about music and hosts folk and "trad" evenings with an inviting vibe (generally Wed, Thu, and Sat at 20:00). Among the local craft beers on tap, the most popular, a pale ale, is Scapa Special. (They say it goes down better than the German fleet.)

Sights in Kirkwall

▲St. Magnus Cathedral

This grand edifice, whose pointy steeple is visible from just about anywhere in town, is one of Scotland's most enjoyable churches to visit (free, Mon-Sat 9:00-18:00, Sun from 14:00). The building dates from the 12th century, back when this was part of the Parish of Trondheim, Norway. Built from vibrant red sandstone by many of the same stonemasons who worked on Durham's showpiece cathedral, St. Magnus is harmonious Romanesque inside and out: stout columns and small, rounded windows  and arches. Inside, it boasts a delightful array of engaging monuments, all well-described by the self-guided tour brochure: a bell from the *Royal Oak* battleship, sunk in Scapa Flow in 1939 (explained later); a reclining monument of arctic explorer John Rae, who appears to be enjoying a very satisfying eternal nap; the likely bones of St. Magnus (a beloved local saint); and many other characteristic flourishes. But the highlight is the gravestones that line the walls of the nave, each one carved with reminders of mortality: skull and crossbones, coffin, hourglass, and the shovel used by the undertaker. Read some of the poignant epitaphs: "She lived regarded and dyed regreted."

Nearby: The **Bishop and Earl's Palaces** (across the street) are a pair of once-grand, now-empty ruined buildings—for most, they're not worth the admission fee.

▲▲Orkney Museum

Just across the street from the cathedral, this museum packs the old parsonage with well-described exhibits covering virtually every dimension of history and life on the island. A visit here (to see the Stone Age, Iron Age, and Viking artifacts) can be good preparation before exploring the islands' archaeological sites. Poking around, you'll see a 1539 map showing how "Orcadia" was part of Scandinavia, an exhibit about the crazy annual brawl called The Ba', and

lots of century-old photos of traditional life (free, Mon-Sat 10:30-17:00, closed Sun, fine book shop, tel. 01856/873-535).

Mercat Cross

In front of the cathedral stands Kirkwall's mercat cross (market cross), which is the starting point for the annual event called The Ba'. Short for "ball," this is a no-holds-barred, citywide rugby match that takes place every Christmas and New Year's Day. Hundreds of Kirkwall's rough-and-tumble young lads team up based on neighborhood (the Uppies and the Doonies), and attempt to deliver the ball to the opposing team's goal by any means necessary. The only rule: There are no rules. While it's usually just one gigantic scrum pushing back and forth through the streets, other tactics are used (such as the recent controversy when one team simply tossed the ball in a car and drove it to the goal). Ask locals about their stories—or scars—from The Ba'.

▲Highland Park Distillery

Outside the town center is a sprawling stone facility that's been distilling whisky since 1789 (legally). They give 75-minute tours similar to other distilleries, but this is one of only six in all of Scotland that malts its own barley—you'll see the malting floor (where the barley is spread and stirred while germinating) and the peat-fired kilns. Guides love to explain how the distillery's well-regarded whiskies get their flavor from Orkney's unique composition of peat (composed mostly of heather on this treeless island) and its high humidity (which minimizes alcohol "lost to the angels" during maturation). While the distillery is "silent" for much of July and August, its tour is good even if the workers are gone (£10, tours Mon-Sat 10:00-16:00, Sun 12:00-16:00, fewer off-season, includes two tasty shots; on the edge of town to the south, toward the Scapa Flow WWII sites; tel. 01856/873-107, www.highlandpark.co.uk).

Sleeping in Kirkwall

These accommodations are in or near Kirkwall. Orkney's B&Bs are not well marked; get specific instructions from your host before you arrive.

In Kirkwall: $$$ Lynnfield Hotel rents 10 rooms that are a bit old-fashioned in decor, but with modern hotel amenities (on Holm Road/A-961, tel. 01856/872-505, www.lynnfieldhotel.com). High up in town, consider **$$ Hildeval B&B,** in a modern home with five contemporary-style rooms (on East Road, tel. 01856/878-840, www.hildeval-orkney.co.uk). With a handy location just behind the cathedral, **$ 2 Dundas Crescent** has three old-fashioned rooms rented by welcoming Ruth, in a big old house that used to be a manse—a preacher's home (tel. 01856/874-805, www.twodundas.co.uk). And ¢ the **SYHA Youth Hostel** rents both dorm beds and private rooms (Old Scapa Road, 15-minute walk from center, tel. 01856/872-243, www.syha.org.uk).

In the Countryside: Just past the airport, **$$ Straigona B&B,** about a five-minute drive outside of Kirkwall, has three rooms in a cozy modern home, run by helpful Julie and Mike (tel. 01856/861-328, www.straigona.co.uk). For more anonymity and grand views over Scapa Flow, the recommended restaurant **$$ The Foveran** has eight rooms, some with contemporary flourish and others more traditional (5 minutes from Kirkwall by car on the A-964, tel. 01856/872-389, www.thefoveran.com).

Eating in Kirkwall

The first three places are near the cathedral; the next two are on the harbor. The main pedestrian street connecting the harbor and cathedral is lined with other options. Hotels along the harbor are also a good bet for dinner.

$$ The Reel Coffee Shop is a music club, café, and pub popular for its light lunches (open daily 9:00-17:00, next to the cathedral). It reopens on many evenings to host live music (Wed, Thu, and Sat evenings from 20:00, 6 Broad Street, tel. 01856/871-000).

$$ Judith Glue Shop is a souvenir-and-craft shop across from the cathedral, with a cutesy café in the back (25 Broad Street, tel. 01856/874-225).

$ Strynd Tea Room, tucked down an alley near the cathedral (just behind The Reel), is a fine choice for coffee and cakes, afternoon tea, or a light lunch (Broad Street, tel. 01856/871-552).

$ The Harbour Fry is best place for fish-and-chips, with both eat-inside or takeaway options (daily 12:00-21:00, half a block off the harbor at 3 Bridge Street, tel. 01856/873-170).

$$ Helgi's Pub, facing the harbor, serves quality food and is popular for its fun menu and burgers. Upstairs is boring, the ground floor is more fun, and you're welcome to sit at the bar if the tables are full. Reservations are smart for dinner (daily 12:00-14:00 & 17:00-21:00, 14 Harbor Street, tel. 01856/879-293, www.helgis.co.uk).

DESTINATION RESTAURANTS NEAR KIRKWALL

With talented chefs working hard to elevate Orcadian cuisine—using traditional local ingredients, but with international flourish, these are considered the best restaurants around.

$$$$ The Foveran, perched on a bluff with smashing views over Scapa Flow, has a cool, contemporary dining room with a wall of windows (dinner nightly May-Sept, weekends-only in winter, southwest of Kirkwall on the A-964, tel. 01856/872-389, www.thefoveran.com).

$$$$ Lynnfield Hotel, near the Highland Park Distillery on the way out of town, has a more traditional feel (open daily for lunch and dinner, reservations smart in the evening, on Holm Road/A-961, tel. 01856/872-505, www.lynnfieldhotel.com).

Sights in the Orkneys

PREHISTORIC SITES

Orkney boasts an astonishing concentration of 5,000-year-old Neolithic monuments worth ▲▲▲—one of the best such collections in Great Britain (and that's saying something). And here on Orkney, there's also a unique Bronze and Iron Age overlay, during which Picts, and then Vikings, built their own monuments to complement the ones they inherited. The best of these sites are easily toured along a single stretch of road, as described below.

Background: Five thousand years ago—centuries before Stonehenge—Orkney had a bustling settlement with some 30,000 people (a population larger than today's). The climate, already milder than most of Scotland thanks to the Gulf Stream, was even warmer then, making this a desirable place to live. Orkney's prehistoric residents left behind structures from every walk of life: humble residential settlements (Skara Brae, Barnhouse Village), mysterious stone circles (Ring of Brodgar, Stenness Stones), more than 100 tombs (Maeshowe, Tomb of the Eagles), and what appears to be a sprawling ensemble of spiritual buildings (the Ness of Brodgar). And, this being the Stone Age, all of this was accomplished using tools made not of metal, but of stone and bone.

Many more sites await excavation. (Any time you see a lump or a bump in a field, it's likely an ancient site—identified with the help of ground-penetrating radar—and protected by the government.) While you could spend days poring over all of Orkney's majestic prehistoric monuments, on a short visit focus on the following highlights. (Actual artifacts from these sites are on display only in the Orkney Museum in Kirkwall.)

Maeshowe

The finest chambered tomb north of the Alps, Maeshowe (mays-HOW) was built around 3500 B.C. From the outside, it looks like

yet another big mound. But inside, the burial chamber is remarkably intact. The only way to go inside is on a fascinating 30-minute tour. You'll squeeze through the entrance tunnel and emerge into a space designed for ancestor worship, surrounded by three smaller cells. At the winter solstice, the setting sun shines through the entrance tunnel, illuminating the entrance to the main cell. How they managed to cut and transport gigantic slabs of sandstone, then assemble this dry-stone, corbeled pyramid—all in an age before metal tools—still puzzles present-day engineers. Adding to this place's mystique, in the 12th century, a band of Norsemen took shelter here for three days during a storm, and entertained themselves by carving runic messages into the walls—many of them still readable (£6, tours daily 10:00-16:00, tel. 01856/761-606, www.historicenvironment.scot/maeshowe). Reservations are required (book in person or online, but not by phone).

Prehistoric Sites near Maeshowe

A narrow spit of land just a few hundred yards from Maeshowe is lined with several stunning, free-to-visit, always-"open" Neolithic sites (from Maeshowe, head south on the A-965 and immediately turn right onto the B-9056, following *Bay of Skaill* signs). Along this road, you'll reach the following sites, in this order (watch for the brown signs). Conveniently, these line up on the way to Skara Brae.

Stones of Stenness: Three-and-a-half standing stones survive from an original 12 that formed a

100-foot-diameter ring. Dating from around 3000 B.C., these are some of the oldest standing stones in Britain (a millennium older than Stonehenge).

Barnhouse Village: From the Stones of Stenness, a footpath continues through the field to the Barnhouse Village. Likely built around the same time as the Stones of Stenness, this was probably a residential area for the priests and custodians of the ceremonial monuments all around. Discovered in 1984, much of what you see today has been reconstructed—making this the least favorite site of archaeological purists. Still, it provides an illuminating contrast to Skara Brae (described later): While those Skara Brae homes were built underground, the ones at Barnhouse were thatched stone huts not unlike ones you still see around Great Britain today. The entire gathering was enclosed by a defensive wall.

Back on the road, just before the **causeway** between two lochs—saltwater on the left and freshwater on the right—two pillars flank the road (one intact, the other stubby). These formed a gateway of sorts to the important Neolithic structures just beyond.

Ness of Brodgar: On the left, look for a busy excavation site in action. The Ness of Brodgar offers an exciting opportunity to

observe an actual archaeological dig in progress (discovered only in 2003). The work site you see covers only one-tenth of the entire complex, which was likely an ensemble of important ceremonial buildings...think of it as the "Orkney Vatican." The biggest foundation, nicknamed "the Cathedral," appears to have been a focal point for pilgrimages. Don't be surprised if there's no action—due to limited funding, archaeologists are likely at work here only in July and August (at other times, it's carefully covered, with nothing to see). The archaeologists hope to raise enough funds to build a permanent visitors center. Free guided tours are sometimes available (July-Aug Mon-Fri at 11:00, 13:00, and 15:00, check www.nessofbrodgar.co.uk for details).

The Ring of Brodgat: Farther along on the left, look for stones capping a ridge above the road. The Ring of Brodgar is more than three times larger than the Stones of Stenness (and about 500 years newer). Of the

original 60 or so stones—creating a circle as wide as a football field—25 still stand. The ring, which sits amidst a marshy moor, was surrounded by a henge (moat) that was 30 feet wide and 20 feet deep. Walking around the ring, notice that some are carved with "graffiti"—names of visitors from the late 19th century to the early 20th century, as well as some faint Norse runes carved by a Viking named Bjorn around A.D. 1150 (park 300 yards away, across the road).

Skara Brae

At the far-eastern reaches of Mainland (about a 20-minute drive from Maeshowe), this remarkable site illustrates how some Neolithic people lived like rabbits in warrens—hunkered down in subterranean homes, connected by tunnels and lit only by whale-oil lamps. Uncovered by an 1850 windstorm, Skara Brae (meaning roughly "village under hills") has been meticulously excavated and is very well presented (£7.50, open daily 9:30-17:30 year-round, café and WCs).

Begin your visit in the small exhibition hall, where you'll watch a short film and see displays on Neolithic life. Then head out and walk inside a reconstructed home from Skara Brae—with a hearth, beds, storage area, and live-bait tanks dug into the floor. Finally, walk across a field to reach the site itself. Museum attendants stand by to answer any questions.

The oldest, standalone homes at Skara Brae were built around 3100 B.C.; a few centuries later, the complex was expanded and con-

nected with tunnels. You'll walk on a grassy ridge just above the complex, peering down into 10 partially ruined homes and the tunnels that connect them. For safety, all of this was covered with turf, with only two or three entrances and exits. Because sandstone is a natural insulator, these spaces—while cramped and dank—would have been warm and cozy during the frequent battering storms. If you see a grate, squint down into the darkness: A primitive sewer system, flushed by a rerouted stream, ran beneath all of the homes, functioning not too differently from modern sewers. And all of this was accomplished without the use of metal tools. They even created an ingenious system of giant stone slabs on pivots, allowing them to be opened and closed like modern doors.

Before leaving, look out over the nearby bay, and consider that this is only about one-third of the entire size of the original Skara Brae. What's now a beach was once a freshwater loch. But with the rising Atlantic, the water became unusable. About 800 years after it was built, the village was abandoned; since then, most of it has been lost to the sea. This area is called Skaill Bay, from the Old Norse *skål*, for "cheers!"—during Viking times, this was a popular place for revelry...but the revelers had no clue they were partying on top of a Neolithic village.

And now for something completely different: Your ticket to Skara Brae also includes the **Skaill House,** the sprawling stone mansion on the nearby hilltop. Here you can tour some lived-in rooms (c. 1950) and see a fascinating hodgepodge of items once important to a leading Orkney family. Some items illustrate Orkney's prime location for passing maritime trade: The dining room proudly displays Captain James Cook's dinner service—bartered by his crew on their return voyage after the captain was killed in Hawaii (Orkney was the first place they made landfall in the UK). You'll also see traditional Orkney chairs (with woven backs); in the library, an Old Norse "calendar"—a wooden stick that you could hold up to the horizon at sunset to determine the exact date; a Redcoat's red coat from the Crimean War; a Spanish chest salvaged

from a shipwreck; and some very "homely" (and supposedly haunted) bedrooms.

Nearby: Just south of Skara Brae, drivers can consider a quick visit to the sightseeing twofer of **Yesnaby** (watch for the turnoff on the B-9056). On a bluff overlooking the sea, you'll find an old antiaircraft artillery battery from World War II, and some of Orkney's most dramatic sea-cliff scenery.

SCAPA FLOW: WORLD WAR II SITES

For a quick and fascinating glimpse of Orkney's World War II locations, worth ▲▲▲, drive 10 minutes south from Kirkwall on the A-961 (leave town toward St. Mary's and St. Margaret's Hope, past the Highland Park Distillery)—to the natural harbor called Scapa Flow (see the sidebar). From the village of St. Mary's, you can cross over all four of the Churchill Barriers, with subtle reminders of war all around. The floor of Scapa Flow is littered with shipwrecks, and if you know where to look, you can still see many of them as you drive by.

Barrier #1 crosses from St. Mary's to the Isle of Burray. This narrow channel is where, in the early days of World War II, the German

U-47 slipped between sunken ships to attack the *Royal Oak*—demonstrating the need to build these barriers. Notice that the Churchill Barriers have two levels: smaller quarried stone down below, and huge concrete blocks on top.

Just over the first barrier, perched on the little rise on the left, is Orkney's most fascinating wartime site: the **Italian Chapel** (£3, daily 9:00-18:30 in summer, shorter hours off-season). Italian POWs who were captured during the North African campaign (and imprisoned here on Orkney to work on the Churchill Barriers) were granted permission to create a Catholic chapel to remind them of their homeland. While the front view is a pretty Baroque facade, if you circle around you'll see that the core of the structure is two prefab Nissen huts (similar to Quonset huts). Inside, you can see the remarkable craftsmanship of the artists who decorated the church. In 1943, Domenico Chiocchetti led the effort to create this house of worship, and personally painted the frescoes that adorn the interior. The ethereal *Madonna*

e Bambino over the main altar is based on a small votive he had brought with him to war. An experienced ironworker named Palumbi used scrap metal (much of it scavenged from sunken WWI ships) to create the gate and chandeliers, while others used whatever basic materials they could to finish the details. (Notice the elegant corkscrew base of the baptismal font near the entrance; it's actually a suspension spring coated in concrete.) These lovingly crafted details are a hope-filled symbol of the gentility and grace that can blossom even during brutal wartime. (And the British military is proud of this structure as an embodiment of Britain's wartime ethic of treating POWs with care and respect.) Spend some time examining the details—such as the stained-glass windows, which are painted rather than leaded. The chapel was completed in 1944, just two months before the men who built it were sent home. Chiocchetti returned for a visit in the 1960s, bringing with him the wood-carved Stations of the Cross that now hang in the nave.

Continuing south along the road, you'll cross over two more barriers in rapid succession. You'll see the masts and hulls of

NORTHERN SCOTLAND

Scapa Flow: Britain's Remote Wartime Naval Base

Orkney's arc of scattered islands form one of the world's largest natural harbors, called Scapa Flow (SKAH-pah flow). The Norsemen named this area *skalpai floi*—"scabbard water," where a sword was sheathed—suggesting that they used this area to store their warships when not in use. And in the 20th century, Scapa Flow was the main base for Britain's Royal Navy.

During World War I, to thwart U-boat attacks, dozens of old ships and fishing vessels were requisitioned and intentionally sunk to block the gaps between the islets that define Scapa Flow. You can still see many of these "block ships" breaking the surface today.

At the end of World War I, a fleet of 74 German battleships surrendered at Scapa Flow. On the morning of June 21, 1919—days before the Treaty of Versailles was formally enacted—the British admiral took most of his navy out on a "victory lap" patrol. Once they were gone, the German commander ordered his men to scuttle the entire fleet, rather than turn them over. By the time the British fleet returned five hours later, 52 German ships littered the bottom of the bay. The British opened fire on the remaining German ships, killing nine Germans—the final casualties of World War I. While most of the ships were later salvaged for scrap, to this day, German crockery washes up on Orkney beaches after a storm. Seven ships remain at a depth of 150 feet, making this one of Eu-

shipwrecks (on the left) scuttled here during World War I to block the harbor. As you cross over the bridges, notice that these are solid barriers, with no water circulation—in fact, the water level on each side of the barrier varies slightly, since the tide differs by an hour and a half.

At the far end of **Barrier #3,** on the left, watch for the huge wooden boxes on the beach. These were used in pre-barrier times (WWI) for boom floats, which supported nets designed to block German submarines.

After Barrier #3, as you climb the hill, watch for the pull-rope's most popular scuba diving destinations.

Scapa Flow also played an important role in World War II. Even before Britain declared war on Germany, Luftwaffe reconnaissance flights had identified a gap in the sunken-ship barriers around the harbor. And on October 14, 1939—just weeks after war was declared—a Nazi U-47 slipped inside the harbor and torpedoed the HMS *Royal Oak,* killing 834 (including 110 seamen-in-training under the age of 15). To this day, the battleship—which had been fully loaded with fuel and ordnance—sits on the bottom of the bay, marked with a green warning buoy.

In April 1940, Luftwaffe planes flew from German-occupied Norway to bomb Orkney for three days straight in what's termed the "Battle of Orkney." But the islands were bulked up with heavy-duty gun batteries and other defenses, turning Orkney into a fortress. A sea of blimps called "barrage balloons"—designed to interfere with air attacks—clogged the air overhead. They even built a false fleet out of wood (also protected by barrage balloons) as a decoy for the Luftwaffe. The local population of 22,000 was joined by some 80,000 troops. Many surviving fragments from the Battle of Orkney can still be seen all over the island.

To ensure that no further surprises would sneak into the bay, First Lord of the Admiralty Winston Churchill visited here (just weeks before becoming prime minister) and hatched a plan to build sturdy barriers spanning the small distances between the islands south of Kirkwall. Throughout the wartime years, British workers and Italian prisoners of war labored to construct the "Churchill Barriers." The roads on top of the barriers opened just a few days after V-E Day, and today tourists use them to island-hop—and to learn about the dramatic history of Scapa Flow.

out on the right with an orientation board. From this **viewpoint,** you can see three of the Churchill Barriers in one grand panorama.

Carrying on south, the next barrier isn't a Churchill Barrier at all—it's an ayre, a causeway that was built during the Viking period.

Finally you'll reach **Barrier #4**—hard to recognize because so much sand has accumulated on its east side (look for the giant breakwater blocks). Surveying the dunes along this barrier, notice the crooked concrete shed poking up—actually the top of a shipwreck.

The far side of this sand dune is one of Orkney's best beaches—sheltered and scenic.

From here, the A-961 continues south past **St. Margaret's Hope** (where the ferry to Gills Bay departs) and all the way to Burwick, at the southern tip of South Ronaldsay. From here you can see the tip of Scotland. Nearby is the **Tomb of the Eagles,** a burial cairn similar to Maeshowe, but less accessible (time-consuming visit, www.tomboftheeagles.co.uk).

More WWII Sites: For those really interested in the World War II scene, consider a ferry trip out to the **Isle of Hoy;** the main settlement, Lyness, has the Scapa Flow Visitors Centre and cemetery (www.scapaflow.co.uk). Near Lyness alone are some 37 Luftwaffe crash sites. A tall hill, called Wee Fea, was hollowed out to hold 100,000 tons of fuel oil. Also on Hoy, you can hike seven miles round-trip to the iconic **Old Man of Hoy**—a 450-foot-high sea stack in front of Britain's tallest vertical sea cliffs. (Or you can see the same thing for free from the deck of the Stromness-Scrabster ferry.)

FERRY PORT TOWNS

With more time, check out these two towns with connections to northern Scotland. **Stromness** is Orkney's "second city," with 3,000 people. It's a stony 17th-century fishing town and worth a look. Equal parts fishing town and tourist depot, its traffic-free main drag has a certain salty charm. If driving, there's easy parking at the harbor. If catching the ferry to Scrabster, get here early to enjoy a stroll.

St. Margaret's Hope—named for a 13th-century Norwegian princess who was briefly Queen of Scots until she died en route to Orkney—is even smaller, with a charming seafront-village atmosphere. Ferries leave here for Gills Bay.

PRACTICALITIES

This section covers just the basics on traveling in Scotland (for much more information, see *Rick Steves Scotland*). You'll find free advice on specific topics at www.ricksteves.com/tips.

MONEY

For currency, Scotland uses the pound sterling (£), also called a "quid": 1 pound (£1) = about $1.30. One pound is broken into 100 pence (p). To convert prices in pounds to dollars, add about 30 percent: £20 = about $26, £50 = about $65. (Check www.oanda.com for the latest exchange rates.)

Like England, Scotland issues its own pound notes. Scottish pounds are technically interchangeable across Great Britain but sometimes are not accepted by businesses in England. Banks in Scotland or England can convert your Scottish pounds into English pounds at no charge.

The standard way for travelers to get pounds is to withdraw money from an ATM (which locals call "cashpoints") using a debit card, ideally with a Visa or MasterCard logo. To keep your cash, cards, and valuables safe, wear a money belt.

Before departing, call your bank or credit-card company: Confirm that your card(s) will work overseas, ask about international transaction fees, and alert them that you'll be making withdrawals in Europe. Also ask for the PIN number for your credit card—you may need it for Europe's "chip-and-PIN" payment machines (see below; allow time for your bank to mail your PIN to you).

Dealing with "Chip and PIN": Most credit and debit cards now have chips that authenticate and secure transactions. European cardholders insert their chip card into the payment slot, then enter a PIN. (Until recently, most US cards required a signature.) Any American card with a chip will work at Europe's hotels, restaurants, and shops—although sometimes the clerk may ask for a signature. But some self-service payment machines—such as those at train stations, toll roads, or unattended gas pumps—may not accept your card, even if you know the PIN. If your card won't work, look for a cashier who can process the transaction manually—or pay in cash.

Dynamic Currency Conversion: If merchants or hoteliers offer to convert your purchase price into dollars (called dynamic currency conversion, or DCC), refuse this "service." You'll pay more in fees for the expensive convenience of seeing your charge in dollars. If an ATM offers to "lock in" or "guarantee" your conversion rate, choose "proceed without conversion." Other prompts might state, "You can be charged in dollars: Press YES for dollars, NO for pounds." Always choose the local currency.

STAYING CONNECTED

The simplest solution is to bring your own device—mobile phone, tablet, or laptop—and use it just as you would at home (following the tips below, such as connecting to free Wi-Fi whenever possible). The following instructions apply in Scotland and across Great Britain.

To call Great Britain from a US or Canadian number: Whether you're phoning from a landline, your own mobile phone, or a Skype account, you're making an international call. Dial 011-44 and then the area code (minus its initial zero) and local number. (The 011 is our international access code, and 44 is Great Britain's country code.) If dialing from a mobile phone, you can enter + in place of the international access code—press and hold the 0 key.

To call Great Britain from a European country: Dial 00-44 followed by the area code (minus its initial zero) and local number. (The 00 is Europe's international access code.)

To call within Great Britain: If you're dialing within an area code, just dial the local number; but if you're calling outside your area code, you have to dial both the area code (which starts with a 0) and the local number.

To call from Great Britain to another country: Dial 00 followed by the country code (for example, 1 for the US or Canada), then the area code and number. If you're calling European countries whose phone numbers begin with 0, you'll usually have to omit that 0 when you dial.

Tips: If you bring your own mobile phone, consider getting an international plan; most providers offer a global calling plan that cuts the per-minute cost of phone calls and texts, and a flat-fee data plan.

Use Wi-Fi whenever possible. Most hotels and many cafés offer free Wi-Fi, and you'll likely also find it at tourist informa-

Sleep Code

Hotels are classified based on the average price of a typical en suite double room with breakfast in high season.

$$$$	**Splurge:** Most rooms over £160
$$$	**Pricier:** £120-160
$$	**Moderate:** £80-120
$	**Budget:** £40-80
¢	**Backpacker:** Under £40
RS%	**Rick Steves discount**

Unless otherwise noted, credit cards are accepted and free Wi-Fi is available. Comparison-shop by checking prices at several hotels (on each hotel's own website, on a booking site, or by email). For the best deal, *always book directly with the hotel.* Ask for a discount if paying in cash; if the listing includes **RS%,** request a Rick Steves discount.

tion offices (TIs), major museums, and public-transit hubs. With Wi-Fi you can use your phone or tablet to make free or inexpensive domestic and international calls via a calling app such as Skype, FaceTime, or Google+ Hangouts. When you can't find Wi-Fi, you can use your cellular network to connect to the Internet, send texts, or make voice calls. When you're done, avoid further charges by manually switching off "data roaming" or "cellular data."

It's possible to stay connected without a mobile device. You can make calls from your hotel (or the rare public phone), and get online using public computers (there's usually one in your hotel lobby). Most hotels charge a high fee for international calls—ask for rates before you dial. For more on phoning, see www.ricksteves.com/phoning. For a one-hour talk on "Traveling with a Mobile Device," see www.ricksteves.com/travel-talks.

SLEEPING

I've categorized my recommended accommodations based on price, indicated with a dollar-sign rating (see sidebar). I recommend reserving rooms in advance, particularly during peak season. Once your dates are set, check the specific price for your preferred stay at several hotels. You can do this either by comparing prices on sites such as Hotels.com or Booking.com, or by checking the hotels' own websites. To get the best deal, contact my family-run hotels directly by phone or email. When you go direct, the owner avoids any third-party commission, giving them wiggle room to offer you a discount, a nicer room, or free breakfast. If you prefer to book online or are considering a hotel chain, it's to your advantage to use the hotel's website.

For complicated requests, send an email with the following information: number and type of rooms; number of nights; arrival date; departure date; and any special requests. Use the European style for writing dates: day/month/year. Hoteliers typically ask for your credit-card number as a deposit. In general, hotel prices can soften if you do any of the following: offer to pay cash, stay at least three nights, or travel off-season.

Know the terminology: An "en suite" room has a bathroom (toilet and shower/tub) actually inside the room; a room with a "private bathroom" can mean that the bathroom is all yours, but it's across the hall. If you want your own bathroom inside the room, request "en suite."

Compared to hotels, B&Bs and guesthouses give you double the cultural intimacy for half the price. Many B&Bs take credit cards, but may add the card service fee to your bill (about 3 percent). If you do need to pay cash for your room, plan ahead to have enough on hand when you check out.

EATING

I've categorized my recommended eateries based on price, indicated with a dollar-sign rating (see sidebar).

The traditional fry-up or full Scottish breakfast, which is usually included at your B&B or hotel, comes with your choice of eggs, Canadian-style bacon and/or sausage, a grilled tomato, sautéed mushrooms, baked beans, and often haggis, black pudding, or a dense potato scone. If it's too much for you, only order the items you want.

To dine affordably at classier restaurants, look for "early-bird specials" (offered about 17:30–19:00, last order by 19:00, sometimes on weekdays only). Smart travelers use pubs (short for "public houses") to eat, drink, and make new friends. Pub grub is Scotland's best eating value. For about $15–20, you'll get a basic hot lunch or dinner. The menu is hearty and traditional: stews, soups, fish-and-chips, meat, cabbage, and potatoes, plus often a few Italian or Indian-style dishes. Meals are usually served from 12:00 to 14:00 and from 18:00 to 20:00, not throughout the day. Order drinks and meals at the bar; they might bring it to you when it's ready, or you'll pick it up at the bar. Pay as you order, and don't tip unless there's full table service.

Most pubs have lagers (cold, refreshing, American-style beer), ales (amber-colored, cellar-temperature beer), bitters (hop-flavored ale, perhaps the most typical British beer), and stouts (dark and somewhat bitter, like Guinness).

While bar-hopping tourists generally think in terms of beer, many Scottish pubs are just as enthusiastic about serving whisky. If you are unfamiliar with whisky (what Americans call "Scotch" and the Irish call "whiskey"), it's a great conversation starter. Pubs often have dozens of whiskies available.

Restaurant Price Code

I've assigned each eatery a price category, based on the average cost of a typical main course. Drinks, desserts, and splurge items (steak and seafood) can raise the price considerably.

$$$$	**Splurge:**	Most main courses over £20
$$$	**Pricier:**	£15-20
$$	**Moderate:**	£10-15
$	**Budget:**	Under £10

In Scotland, carryout fish-and-chips and other takeout food is **$**; a basic pub or sit-down eatery is **$$**; a gastropub or casual but more upscale restaurant is **$$$**; and a swanky splurge is **$$$$**.

Tipping: If a service charge is included in the bill, it's not necessary to tip. Otherwise, it's appropriate to tip about 10-12 percent for good service.

TRANSPORTATION

By Train: Great Britain's 100-mph train system is one of Europe's best...and most expensive. To see if a rail pass could save you money—as it often does in Britain—check www.ricksteves.com/rail. If you're buying point-to-point tickets, you'll get the best deals if you book in advance, leave after rush hour (after 9:30), or ride the bus. Train reservations are free and recommended for long journeys or any trip on Sundays (reserve at any train station or online). For train schedules, see www.nationalrail.co.uk or Germany's excellent all-Europe website, www.bahn.com.

By Car: A car is useful for scouring the remote rural sights, but it's an expensive headache in big cities. It's cheaper to arrange most car rentals from the US. For tips on your insurance options, see www.ricksteves.com/cdw, and for route planning, consult www.viamichelin.com. Bring your driver's license. Speedy motorways (comparable to our freeways) let you cover long distances in a snap. Remember that the Scottish drive on the left side of the road (and the driver sits on the right side of the car). You'll quickly master Scotland's many roundabouts: Traffic moves clockwise, cars inside the roundabout have the right-of-way, and entering traffic yields (look to your right as you merge). Note that "camera cops" strictly enforce speed limits by automatically snapping photos of speeders' license plates, then mailing them a ticket.

Local road etiquette is similar to that in the US. Ask your car-rental company about the rules of the road, read the UK Department for Transport's *Highway Code* (www.gov.uk/highway-code), or check the US State Department website (www.

travel.state.gov, select "International Travel," then "Country Information," then search for your destination and click "Travel and Transportation").

By Bus: Most long-haul domestic routes in Scotland are operated by Scottish Citylink (www.citylink.co.uk). Longer-distance routes (especially those to England) are operated by National Express (www.nationalexpress.com) or Megabus (www.megabus.com).

HELPFUL HINTS

Emergency Help: To summon the **police** or an **ambulance**, call 999 or 112. For passport problems, call the **US Consulate in Edinburgh** (tel. 0131/556-8315, https://uk.usembassy.gov/embassy-consulates/edinburgh) or the Canadian Consulate in Edinburgh (mobile 0770-235-9916, www.unitedkingdom.gc.ca).

Theft or Loss: To replace a passport, you'll need to go in person to an embassy or consulate (see above). Cancel and replace your credit and debit cards by calling these 24-hour US numbers collect: Visa: tel. 303/967-1096, MasterCard: tel. 636/722-7111, American Express: tel. 336/393-1111. In Britain, to make a collect call to the US, dial 0-800-89-0011; press zero or stay on the line for an operator. File a police report either on the spot or within a day or two; you'll need it to submit an insurance claim for lost or stolen rail passes or travel gear, and it can help with replacing your passport or credit and debit cards. For more information, see www.ricksteves.com/help.

Time: Scotland uses the 24-hour clock. It's the same through 12:00 noon, then keep going: 13:00, 14:00, and so on. Scotland, like the rest of Great Britain, is five/eight hours ahead of the East/West Coasts of the US (and one hour earlier than most of continental Europe).

Holidays and Festivals: Great Britain celebrates many holidays, which can close sights and attract crowds (book hotel rooms ahead). For information on holidays and festivals, check Scotland's tourism website: www.visitscotland.com. For a simple list showing major—though not all—events, see www.ricksteves.com/festivals.

Numbers and Stumblers: What Americans call the second floor of a building is the first floor in Europe. Europeans write dates as day/month/year, so Christmas 2020 is 25/12/20. For most measurements, Great Britain uses the metric system: A kilogram is 2.2 pounds, and a liter is about a quart. For driving distances, they use miles.

RESOURCES FROM RICK STEVES

This Snapshot guide is excerpted from my latest edition of *Rick Steves Scotland,* one of many titles in my ever-expanding series of guidebooks on European travel. I also produce a public television series, *Rick Steves' Europe,* and a public radio show, *Travel with Rick Steves.* My website, www.ricksteves.com, offers free travel information, a forum for travelers' comments, guidebook updates, my travel blog, an online travel store, and information on European rail passes and our tours of Europe. If you're bringing a mobile device on your trip, you can download my free Rick Steves Audio Europe app, featuring podcasts of my radio shows, my Edinburgh Royal Mile Walk audio tour, and travel interviews about Scotland. You can get Rick Steves Audio Europe via Apple's App Store, Google Play, or the Amazon Appstore. For more information, see www.ricksteves.com/audioeurope.

ADDITIONAL RESOURCES

Tourist Information: www.visitscotland.com
Passports and Red Tape: www.travel.state.gov
Packing List: www.ricksteves.com/packing
Travel Insurance: www.ricksteves.com/insurance
Cheap Flights: www.kayak.com or www.google.com/flights
Airplane Carry-on Restrictions: www.tsa.gov
Updates for This Book: www.ricksteves.com/update

HOW WAS YOUR TRIP?

To share your tips, concerns, and discoveries after using this book, please fill out the survey at www.ricksteves.com/feedback. Thanks in advance—it helps a lot.

INDEX

INDEX

INDEX

Explore Europe

At ricksteves.com you can browse through thousands of articles, videos, photos and radio interviews, plus find a wealth of money-saving travel tips for planning your dream trip. And with our mobile-friendly website, you can easily access all this great travel information anywhere you go.

TV Shows

Preview the places you'll visit by watching entire half-hour episodes of Rick Steves' Europe (choose from all 100 shows) on-demand, for free.

your travel dreams into affordable reality

Radio Interviews

Enjoy ready access to Rick's vast library of radio interviews covering travel

tips and cultural insights that relate specifically to your Europe travel plans.

Travel Forums

Learn, ask, share! Our online community of savvy travelers is a great resource for first-time travelers to Europe, as well as seasoned pros. You'll find forums on each country, plus travel tips and restaurant/hotel reviews. You can even ask one of our well-traveled staff to chime in with an opinion.

Travel News

Subscribe to our free Travel News e-newsletter, and get monthly updates from Rick on what's happening in Europe.

Audio Europe™

Rick's Free Travel App

Get your FREE **Rick Steves Audio Europe**™ app to enjoy…

- Dozens of self-guided tours of Europe's top museums, sights and historic walks
- Hundreds of tracks filled with cultural insights and sightseeing tips from Rick's radio interviews
- All organized into handy geographic playlists
- For Apple and Android

With Rick whispering in your ear, Europe gets even better.

Find out more at ricksteves.com

Pack Light and Right

Save time and energy

This guidebook is your independent-travel toolkit. But for all it delivers, it's still up to you to devote the time and energy it takes to manage the preparation and logistics that are essential for a happy trip. If that's a hassle, there's a solution.

Rick Steves Tours

A Rick Steves tour takes you to Europe's most interesting places with great

with minimum stress

guides and small groups of 28 or less. We follow Rick's favorite itineraries, ride in comfy buses, stay in family-run hotels, and bring you intimately close to the Europe you've traveled so far to see. Most importantly, we take away the logistical headaches so you can focus on the fun.

travelers—nearly half of them repeat customers— along with us on four dozen different itineraries, from Ireland to Italy to Athens. Is a Rick Steves tour the right fit for your travel dreams? Find out at ricksteves.com, where you can also request Rick's latest tour catalog. Europe is best experienced with happy travel partners. We hope you can join us.

Join the fun

This year we'll take thousands of free-spirited

BEST OF GUIDES

Full color easy-to-scan format, focusing on Europe's most popular destinations and sights.

Best of England
Best of Europe
Best of France
Best of Germany
Best of Ireland
Best of Italy
Best of Spain

COMPREHENSIVE GUIDES

City, country, and regional guides with detailed coverage for a multi-week trip exploring the most iconic sights and venturing off the beaten track.

Amsterdam & the Netherlands
Barcelona
Belgium: Bruges, Brussels, Antwerp & Ghent
Berlin
Budapest
Croatia & Slovenia
Eastern Europe
England
Florence & Tuscany
France
Germany
Great Britain
Greece: Athens & the Peloponnese
Iceland
Ireland
Istanbul
Italy
London
Paris
Portugal
Prague & the Czech Republic
Provence & the French Riviera
Rome
Scandinavia
Scotland
Spain
Switzerland
Venice
Vienna, Salzburg & Tirol

HE BEST OF ROME

e, Italy's capital, is studded with
an remnants and floodlit-fountain
es. From the Vatican to the Colos-
with crazy traffic in between, Rome
derful, huge, and exhausting. The
s, the heat, and the weighty history

of the Eternal City where Caesars walked
can make tourists wilt. Recharge by taking siestas, gelato breaks, and after-dark
walks, strolling from one atmospheric
square to another in the refreshing evening air.

Pantheon—which
dome until the
2,000 years old
over 1,500).

Athens in the Vat-
es the humanistic

diators fought
her, entertaining

ome *ristorante.*
st St. Peter's
riously.

oks in a café

Rick Steves guidebooks are published by Avalon Travel,
an imprint of Perseus Books, a Hachette Book Group company.

with minimum stress

guides and small groups of 28 or less. We follow Rick's favorite itineraries, ride in comfy buses, stay in family-run hotels, and bring you intimately

close to the Europe you've traveled so far to see. Most importantly, we take away the logistical headaches so you can focus on the fun.

Join the fun

This year we'll take thousands of free-spirited travelers—nearly half of them repeat customers— along with us on four dozen different itineraries, from Ireland to Italy to Athens. Is a Rick Steves tour the right fit for your travel dreams? Find out at ricksteves.com, where you can also request Rick's latest tour catalog.

Europe is best experienced with happy travel partners. We hope you can join us.

See our itineraries at ricksteves.com

BEST OF GUIDES

Full color easy-to-scan format, focusing on Europe's most popular destinations and sights.

Best of England
Best of Europe
Best of France
Best of Germany
Best of Ireland
Best of Italy
Best of Spain

COMPREHENSIVE GUIDES

City, country, and regional guides with detailed coverage for a multi-week trip exploring the most iconic sights and venturing off the beaten track.

Amsterdam & the Netherlands
Barcelona
Belgium: Bruges, Brussels, Antwerp & Ghent
Berlin
Budapest
Croatia & Slovenia
Eastern Europe
England
Florence & Tuscany
France
Germany
Great Britain
Greece: Athens & the Peloponnese
Iceland
Ireland
Istanbul
Italy
London
Paris
Portugal
Prague & the Czech Republic
Provence & the French Riviera
Rome
Scandinavia
Scotland
Spain
Switzerland
Venice
Vienna, Salzburg & Tirol

HE BEST OF ROME

e, Italy's capital, is studded with
n remnants and floodlit-fountain
es. From the Vatican to the Colos-
with crazy traffic in between, Rome
erful, huge, and exhausting. The
, the heat, and the weighty history

of the Eternal City where Caesars walked
can make tourists wilt. Recharge by taking siestas, gelato breaks, and after-dark
walks, strolling from one atmospheric
square to another in the refreshing evening air.

*Pantheon—which
dome until the
2,000 years old
over 1,500).*
Athens in the Vat-
s the humanistic

*diators fought
ther, entertaining*

*ome ristorante.
t St. Peter's
rtously.
us in a coin*

Rick Steves guidebooks are published by Avalon Travel, an imprint of Perseus Books, a Hachette Book Group company.

POCKET GUIDES

Compact, full color city guides with the essentials for shorter trips.

Amsterdam
Athens
Barcelona
Florence
Italy's Cinque Terre
London
Munich & Salzburg
Paris
Prague
Rome
Venice
Vienna

SNAPSHOT GUIDES

Focused single-destination coverage.

Basque Country: Spain & France
Copenhagen & the Best of Denmark
Dublin
Dubrovnik
Edinburgh
Hill Towns of Central Italy
Krakow, Warsaw & Gdansk
Lisbon
Loire Valley
Madrid & Toledo
Milan & the Italian Lakes District
Naples & the Amalfi Coast
Normandy
Northern Ireland
Norway
Reykjavík
Sevilla, Granada & Southern Spain
St. Petersburg, Helsinki & Tallinn
Stockholm

CRUISE PORTS GUIDES

Reference for cruise ports of call.

Mediterranean Cruise Ports
Scandinavian & Northern European
Cruise Ports

Complete your library with...

TRAVEL SKILLS & CULTURE

Study up on travel skills and gain insight on history and culture.

Europe 101
Europe Through the Back Door
European Christmas
European Easter
European Festivals
Postcards from Europe
Travel as a Political Act

PHRASE BOOKS & DICTIONARIES

French
French, Italian & German
German
Italian
Portuguese
Spanish

PLANNING MAPS

Britain, Ireland & London
Europe
France & Paris
Germany, Austria & Switzerland
Ireland
Italy
Spain & Portugal

Avalon Travel
Hachette Book Group
1700 Fourth Street
Berkeley, CA 94710

Printed in Canada by Friesens.
First Edition. First printing May 2018.

ISBN 978-1-64171-168-5

For the latest on Rick's lectures, guidebooks, tours, public television series, and public radio show, contact Rick Steves' Europe, 130 Fourth Avenue North, Edmonds, WA 98020, 425/771-8303, www.ricksteves.com, rick@ricksteves.com.

Rick Steves' Europe

Managing Editor: Jennifer Madison Davis
Special Publications Manager: Risa Laib
Assistant Managing Editor: Cathy Lu
Editors: Glenn Eriksen, Julie Fanselow, Tom Griffin, Katherine Gustafson, Mary Keils, Suzanne Kotz, Rosie Leutzinger, Carrie Shepherd
Editorial & Production Assistant: Jessica Shaw
Editorial Intern: Kevin Teeter
Researcher: Cathy Lu
Contributor: Gene Openshaw
Graphic Content Director: Sandra Hundacker
Maps & Graphics: David C. Hoerlein, Lauren Mills, Mary Rostad

Avalon Travel

Senior Editor and Series Manager: Maddy McFrasher
Editor: Jamie Andrade
Editor: Sierra Machado
Copy Editor: Maggie Ryan
Proofreaders: Kelly Lydick and Patrick Collins
Indexer: Stephen Callahan
Production & Typesetting: Christine DeLorenzo, Kit Anderson, Lisi Baldwin, Rue Flaherty, Jane Musser, Sarah Wildfang
Cover Design: Kimberly Glyder Design
Maps & Graphics: Kat Bennett, Lohnes & Wright

Front Cover: Glen Coe © Irimaxim | Dreamstime.com

Title Page: © Dominic Arizona Bonuccelli

Additional Photography: Dominic Arizona Bonuccelli, Rich Earl, Jennifer Hauseman, Cameron Hewitt, David C. Hoerlein, Lauren Mills, Rhonda Pelikan, Jennifer Schutte, Rick Steves, Gretchen Strauch, Wikimedia Commons(PD-Art/PD-US), © Stephen C. Dickson cc BY-SA 4.0. Photos are used by permission and are the property of the original copyright owners.

Let's Keep on Travelin'

Your trip doesn't need to end.

Follow Rick on social media!

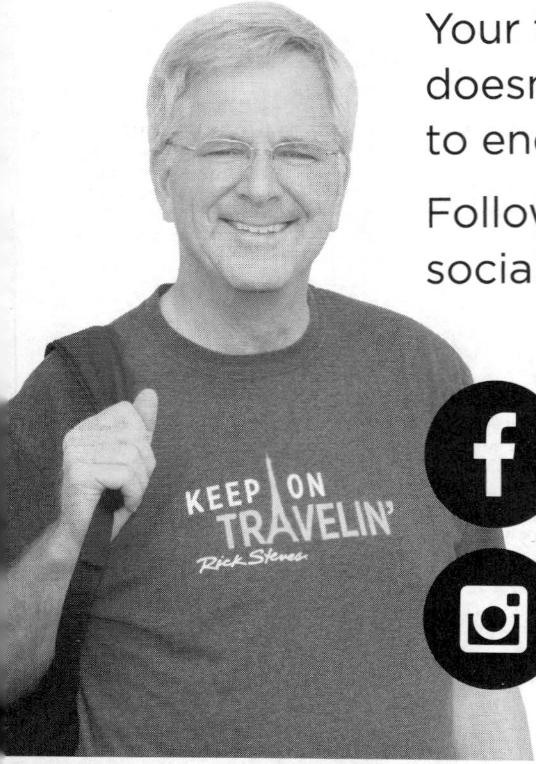

KEEP ON TRAVELIN'
Rick Steves